THE
DIVINE
NEW ORDER

by

GABRIEL OF SEDONA

The Extension Schools
of Melchizedek Publishing

Although the author of this book claims to be a vessel for bringing through the Continuing Fifth Epochal Revelation the interpretations and opinions expressed are not those of the Trustees of the URANTIA Foundation, nor do the publishers claim any affiliation with any organized URANTIA group.

© 1992, 1995 by Gabriel of Sedona
of
Aquarian Concepts Community
as mandated by
The Bright and Morning Star of Salvington

The Extension Schools
of
Melchizedek Publishing
P.O. Box 3946
West Sedona, AZ, U.S.A. 86340

Printed in the United States of America

ISBN 0-9647357-0-9

TABLE OF CONTENTS

ACKNOWLEDGMENTS

I first would like to thank Niánn, who typed and retyped my first drafts, corrected misspellings, grammar and so on. Not only am I blessed to have such a wonderful, spiritual complement as Niánn with me, but it is also a fact that, with a masters degree in education and literature and fifteen years of teaching experience, she has also been a great blessing in assisting me in the preparation of this book and the transmissions which will be presented in *The Cosmic Family* volumes.

My thanks also to Lexia, for proofreading and other labors of love, and to Desmond, for all of his labors of love in doing the little things that he does that frees me and enables me to make things like this book possible.

Thanks to Taleon and Delphius for editing.

Thanks to Santeen for helping with the business end of getting it published in book form.

Thanks for all the donors who so generously gave to help finance the cost.

Thanks to all present Cosmic Family community members for showing up here at Planetary Headquarters from all over the world to help in this great spiritual work.

Finally, my heartfelt thanks and gratitude to all my unseen but ever present celestial family and friends who have taught us so much in such a short period of time, and have truly set me on a higher path to our Universal Father.

Gabriel Of Sedona

INTRODUCTION

In a time and space continuum what is has already been and what will be has been already. A quote from Ecclesiastes says the same thing. "That which is has been already, and that which will be has already been, for God seeks what has passed by." (Ec. 3:15, New American Standard Bible)

Many of the prophecies that have been written in the Bible and other sacred writings have come to pass or are happening now as you read this book. Some of this book is prophecy. The outcome is in your hands.

The purpose of this book is to introduce new cosmic concepts in words that will be part of one planetary language in the understanding of spiritual reality in which our planet, Urantia/Earth,* will be operating when the **change point**[1] and shift from **third dimension** to **fourth dimension**, and above, occurs, and a new divine government of **Christ Michael** (Jesus) is appropriated. Perhaps an **auhter energy** shift will also occur if these two events do not transpire in May of 2000 or 2001 AD. A lower term for this consciousness shift or change point is quantum leap. It is not a government of arms or military power. We do not teach rule by force of arms, nor do we stock weapons of any kind. We teach only the fatherhood of God and the brotherhood of man/woman; we teach love.

With these thoughts, let this be the hope for our planet: that after individuals read this book they can join in the GREAT CELEBRATION once they, as individuals, have practiced the answers.

The Author

---

[1]Terms in **bold type** are new words or concepts introduced in Continuing Fifth Epochal Revelation or words that were introduced in the Fifth Epochal Revelation, *The URANTIA Book*, with updated information. These are defined in the Glossary at the back of the book.

*Terms marked with an asterisk are mostly from *The URANTIA Book* or are terms used in science or New-Age terminology. These are also defined in the Glossary at the back of this book.

STATEMENT BY THE AUTHOR

I began this book in April, 1989, and finished it in November, 1991. It was first printed in July 1992, re-edited and reprinted in March 1993. Following the advice of **Celestial Overcontrol** I wrote another two chapters as an appendix to this book in July 1993 and it saw its third printing in September 1993, when it also received its new title *The Divine New Order*. We did not want to be confused with "The New Order" of the world or third-dimensional government. In March 1994 it was reedited and updated as to the changes within our community. In April 1995 I wrote another chapter and it was again reedited and updated.

This book is an attempt to explain how I became a **Continuing Fifth Epochal Revelation** vessel or **Audio Fusion Material Complement (AFMC)**[2] and is based on certain events in my life. As strange as it may seem, all events are true with the exception of future events which have a high probability of happening according to our Celestial Overseers who told me of them. We, as individuals and as a mass consciousness, must determine our own future and the history of our planet. Certain names of people were changed; others I left, as I wanted to honor them because I respect and love them.

As to the return of certain **cosmic family** members who were with us and left, it is our sincere hope that they will one day rejoin us. I projected their return and future destinies according to what Celestial Overcontrol said. The choice, however, is theirs.

Gabriel of Sedona, MBMS

---

[2]The publishers would like to stress the difference between a "channel" and an audio fusion material complement. For definitions see Glossary. We strongly advise your further study by reading Paper 209 in *The Cosmic Family, Volume I*, or *So Who Is Really Speaking?* in *The Salvington Circuit, Volume I, No 2, July/August 1993*.

FOREWORD

I dedicate this book to Niánn, Alcyone, Sonta-An and **Amadon**, my immediate family, and to all my cosmic family, some who are with us now, and some who will be coming. I personally feel that the truest evidence of the reality of all the experiences mentioned in this book, and in particular of our celestial friends, are my immediate family. This is because before I knew them, I first met Sky Hawk (**Paladin**), whom you will come to know in this book, and it was he who told me that Niánn, Alcyone, Sonta-An and Amadon would be coming. To me they are the best evidence of the reality that God is, indeed, with me.

Further in the book is the detailed account of how I met Niánn. All I would like to say here is that shortly after Sky Hawk told me she was coming, she appeared in my life. I was also told that I would first have a daughter and that I would name her Alcyone because she was coming from the **Pleiades**. My guides also said that I was to have a boy and that I should name him Amadon. When Niánn was three months pregnant with the twin girls, I felt intuitively that she was having more than one child. I naturally thought that it must be Alcyone and Amadon. In Pittsburgh she had her first doctor's checkup, and I asked the doctor to check thoroughly for twins. The doctor said, "No way! There is only one head and only one heartbeat." We decided against an ultrasound because we felt it could be dangerous to the baby. When we arrived back in Arizona I asked the midwives to check thoroughly because I thought she was having twins. They did not detect another heartbeat. During the following months, a very capable midwife and her assistant checked for twins. Nothing was discovered. During this time neither Paladin nor our **midwayers** would confirm that Niánn was having twins, but Paladin would joke with me about it, and at times would admit she was having twins and then retract his statement. In the ninth month, right before her delivery, we went for a final medical checkup in Cotton-

3

wood, Arizona, and I asked the doctor to please check for twins. After he checked, he laughed at me and said that Niánn was too small and he could only find one head and one heartbeat. When I went into the circles of other clairvoyants, some would touch Niánn's stomach and say, "It's a boy!" Since Paladin did tell me that Alcyone was coming, I was ready to explode with frustration. When I would ask Paladin if it was a boy, he would assure me that it was Alcyone but never would confirm the twins.

On December 3, 1988, at home in Prescott, Arizona, Alcyone was born. A few moments later it was determined that a second baby was indeed inside. Now, even I was surprised, since I had accepted everyone else's opinions. When they said another heartbeat was there I thought, "Well, there's Amadon!" Niánn had to be taken to the hospital to have a caesarian. If I had not been so shocked with the second baby and had allowed myself time to tune in, I probably would have realized it was a female essence. Since Paladin had told me we would also have a boy, I thought for sure it was Amadon. After sitting in the waiting room for no more than twenty minutes (they wouldn't let me in the operating room), the nurse came in and told me that the second baby was born and was fine. I said, "I know, it's a boy!" She said with a knowing smile on her face, "Go see; your second baby is with your first girl baby." I literally ran to the nursery where several nurses were gathered. They had me put on a white jacket (it should have been a straight jacket), and I told them, "I know, it's a boy!" They giggled and said, "Go see." So I went in and I saw two tags, "Girl A" and "Girl B." By now I believed completely in the validity of the guides, so I turned around and said to them, "Where is my son?" I was quite shocked when they said it was another girl. Did I have a bone to pick with Paladin and Company!!! We could hardly wait until Niánn was better so that we could contact them again. For three days, until Niánn came home, I refused to name her. Finally, Paladin told me that I should name her Sonta-An, after the first human male on Urantia, one of the twins, Andon and Fonta, a name which means "loved by mother." Paladin also explained that she came from Alcyone of the Pleiades. She was an extra blessing that had been kept secret from me until the very end. I had lost my first daughter, Dina, at the age of seven, but now I had two little girls, a double gift from God. They gave more information about both of these children which would not be appropriate in the context of this foreword.

When Niánn told me ten months later that she was pregnant again, I was angry, shocked and wondered why God couldn't wait a few years; but Niánn's childbearing years were slipping away. She had all three of these children in her forties. Immediately, I asked Paladin, "Is this Amadon?" Naturally he would dangle the carrot. I was determined that if this were a girl I would never allow myself to be used as an **interplanetary receiver** again! When **the Bright and Morning Star** fused with me for three days in 1989 before Amadon was born, he made a clear statement that Niánn was pregnant with a male child, and that it was the Amadon of *The URANTIA Book*. Again, some clairvoyants would touch Niánn's belly and declare, "It's a girl!" This would upset me greatly! On July 17, 1990, at our home in Prescott, Arizona, a very male child, Amadon, was born.

To these children, my wife, Niánn, and all the children of my past and all Urantia relatives and cosmic family, I dedicate this book. Someday, all of us will be together, of one mind and purpose, all sharing our talents for one true community—the Father/Motherhood of God and the brotherhood of man.

CHAPTER 1

COMING BACK TO EARTH (URANTIA)—REFLECTIONS

We were at last coming back to Urantia, the earth we so loved. Looking through the view screen at outer space in the inter-planetary transport craft called *The Star of Bethlehem*, I marvelled at the awesome sight of our planet. It looked so lonely and blue. Maybe I felt the essence of the Mother within and her cries to be repopulated by her children. The earth was about to give birth to a new seed, and we were the offspring. As we got closer I could see that the blue was the clear water, void of pollution now after three years of cleansing. We could actually see the rivers cut through the newly formed land areas. It was hard to believe that America looked so different. What used to be California and up through Washington was now ocean, and a tremendous land mass extended from Hawaii to a few miles from what formerly was the California coast. We were told how many survivors were left on the earth, and we knew that the majority of them would be insane. Had we not been evacuated, I too, along with so many others who were in the ship with me now, would have also gone off the deep end. I could never have imagined just how terrible the destruction of our planet would be. First, man destroyed man in the final conventional wars that led to nuclear holocaust in the late nineties, and then the earth answered back with her own cleansing. Earthquakes, volcanic eruptions and storms, on a scale previously unknown to man, were a daily experience on every continent, killing millions and leaving doom and despair with every soul upon the planet. After the great plate shift, that took the west coast, we wondered for one solid year if we were going to be killed by another great earth shift or by the bands of half insane and starved Americans, or by Chinese invaders who had forgotten that war no longer mattered and that individual survival was the name of the game. Both governments had long since fallen and so had just about every other form of governmental rule on the planet. It was "survival of the fittest," and each man was at war with the other. Food, water and shelter were the goal of every soul upon Urantia. All human decency seemed to be lost to the animal instinct of taking what you needed from those who were weaker. They had not yet learned the true heart of man with a personal God as ruler.

I remember the first time I ever heard about the change point/-Christian tribulation/New-Age prophecies/Hopi's Fifth World, *call it what you may, was in 1971 in a place called Pittsburgh Power and Light Company, a Christian coffee house run by a Presbyterian minister who seemed to believe what he was saying. He quoted from *The Book of Revelation*, chapter 16, of the Bible, reading the entire passage. I was going through my first divorce, which not only included a wife but also a two-year-old daughter; so the pain over the loss of two people I deeply loved was great. Somehow this minister's words rang true, as if coming from a higher authority.

1   And I heard a great voice out of the temple, saying to the seven angels, Go your ways, and pour out the vials of the wrath of God upon the earth.

2   And the first went, and poured out his vial upon the earth; and there fell a noisome and grievous sore upon the men which had the mark of the beast, and *upon* them which worshipped his image.

3   And the second angel poured out his vial upon the sea; and it became as the blood of a dead man; and every living soul died in the sea.

4   And the third angel poured out his vial upon the rivers and fountains of waters; and they became blood.

5   And I heard the angel of the waters say, Thou art righteous, O Lord, which art, and wast, and shalt be, because thou hast judged thus.

6   For they have shed the blood of saints and prophets, and thou hast given them blood to drink; for they are worthy.

7   And I heard another out of the altar say, Even so, Lord God, Almighty, true and righteous are thy judgments.

8   And the fourth angel poured out his vial upon the sun; and power was given unto him to scorch men with fire.

9   And men were scorched with great heat, and blasphemed the name of God, which hath power over these plagues; and they repented not to give him glory.

10   And the fifth angel poured out his vial upon the seat of the beast; and his kingdom was full of darkness; and they gnawed their tongues for pain,

11   And blasphemed the God of heaven because of their pains and their sores, and repented not of their deeds.

12   And the sixth angel poured out his vial upon the great river Euphrates; and the water thereof was dried up, that the way of the kings of the east might be prepared.

13   And I saw three unclean spirits like frogs come out of the mouth of the dragon, and out of the mouth of the beast, and out of the mouth of the false prophet.

14   For they are the spirits of devils, working miracles, which go forth unto the kings of the earth and of the whole world, to gather them to the battle of that great day of God Almighty.

15   Behold, I come as a thief. Blessed is he that watches, and keepeth his garments, lest he walk naked, and they see his shame.

16   And he gathered them together into a place called in the Hebrew tongue Armageddon.

17   And the seventh angel poured out his vial into the air; and there came a great voice out of the temple of heaven, from the throne, saying, It is done.

18   And there were voices, and thunders, and lightnings; and there was a great earthquake, such as was not since men were upon the earth, so mighty an earthquake, and so great.

19   And the great city was divided into three parts, and the cities of the nations fell: and great Babylon came in remembrance before God, to give unto her the cup of the wine of the fierceness of his wrath.

20   And every island fled away, and the mountains were not found.

21   And there fell upon men a great hail out of heaven, every stone about the weight of a talent: and men blasphemed God because of the plague of the hail, for the plague thereof was exceedingly great.

After the reading and preaching about being right with God before these things took place, I gained my first insight into the reality of those who believed and those who did not, by mingling with the crowd. I had come to believe in the existence of a personal God, for surely God was carrying me and my sufferings through this divorce. My simple honest thoughts were that if these words were true, the only way to survive was to be on good terms with my Creator. My thoughts were interrupted by people commenting on the sermon. "You don't believe any of that nonsense do you?" "I don't know," was my reply, "but I think I would act as though it could be a possibility and conduct my life with survival in mind." Whatever that meant, I honestly did not know.

Little did I realize that for the next 27 years I would spend my life preparing for survival into the twenty-first century, as many others did who listened. I had no idea, at that time, I would become an interplanetary communicator with celestial beings, some who were at one time from the Pleiades and other architectural worlds closer to our planet they called *Urantia*. I did not know that I would eventually also be a voice for interdimensional nonmaterial beings from many systems and worlds. These nonmaterial beings from other worlds , including former mortals called **finaliters,** all believed that Urantia was about to be destroyed and replaced by a Divine New Order of reality they called the fourth dimension. I had much to learn, and my journey was about to begin.

CHAPTER 2

SOLUTIONS—THE BEGINNING

I began reading all that I could get my hands on concerning the scientific view of the physical state of our planet due to pollution and greed. Maybe my new-found spiritual beliefs had no factual reality in regard to a dying planet. So many who believed that man would never use nuclear weapons to the magnitude of destroying our planet seemed to be oblivious to the other dangers of environmental concern. I began to see Earth as a much more complex, interdependent system in which oceans, atmosphere and all life affect one another, and all help to shape the face of the planet. Among my new discoveries at that time were:

1. The world's worst ecological disaster had made human life possible. Tiny organisms from the ocean had dumped huge amounts of toxic waste into the environment. It had killed most of the life on the planet. That deadly substance was our precious oxygen.

2. Sudden shifts in currents, such as the Gulf Stream, can trigger mini ice ages that last for centuries.

3. Tiny fluctuations in the earth's orbit, augmented by changes in the proportions of atmospheric gases, control the advance and retreat of glaciers.

4. Deforestation is endangering all life on this planet.

5. Global warming is increasing the carbon dioxide in the atmosphere, which brings about multiple changes.

6. Depletion of the earth's protective ozone shield is endangering us.

7. Overpopulation is creating and will continue to cause major problems, such as food shortage, deforestation, global warming, etc.

8. An increase in earthquakes and erupting volcanoes had begun, due to the shifting of the plates in the earth.

9. There is a possibility of the earth shifting on its axis.

10. Powerful energies are now coming to the earth as a result of the configuration and alignment of 7 planets in our system of Satania.*

11. Diseases could increase to epidemic proportions, due to the pollution in all areas of life, including pollution of the mind.

After any serious study of the problems of ecological concern on a global scale, even the most optimistic view of the chances for survival of our planet into the twenty-first century would have to change. Many scientists gave our planet until 2020 before it would be depleted of all natural resources. Some were more optimistic and said that we could heal all of our environmental ills by 2040, giving us another twenty years to get our act together as a united people of this earth. One thing was plain to me, God didn't have to use his wrath to destroy the earth, as some religious sects believed, we were on our way out due to our own actions, regardless of what God did. I didn't see God as so wrathful anyway. If anything, I was sure he and all the helpers of the grand universe* were trying their best to buy us more time by doing their invisible healing of Mother Nature. I would later learn that they could only do so much, and time would run out. The clock had been set by our universe* government when our planet and 36 others in our local system of Satania fell in the Lucifer rebellion.* I had to laugh at those who thought recycling would get the job done. They should have started that at the beginning of the industrial revolution. Some experts said pollution prevention via controlling methods of production was the key. Others said that energy conservation was the answer. In production technology we ran into a case of political problems. In our economic system, that decision process was totally under private control. A corporation's legal obligation was not to the nation or the planet but to its stockholders—to the profit motive.

Motive! This was a word that jumped out at me and struck my heart. Did any wrong motive of mine add to the pollution of our planet? In what way did I compromise with materialistic values? Perhaps I already was a part of the problem. Perhaps I too was part of the profit motive. How would life go if my every decision was for the good of my neighbor and not just for myself? I, the individual, would have to change in order for the corporation, made up of individuals, to change. The mass consciousness as a whole had to be enlightened as to the real problem, and the problem was the individuals, each one of them, Mr. and Mrs. Planetary Citizen.

It took me many years before I discovered we all were actually universe citizens with a cosmic responsibility for the life on other planets as well as our own. The nationalistic view of many Americans was at the "still swinging in the trees" stage.

CHAPTER 3

MY FIRST EXPERIENCE WITH SURVIVAL PREPARATION AND MY REVEREND AND MONASTERY DAYS

In 1973, about a year after my search for solutions began, I found myself in a young Christian minister's basement in Pittsburgh, my hometown. He and his group were preparing physically and spiritually for the coming tribulation on the planet. I listened intently as they told me their view of the coming food shortage in our country, while I stuffed my face with a big sandwich prepared by one of the community members. Being already about 15 pounds overweight at that time, food shortage didn't seem to be the problem. How could America ever have that problem? I thought this young man was overly concerned. (Years later I found myself praying that God would send to our community people who knew how to store and preserve food.) This young man intrigued me; he and his wife both under thirty, were both intelligent and wise. They had a following of about forty individuals, mostly under thirty also. I was impressed at the organization of their food storage and the different foods they had available plus outdoor survival equipment. They were post-tribulationists, believing that they, as true Christians, would have to go through the years of war, earth changes and famine that would be upcoming. They said that Christians, with an ear to hear from God, like Joseph in Egypt of old, should prepare themselves for seven years of hardship. I admired them at the time for what that young minister, his wife and community were able to accomplish. There was enough food to feed several hundred people for several months and fewer people for several years. I didn't realize at the time what tremendous organization it required to get people with various talents to join to accomplish such a task.

It was seven years later in Tucson, Arizona, where I had become an ordained Christian nondenominational minister, that I truly began to see the real problems of trying to live in godly reality. Many of the ministers of the city had decided to come together to pray for the "peace of the city." Although I was very unorthodox by their standards, I was asked to participate. I think they invited me because I sent many new converts to their churches, but they knew I didn't believe in many of their doctrines or interpretations of the Bible. On Sundays, all preached sermons of the coming doom to our planet, the tribulation period. They all believed in what they called the rapture, the taking away of all true believers. They strongly disagreed about exactly when they would be taken. Even though we came together to pray for the peace of the city, (we should have prayed for peace on the planet) it didn't take long before war broke out among them. They were divided over three streams of thought:

The pre-tribulationists believed that Jesus would come back riding a white horse with all the angels in heaven and call up (rapture) the true Christians (*Christian* according to their definition of course) before the tribulation. Rev. Rap would even pick a date in a few years and draw national attention when his date did not come to pass. "God would not allow His children to suffer the kind of pains that were coming; famine and plague would not touch His bride." I guess he considered all the starving children in Bangladesh at that time as the devil's children. I thought this man was quite off track, but many believed this doctrine.

Rev. Meters was a mid-tribulationist. "Many so-called Christians are lukewarm today; they will have to endure some suffering to wake them up. I believe that three years will transpire into the tribulation period before the rapture takes place. I have the word of God in *Revelations* to back me up." I hated it when they would use that line. They all did it. Each used the Bible to confirm his individual doctrines. One would think they would realize the truth probably existed somewhere in between.

Unlike the young minister in Pittsburgh, these self-righteous men went on about the stupidity of storing food, gasoline and water. God would supply all of their needs. "If God dropped manna from the sky for the ancient Israelites, why not for us?" spoke Rev. Meters. I wondered why God wasn't dropping bread down now in many parts of the world. Surely tribulation was happening to many people on the planet right then. The bread that was being sent to them was being destroyed by their own governments or confiscated before many of the starving ever saw it, but Rev. Meters did seem to possess some kind of unusual faith, however misconstrued. It was years later that I understood why this kind of faith was needed.

Rev. State was a post-tribulationist. "True Christians will be needed on the earth to help all those suffering souls to find God during those seven years of testing. Right before the final destruction of the earth, God will take away the elect." My thoughts were, "Isn't life itself enough of a test? If those men who are supposed to be praying for peace are part of God's elect, then God help us." I saw more peace among street gangs back in my old neighborhood in Pittsburgh than I saw there, but I felt I shouldn't express that among these self-righteous men.

There was so much I had to learn at that point in my life, and I knew it; but I didn't feel the other men who called themselves ministers really believed that they had more to learn about what's out there in the grand universe, about the God they so smugly defined, and about those trillions of worlds and creatures beyond our planet.

A few years after that prayer meeting, my second wife left me for a close friend and was remarried. I was grief stricken. I decided to look for the solutions to the world's problems in another religious and intellectual avenue. I considered becoming a Catholic priest; you might say I was going back to my roots. This surely would make my mother, who never thought I was part of the establishment, very happy. Of course, I hadn't listened to my parents since I was about 17 years old. While in two Benedictine monasteries and a Third Order Franciscan community, all in the southwestern United States, I did find out in the next several years that there were many happy Catholic mothers and many unhappy priests.

In these monasteries there were many enlightening subjects talked about by the brothers at night. Men will be men. Unfortunately, masturbation, fornication (that terrible sin of sex before marriage) and masturbation again, were also discussed. So I decided to hang out with the older priests for more meaningful conversation since I wanted to learn about some possible way to solve the world's problems. A few of these priests told me that I was an old soul. They secretly believed in reincarnation but never voiced their beliefs openly. They were environmentally conscious and had an elaborate solar-energy setup, which had been designed by one of the priests, that heated the majority of the monastery. The abbot served as the voice of God for over 150 men and women who stayed in this experimental monastery with priests, nuns and lay people. He was threatened by anyone who questioned his views. He was really into saving the world by educating people about Jungian psychology and placing everybody into personality types. If we understood each other better, maybe we would cooperate with each other more. I'm OK, you're OK. This sounded great, but in the six months I was there I never heard him listening to anybody else's suggestions. He also spoke about the inequality between men and women and how women needed to be liberated. But at the same time no woman in the community was given any authority or allowed to teach.

The Franciscan community was run by a strong wife of a not-so-strong husband. I would later learn that many males and females on this planet had an imbalance in the Father/Mother circuits of the personality, but I'll get into that later. If we wanted to go to the bathroom we had better ask her permission. They were environmentally aware and they were decent people, but the imbalance there was too much for me. I prayed that her husband would assume his proper role in the home as a **Father-circuited** leader and protector.

From one of the tests[3] that the abbot had everybody take, it was discovered that I was an INFP with ENFP tendencies and gifts, a very unusual personality, which is true of only 1% of the world's population: very intuitive, had extrasensory perception, I liked my solitude, but was a natural born leader. That was a shock to me. I always thought I was slightly different, but this was a little too much. He said that the majority of people like me choose monastic life to escape the world, or become famous so that they could escape the world through their wealth. Because so much of what he said about me was true, I knew that he was onto something supernatural, something beyond man's explanation. It was true that I was able to foreknow certain things, particularly deaths in my family and certain world events. But I never thought it was special nor had I tried to develop it. This was my first understanding of my paranormal gifts.

One day, the abbot asked me to leave the monastery in the dead of winter in a snowstorm because I questioned one of his decisions. I then decided to try Native American spirituality. I went to visit the Native American tribes in Arizona.

---

[3]Meyer-Briggs Type Indicator is a measure of personality dispositions and interests based on Jung's theory of types. It provides four bipolar scales: Introversion/Extroversion, Sensing/Intuition, Thinking/Feeling, and Judging/Perceiving. Scores are reported by a four-letter type code.

CHAPTER 4

WANDERING IN THE SOUTHWEST AND MEXICO

I left the Benedictine monastery feeling very much like a lost soul. I did not know where I belonged or to what spiritual reality I could devote my life. I even doubted the existence of God at times.

One place I had wanted to go to for a new vision quest was San Carlos Lake, on the San Carlos Apache Reservation where I had spent many weekends when I lived in Tucson. When I arrived I tried to find the spot where my ex-wife and I had spent so many happy times, but for some reason I could not find it even though I was determined to do so. I quieted myself down long enough to begin to pray and felt at the time that the reason I could not find it was because God was telling me that this woman was out of my life and I had to begin anew.

As I settled in at another location I became very poetically inspired and began to write. I also felt, as I had at certain times in previous years, another presence near me, unseen, yet real. This experience frightened me at first, so I broke camp and went into a reservation town and had a cup of Indian coffee. It was strong enough to put hair on my chest. Little did I know that just a few hundred yards away was the very home in which Niánn grew up as a young girl, and I would meet her in a few years. I did not know it then, but I was led back to the reservation and within the radius of where Niánn had actually grown up so that my vibrations could connect once again with hers. Though Niánn was at that time teaching in Globe, Arizona, about ten miles away from the reservation, her essence and life force was still very much a part of the area to which I had been led. It also enabled my contact with the midwayers, although I did not know what a midwayer was at that time and they did not come into my reality strong enough to tell me who they were. After I had my coffee, I felt a new peace about what I had experienced down by the lake and decided to go back out there and tune in again. I called upon Jesus. A few moments later I again felt a presence nearby, and I heard for the first time within me a name which was, Gentle Eagle. I did not know then, nor was the communication from the midwayers clear enough, but that had been my Apache name, and I had lived on this reservation approximately 186 years ago with Niánn. They also gave me a song which is called "Makes You Wonder Why," the first line of which says, "It takes a lifetime to learn how to live and then you die; makes you wonder why." Because of the song I began thinking of life and death and the afterlife. My Christian background made it very difficult for me to think of myself as having lived before. I erased the whole experience as grieving for my second wife and again became frightened of those voices and immediately left the area, thinking that I was missing her so much that I was hallucinating. What I did not realize was that it was the result of an increasing opening of my **circuits** by the midwayers and a beginning into the Continuing Fifth Epochal Revelation. At the time I had not even come to the first part of this revelation, *The URANTIA Book.*

I decided to visit the Hopi reservation. My second wife and I had never been there together so I did not think I would be affected as much with memories of her. I was greatly impressed by the Hopi religion and traditions. It was the first time that I had heard about the Hopi Fifth World. Later I would understand the concept to be the complement of the **Fifth Epochal Revelation.** Some Hopi believe that many of their ancestors came from the stars and had intermarried with their race. They also believe that the time of purification on the planet is near and that in the earth changes to come, a new dimensional shift is about to occur. I spent many nights camping out, and in the quiet of the nights I somehow felt an inner desire to stay there and become a part of the Hopi; but I also felt another inner calling to move on, so I headed toward the Grand Canyon and discovered that there was an Indian tribe, called the Havasupai, living at the bottom of the canyon. I took the four-

mile mule ride down to the floor of the canyon only to discover
that the Havasupai were miles away; and so I came right back up,
sore butt and all. I acquired more factual information and again
went to find the Havasupai Indians. I decided to hike down the
canyon this time, which took approximately four hours one way.
As I neared the bottom I noticed what seemed to be an oasis with
green fields, trees and Indian children riding bareback on horses.
Strangely, I felt as if I were one of them and could not understand
those feelings. After talking to several Indian children, I discovered that some as old as fourteen, had never been to the top of
the canyon. In talking to a number of the elders, I was told that
they believed very strongly in extraterrestrial spacecrafts, but they
would not tell me why. This increased my interest even more.
Although I did not look like the average white man, I cannot blame
them for not opening up to me completely. They told me they
were afraid their lifestyle would be greatly changed by the plans of
the white man for certain mines and other factories around that
area. I have never seen such clear water as I saw at the bottom of
the Grand Canyon. The steady stream of tourists were beginning
to destroy their environment. I would become very saddened years
later, approximately 1991, when I discovered that this clear water
was now polluted by the very mines they had feared years earlier.

I decided I wanted to see Mexico again. I had been there
several times with a Mexican chaplain by the name of José. As I
drove to the Nogales border I remembered an incident we had
once, while trying to cross over. We would always have to give
the border guards a few dollars because we were carrying food and
other supplies to the poor people and prisoners, and it was illegal
to do so. This particular time, there were guards that José did not
know, and they wanted more money. They came around the van
to talk to me because they saw I was an American. I was wearing
a black turtleneck and had a big cross hanging around my neck.
They thought I was a priest. They called me Padre, excused
themselves and let us pass. José and I laughed all the way to
Hermosillo where we intended to visit the inmates at the state
prison. We learned there had just been a riot and the Commandant

advised us not to go in for fear of our lives, as several had been killed, including an American. It is strange how brave one can become when one knows that God is with him, so I decided to do the same "Father Tony" routine I had done back at the border. As we walked through the open courtyard where all the prisoners, murderers mixed with burglars, were free to roam, they all called me Padre and wanted to be blessed. I didn't know, but I felt that I was a Catholic priest. I didn't feel I was pretending and maybe that is why it came off so well. In later years, I found out in some of the personal transmissions by Paladin, I had been a Franciscan in the thirteenth century.

After leaving the prison, I decided to go to the ocean beach in Guaymas where José and I had been before. Though I was quite alone, I felt no fear. I sensed the reality of unseen beings with me. As I sat on the beach and reflected, I remembered an incident in my life when José and I had lost a whole day. We thought we were returning to Tucson on Sunday evening, but it was already Monday evening! My second wife, was quite distraught and wondered why we hadn't called. All I could remember was that I was anxious to be with her and didn't realize I had lost a whole day. It is still a blank, which is why I am now going to let Paladin come in and tell exactly what happened.

TRANSMISSION FROM PALADIN

"As Gabriel was sitting on the Guaymas beach trying to find his soul, we had decided to take it! It is quite true that he has little or no memory of this except for the lost time period; however, if he did he would no longer want to remain on Urantia and deal with the mundane realities of living, and more specifically trying to bring souls into Continuing Fifth Epochal Revelation. We used projector beams that broke down the molecular structure much like those seen on the starship Enterprise in *Star Trek*. Present upon the smaller disc-shaped craft, the size of which was approximately one acre, was myself, Paladin, and Gabriel's grandmother who was allowed this extraordinary visit from the first mansion world* on which she is presently located, having been a **first-time Urantian**. She appeared young, approximately 29, and quite beautiful. He was awakened to see her and recognized her completely. That is why he had thoughts of her as being young throughout the years afterwards. If he remembers, it was her he asked for when I came to him as Sky Hawk years later in the Arizona mountains. She spoke to him as a grandmother and told him some things about the future. First she told him of his soon-to-come divorce from his second wife whom he loved very much and she knew the emotional pain would almost kill him. She asked him to be strong of faith and to persevere through the various afflictions in body that his emotional state would cause him. Then she told him that Christ Michael indeed had a wonderful plan for him and that he was to become Gabriel, a name that he would take when he was again in the presence of her former life force back in Pittsburgh, Pennsylvania. She wanted him to see her husband, Gabriel's grandfather, who was still living on Urantia, and to let him know that she was alive and soon they would be together again. She also told Gabriel that she was greatly appreciative of the faith he had here while she was alive and that it helped her become part of her new home on the first mansion world of Satania. She wanted to give him a favor, and told him that he had been chosen by God to be a vessel of communication for bringing in the Continuing Fifth Epochal Revelation, and that he had to learn the first part of it, already in print, so that he could assimilate the language within and thus could become the chosen vessel. She said that the book would come to him in his hometown of Pittsburgh, near the **energy reflective circuit** of some of his ancient relatives from other planets. The name of the book was called *The URANTIA Book.* She said that he had heard of the book before but that he had refused it, for he was a Christian minister at that time, but now he must accept it, learn it and then become an Audio Fusion Material Complement for the next nine tenths of it. She said that no one else on the planet could take this position, for there was not time left before the change point on Urantia to bring a soul to the place of being chosen for this work and responsibility. She added that he had been part of other renaissances of this planet and that she and all his relatives on her side were counting on him. As she mentioned these relatives he saw people, as on a large television screen, each one of them young, vibrant and smiling; it was as if they were smiling at him because of the tasks he had already accomplished, some of which he remembers. There was Grandmother and Grandfather Dell Erba, Godfather Mundo, Great Grandmother Cottrell, Sonny Malatesta, Uncle Joseph, Uncle Salvatore, Uncle Fred, Cousin Johnny Mancini, Jimmy Ferrera and others." (End of transmission).

I regained my consciousness and was returned to the beach, but I remembered nothing that had transpired. I returned to Tucson and my wife, very naive about the divorce that was to take place and the events that would bring me back to Pittsburgh.

CHAPTER 5

RETURN TO WHERE THE THREE RIVERS MEET[4]

I had no memories of what had happened in Guaymas, Mexico. I just knew that with my experience I gained a new mission. This time I thought I was to record a spiritual album and reach the world with higher-consciousness music. At this time I was what you might call a New-Age Catholic.

I had been home to Pittsburgh several times throughout the years, but this was the longest time period in which I had not seen most of my family—over eight years. I did not realize then that I was to be the leader of a great cosmic family and that anytime I felt separate from others at any level, grief became part of my reality. When I first became a God-seeking soul I lost many of my friends and family members because I could no longer relate to them. It was sad, for I love them all very much. It was grief that caused my death on this planet in one lifetime as a Franciscan.

I got along well with all my Catholic relatives as long as I did not talk too strongly about religion, something I found very difficult. I went to visit a Catholic charismatic prayer group that I used to attend in the seventies to see what kind of growth had taken place. The leader was not there that night, and nobody knew

---

[4]"Where the three rivers meet" was the home of several Native American nations which extended to Canada at the time of the French and English wars in the New World. The five Iroquois nations came together to develop a common spiritual language. This was a precursor to the Fifth Epochal Revelation. There is an energy reflective circuit "where the three rivers meet." Gabriel of Sedona was born in this area. In 1992 an elder from the Iroquois nation, Great Bear, met with Gabriel in Sedona. He was told of the ancient Iroquois prophecy about a prophet who would come from the East at the end times. Gabriel of Sedona is that prophet.

that I had been there years before. I was surprised they had no
new revelation. The teaching was pretty much the same as it was
in the seventies. At that time I was studying at Duquesne University, the place where the spiritual renewal first started. I was one
of the first Catholic charismatics in the modern era to receive the
baptism of the Holy Spirit,* with certain evidence of this baptism
being the "word of knowledge," "tongues," and "prophecy." (I
talk about this later in the book) There were just a few dozen Duquesne charismatics at the time, and the administration asked some
to leave the school, including a priest. I went to a convention in
Notre Dame stadium in 1973, and there were thirty thousand
charismatic Catholics. I experienced this tremendous growth in the
"renewal" in just a few short years. The URANTIA Book movement should have experienced the Baptism of the Holy Spirit and
the charismatics, Catholics and Protestants, should have come to
The URANTIA Book and eventually to Continuing Fifth Epochal
Revelation. But unfortunately they didn't, and no new growth has
taken place in the charismatic movement as far as acceptance of
new revelation. To simplify, one is mind, the other is heart. Both
mind and heart are needed for true wholeness and ascension. I
have many fond memories of my charismatic days in Pittsburgh
and other cities, one of which is meeting a special soul. She was
Agatha von Trapp, whom I met together with her mother Maria
and another sister. This was the famous family about which the
film, *The Sound of Music*, was made. As a little girl in the forties,
Agatha was one of the singing daughters of the Baron von Trapp
family. I had lunch with Agatha on several occasions and with a
Jewish evangelist friend who knew her. These were the days when
people of different denominations all came together to worship the
same God. The movement should have evolved into the present
Divine New Order and the Divine Planetary Government. Many
left and became involved in the New Age, but when they found
that their Jesus was not there, they had nowhere else to go. Many
went back to their former denominations. Agatha's love for Jesus
was so beautiful. I even considered going to New Guinea with her
as a missionary, as she had been serving her Lord there for many
years. Oh, to have that kind of heart and love for God, fused with

the mindal knowledge of higher cosmic truth! That's what my later work would do for the planet, and many souls would join our community with this kind of combination. Today the charismatic renewal is just another branch of the Catholic Church. The revelation stopped when most people in the Catholic Church didn't join the renewal. As it was in the thirteenth century with Francis of Assisi, the modern renewal didn't go far enough. It could have led the way to the first stage of light and life on Urantia.

One day, while still in Pittsburgh, I went to a Wendy's Restaurant and there I ran into a close friend from the past. I had not seen her in twelve years. I was not planning on seeing her or her husband, although next to my human parents I had loved them more than any other people on the planet. I did not understand why I loved them so much, particularly the husband, who I felt at times took advantage of my love for him. In the past when I had become a born-again Christian they rejected me and my new philosophy. I don't blame them for that. Now here I was a Catholic again, but a New-Age Catholic with some beliefs that they wouldn't accept. However, God had other plans for us and having met again, they were my closest friends for the next year.

When I went to their home it brought back many memories, one of which is most important to this book. After the divorce from my first wife, at a time when my daughter Dina was three years old and still alive, I felt tremendous pain and grief. I was living upstairs in their home and praying to God for a reconciliation with my wife. Downstairs I heard voices of laughter. It sounded like my wife, my daughter Dina and then my parents and my in-laws. In my mind I felt that this terrible separation from them was over. I heard footsteps coming up the stairs, and I thought I heard a little girl laughing and giggling who I thought to be Dina. I waited and I heard a knock on the door three times... rap, rap, rap. I quickly opened the door because I was standing so close to it. When I opened it, no one was there! I stood there in disbelief and was quite frightened. I listened to hear if there was still noise downstairs, and I heard none. I thought I was going out of my mind and felt tremendous pain in my heart. At that moment I felt a presence near me, and it actually put its hand on my shoulder. This also frightened me, and I literally ran down the stairs. I felt this presence follow me. I pounded on the door downstairs and asked for my friends to come; and when the husband came, I asked, "Where is everybody?" and he said, "Who?" It was then that I realized that something supernatural was going on. The familiar voices weren't real, obviously, but who was the being with me? It was years later, and because of Continuing Fifth Epochal Revelation, when I realized that because these close friends were part of my cosmic family and had been my human parents in a past life on this planet, and because their home was located very near the energy reflective circuit of Mount Washington, that these combined energies had allowed the midwayers to come into closer contact with me. I gave my life to God and Christ Michael that evening. In this lifetime that's where it began. I also learned that I would become their teacher-son, a role that has become very difficult for me as I am also teacher-son to my first-time Urantian parents Mary and Anthony. I could never understand why Mary and Anthony were a little jealous of these friends. What none of us understood then is that these dear friends were also once my human parents, but not my **cosmic parents**. On another occasion when I went back to Pittsburgh, the first thing that the husband would say to me was, "I'm Catholic, born Catholic and will die Catholic." For the two weeks that Niánn and I stayed with them in 1988 there was very little spiritual conversation that we could have, as he closed the door immediately. The wife was more open, but at the time of this writing I have no contact with them. I have tried but they have not responded.

Another cosmic family member that I met in Pittsburgh was the brother of two old friends from my childhood. I had not seen him for fifteen years, and he was now nearing thirty. I was to be closest to him on a spiritual level during the whole year I was in Pittsburgh. There was an immediate kinship between us, and we understood spiritual things on a very high level. He was also deeply involved in Native American spirituality. He was making films and had just met Will Sampson, a Native American actor, now deceased, from *One Flew Over the Cuckoo's Nest*. He took me to a ceremony of a Central American Indian tribe called the Caney, and during the year, I visited the Caney circle many times and had open discussions with their shaman leader. I would later find out from Paladin that he was my cosmic son and this shaman leader, a cosmic brother. In the shaman's group I met a Caney woman by the name of Tenache. When I first heard her name my heart leapt. I was later to learn from Paladin that Tenache was the name of one of my Apache Indian loves and wives and that this Tenache was my cosmic daughter. I didn't understand all that was happening at the time, just that I loved these people; but we were all on different paths then and couldn't quite connect.

One evening this cosmic son and I went to Mount Washington. I would find out from Paladin years later that it was an energy reflective circuit. This was not known to the public until this writing. Up till then, I just knew it to be a beautiful view overlooking the three rivers of Pittsburgh. While I was there in meditation, a vision came to me and once again I felt a close presence of an unseen personality. This was made possible by being with my cosmic son. The name Gabriel came to me. At first I thought that the presence might be an angel called Gabriel. Then a vision of a circle came to me with dots in the middle of it. I shared with my cosmic son that I felt a presence nearby, but he wasn't "into it" so much, so I didn't get deep into the experience with him at the time. I went home by myself, prayed about the vision, and felt that I was to change my name to Gabriel and that I was to return to my original Italian surname which was Dell Erba. I sensed I was to name my future children Dell Erba, which means "of the earth." Amadon, my future son, would be named "Dell Erba", and he certainly was of the earth, the loyal one of Urantia. (See *The URANTIA Book*, p. 761) As time passed, the dots that I saw came to be positioned in specific locations within the circle. I also saw a triangle within the circle and a solar cross connecting four points on the circle. Outside the circle I saw a smaller triangle. This is the logo used by the Aquarian Concepts

Community. I had no idea at the time what it meant. In my limited thinking at that time, I thought it symbolized the seven locations around the planet where I would have offices for my spiritual musical ministry in which I was to become Gabriel, a messenger through music. It was four years later, as I was reading a book by Billy Meier, a contact for the Pleiadians living in Switzerland, that I saw the seven dots within the circle was an ancient symbol of the seven sisters of the Pleiades. I would later be told by Paladin that these seven dots would actually be seven **sacred/protected areas** on Urantia that would be **Divine New Order communities**, the first of which would be in Sedona, Arizona. Then I, as the leader, and the eldership of Aquarian Concepts Community at **Planetary Headquarters** in Sedona would help establish the other six communities on Urantia.

One day I received a phone call from a friend who owned a metaphysical bookstore. He said a young artist, upon hearing the music I had recorded, wished to trade me *The URANTIA Book* for my album. When he said the word, *Urantia*, something leaped within me. I thought I had remembered it from when I was a Christian minister eleven years previously and had rejected it. Actually, it had been programmed into me by my grandmother that time in Guaymas, Mexico, when I was beamed up on a space vessel; so I immediately said yes, I would make the trade, and went down to the shop about a block away. The first thing the young artist said to me was, "You have to read about Gabriel." I told him my album was only ten dollars and I believed the book cost much more. He said I should have the book without paying anything for it and that it was the clearest direction that he had ever received from God about anything and for me to please take it immediately. That is how I received *The URANTIA Book*.

I decided to record my album in Pittsburgh and I used all the savings I had accumulated over the years to produce this spiritual/-New Age/pop album myself. It was, and is, meant to reach the mass consciousness and those who listen to rhythm and blues, pop, folk, and jazz. All the musicians who played were spiritually-minded, and we prayed before each session. The experience over the months of making this album was one of the most exhilarating of my life. I was glad the musicians did not recognize it as contemporary Christian music, but they certainly recognized it as something different and quite spiritual. I did not tell them of my other spiritual beliefs; as far as they knew, I was a Christian, expressing an art form different from the usual contemporary Christian music. I was a pioneer in New-Age pop vocal. The album was ahead of its time.

I had become quite settled in Pittsburgh with a nice apartment on the South Side. I had renewed friendships and made new acquaintances, including my cosmic son, who was very close to me and whom I loved very much. Yet I felt this tug and pull to go to Los Angeles. Right before I left, a producer from Hollywood was in Pittsburgh and offered me $30,000 cash and a five-year contract with his company which was open to recording commercial spiritual music. After praying about this I felt that it was not God's will to accept this offer, as it would have tied me down for the next five years. I also felt drawn to Los Angeles because I had met a female rock star and her manager at a songwriter's home in Beverly Hills in 1981; the manager and I seemed to click. My plans were to marry her. Actually I didn't understand the love I had for her until years later, when I found out she had been a wife in a previous life. God used my love for her to get me to Los Angeles (he does that). I didn't know that success in music would escape me as would this woman. If I had remained in Pittsburgh I could never have met my destiny as the Audio Fusion Material Complement of the Bright and Morning Star, Paladin, and many other celestial friends, in order to bring Continuing Fifth Epochal Revelation to this planet. With much pain in my heart and tears in my eyes, I left for Los Angeles. I bid my farewell to all four of my Urantian parents, my dear sister and her children, to my cosmic son, and many others for whom I felt more than an earthly love.

CHAPTER 6

LOS ANGELES, THE DISEASED HEARTBEAT OF AMERICA AND THE PLANET

I had been to L.A. before to learn about the music business and try to have my music heard by someone who could appreciate both art and talent. All three times before, I was defeated by the smog, traffic, and working minimum-wage jobs to survive. The abbot was right. I would have to become famous quickly, or I would end up in isolation somewhere as years before, I had escaped to the monasteries. I tried not to think of failure. I was still naive enough to believe that if the right person heard my music and recognized its spiritual value in helping to change the planet, that commercial success was possible.

I decided to live by the ocean to get away from the pollution. I rented from a ninety-two-year-old Jewish man in Santa Monica, who still chased women. Saul Weck said he knew a lot of famous people but outlived them all.

"You can't trust people who have money or power; don't even trust me," was his first advice.

"They will do anything to protect what they have, whatever the cost to you. When I first came here sixty years ago, the ocean was clean, and there was room to breathe on the beaches. What do you see now? Apartment buildings everywhere and places to feed the fat people who spend too much for the food they eat." He had a real way with words.

"I sold out too; I'm no better than the rest; sold most of this land to developers so that I could wine and dine women. I'm still a dirty old man. Unfortunately the environment that used to be so beautiful is dirtier, and I pray the Lord will forgive me. The weather's not the same here as it was sixty years ago. It's fifteen degrees cooler in the winter months, much hotter in the summer,

31

and too humid on the beach. Only a fool would lie out in the sun. I lost track of the young people who contracted skin cancer. You don't hear the real statistics. Do you think the rich want the tourist-and-beach business ruined? They pay off big to keep it low key."

It sounded as though he was very aware of the condition of the ozone layer without reading scientific reports. Saul was an interesting diversion while I pursued my music career.

Some artists who claimed to be doing New-Age vocal sounded just like gospel; my music didn't. Others just chanted and made unusual sounds with their voices, and that was supposed to be "spiritual." I had real lyrics that brought the listener to a point of truth that some did not want to hear. I told people that it wasn't the planet that needed cleaning up, it was their own minds and hearts that needed a major overhaul. I sang about greed, envy, power, lust, false pride, and materialism, to name a few subjects. I spent all my time either creating new forms of spiritual music on the Santa Monica beach or fighting the rat race of the Hollywood music machine. I wrote spiritual folk, pop, rock and even country western. I told it like it was, but none of the music executives seemed to really care about making a change for the spiritual good of the planet. They liked things just the way they were. They were happy cheating on their wives and snorting cocaine. A few in the business, who were removed from the Hollywood machine, were willing to give me a positive review: several DJs who liked the album but couldn't play it because they would get fired; a top producer who at the time led a famous TV orchestra but was out of the record business; an academy-award-winning songwriter who gave my album a good review, but wouldn't pick up the phone to make the right connections for me. Oh, he gave me names to call, but I could have gotten better contacts from Joe Blow on the streets of Hollywood.

Envy and Greed, the Dark Soul's Needs

I was learning firsthand the real problem with our planet, and it had nothing to do with environmental issues, at least not directly. The songwriter hurt me the most because he was supposed to be a spiritual man, a teacher and leader. I found him to be no better than the rest of the glory hounds. What was he afraid of, that I might beat him for next year's best song award? I found out that the more talented one was, the harder it was to break in, unless they could own and operate you and mold you into one of their clones. People in L.A. would actually go out of their way to destroy you if they thought you were a threat to their career or inflated egos. One female executive of a so-called spiritual record label actually saw to it that I would not receive a record contract from her parent company who wanted me at that time. She blocked a major contract for me by outright lying to her superiors about my personality. She didn't know me from Adam, but I wouldn't jump when she barked and she didn't like my independence. When I had to work minimum-wage jobs to survive, one lousy job after another, I often wondered if I should have jumped just a little for that power-hungry soul, but I knew I would have failed the greater test I had yet to pass.

To keep my sanity I joined a black church and their gospel choir. I had done this before, and loved it. I was even picked to sing lead a few weeks after joining. There were a hundred black people in the choir, and I was honored. Deserved recognition of one's talents is always a blessing on this planet, and when it comes your way, treasure it with humility and thankfulness. I felt outside of the Hollywood jungle with these simple folks who "just loved their Jesus."

Confusion and Delusion

I attended all the help-save-the-planet and New-Age groups I could work into my busy schedule. Most of them were pretty weird even for me. One group believed in the coming earth changes and that California was going to disappear in a great tidal wave. They believed that the Deva forces, whatever they were, were calling the souls who had died in Atlantis back to California to drown all over again. Karma, you know! Another group said that when the planet was about to explode, that they who had grown spiritually, would concentrate and use their mind energy to walk out of their bodies into the glorious new world to come. These were the same people who wouldn't give you a ride home if you needed it or smile at you when you looked at them.

One Sunday a friend and I went to see a channel in a New-Age church. Channeling was unusual then and just getting started. The voice that came out of this young man's mouth sounded like a drunken Irish man who told everybody that God was love and love was God. La-di-da. We laughed so hard we were almost asked to leave. This guy had to be a hopeful actor. If he wasn't, he sure was missing his true calling.

Many of the men who had the energy gift in their hands to heal—Reiki, they called it—wanted to touch all the pretty, sick, un-balanced females for nothing, no charge. The poor men and older or less attractive women would either have to pay or stay forever in an unbalanced body with their unaligned energies shooting all over the place. Psychics were a dime a dozen, and I did not want to be identified with them. One day, just for kicks, I paid one five dollars to read my fortune. It was on the walk at Venice Beach. She used a Tarot deck; and while she was telling me that I would be rich and famous, would soon marry the woman of my dreams and travel a lot in my life, I decided to "read" her. I concentrated and heard a voice that said she was from Indiana, that she was divorced and had two children, two boys. I spoke up and repeated what the voice said. "How in God's name did you know that?" she yelled. I answered, "You're the psychic, you tell me."

I began to practice learning how to listen and see how accurate I could be with people and events. I was amazed myself at the things I was able to determine by listening to that voice. But I had a long way to go before I really learned what was happening and exactly what this gift was.

I was guided to a spiritual group who studied the teachings of the ascended Tibetan Master, Djwal Khul. This group was one of the few that made any sense to me. They talked about being a world server and about the shift that was about to come upon the planet. They taught that our body was really astral and that it had a central channel from the head to the pelvis that had seven spiritual centers they called chakras.* I spent many hours reading all I could about these centers and how to clear this channel, which was called the Antakarana* and was the link with the unseen beings who wished to communicate with all who spiritually advanced to this level. This was available to all souls who were open and willing to learn and venture into the unknown, unknown in today's age, but once very common among the higher civilizations, which they identified as Atlantis and Lemuria. It was this disciplined practice that opened the way for the inner voices to come more often and for other voices to come, all more clearly than my initial contact. Eventually I was able to fuse with some of these entities, as a "walk-in" of these celestial beings.

It didn't take long to discover that most of the New-Age spiritual thought was actually ancient evolutionary religions with new names, nothing really new at all, a lot of it just rediscovered. That a New Age was coming I had no doubt, but bringing most of the old into "the new hip consciousness" I knew was a big mistake. Most of the old concepts that people were accepting as the new answers to their lives and to the world's problems hadn't worked for the past two hundred thousand years and could not work now. Even if the world would be fresh and clean from a future holocaust, I remembered what Christ said about new wine skins being needed for new wine. Our planet needed a complete overhaul. I was about to be given some real answers via a book that the voices said was already in my possession, *The URANTIA Book*. These voices said that this book contained part of a revelation that was given to a channel, actually an interplanetary receiver, over a period of years. I could not deny all channeling because of some corrupt ones. Something was definitely happening to me and I looked forward to studying this revelation.

Hope Begins To Come

The book was fascinating and intellectually above any I had ever read before. Upon reading it, one had to come to the conclusion that no human could have written such concepts with such clarity and consistency. The language was new, at least for Urantia, which is the cosmic name for our planet. The beings who authored the book were of various orders, planes and worlds. Some were angelic, some of higher spiritual orders than even angels, some semimaterial and some nonmaterial. I would later find out that it was the midwayers who were responsible for our planet having the Fifth Epochal Revelation, of which this two thousand page book contained just a small part. Continuing Revelation would come through me. I could be used because of the language I had acquired by studying *The URANTIA Book* and by spiritually advancing to what is called the third **psychic circle**. That I would be chosen was an honor that was little appreciated by many of the people that I would try to reach with its message. It became a trial for me and my wife, Niánn, for many years, up until the final physical evacuation of our planet and the first appearance of our unseen friends to human eyes.

One day I made a phone call, trying to find a record producer. A man answered and told me his name. I had dialed the wrong number, but the kind gentleman talked to me and said that he had a *URANTIA Book* study group in his home each Tuesday night. I told him I was reading the book but didn't know study groups existed. I also realized that some unseen hand had dialed that number. He was a remarkable man. He was a retired brigadier general of the Marine Corps, attorney, and a Bible teacher in his Lutheran church for over thirty years. He was one of the world's leading authorities on *The URANTIA Book*. I was committed to learning this revelation, and I was blessed to be his student. Many times I have been led by God to reconsider decisions I had made previously. One of these decisions affected my music career because I had to devote more time to reading the book, and the black choir I was part of rehearsed on the same night as the Urantia Book study. And so, after a tearful goodbye I left the choir to join the study group. I left with a bang you might say. On Sunday the director had me sing a lead song, called *Waymaker*. It was a hand-clapping, foot-stomping gospel tune that had the whole church standing and shouting. I wondered why God asks us at times to make so difficult a sacrifice, in following what we believe to be God's will for us. Why couldn't I have both? Leaving that choir was one of the most difficult things I ever had to do. I prayed the Waymaker I was following appreciated my loyalty.

The Big Test

One day I received a phone call from one of the major record labels to which I had sent my album. A secretary said that they would like to make an appointment with me to talk to one of their big brass about my music. I was very excited for the next three days, until I went to the plush offices of the music kingdom at Universal City Plaza. I met with a man who introduced himself and told me he had been involved with many of the big names in music in the seventies as a personal manager and now with many as a record executive. The conversation went something like this:

"We really like your music and style and you've got a great selling voice."

Then he completely changed the subject.

"My wife and I belong to St. Mel's Catholic Church in Woodland Hills. I'm a deacon there."

My hopes were up. Maybe he was going to tell me next how badly our nation needed music that could raise the consciousness of its citizens. I thought the best of him and my heart ticked faster than normal.

"We think the spiritual aspect of your music is not for the general public. We don't think they would buy it."

"How do you know for sure unless you try it and give the music air play?", I shot back. He didn't answer but went ahead with his programmed speech.

"Our company is prepared to give you $100,000 in advance and produce two albums a year for you for the next five years. All we ask of you is that you change a few of the words in your songs and take out all that spiritual jargon. What's a few words here or there, and who really cares about our planet?"

Before I answered back, I thought for a few moments. I considered the lousy job I had as a message driver, wearing a funny red suit and fighting the L.A. traffic eight to ten hours a day, delivering messages to people who had "made it" in the system by compromising their values, never thinking they needed morality in their greedy world. I thought of how they treated me and others below them, as pieces of dung or objects to be used or bought. Some of them were musicians like me who didn't have half my talent. I thought of the people who looked at me as though I were a failure because I wasn't making the money they were, or wasn't locked into the system they were or didn't have the things they had. I thought of some of my closest friends and even my parents, who saw me as strange because I didn't do it their way. They never saw the nobility of my motives or that I was trying to make a difference on the planet. I thought of all the years as a kid that I spent alone practicing. I thought of the many heartbreaks along the way to get me to this offer. And then I silently asked God to give me an answer. It came to me quickly; the riches of the world that Satan[*] offered Christ and how he rejected them. I knew what I had to do.

"Sir, I truly appreciate your company's offer, but the world doesn't need another John Lennon or Elvis Presley. They really did nothing to uplift our troubled planet or bring about any real spiritual change. The world needs a Gabriel and with God's help and in his time that's what the world will get."

The big wheel shot back, "Kid, you're crazy. You may never get an opportunity like this again."

I knew he might be right. I had hoped to teach this older man that there was something to look forward to that had nothing to do with this corrupt and greedy world, and I very sincerely said,

"Sir, a Divine New Order is coming upon this planet, a just order, you might say, where all dreams come true if they include the common good of your fellow brothers and sisters. One day you will hear my music being played around this planet on all of the radio stations and television networks, for they will be owned by the administration of a just system and operated by people with concern for our planet and the people on it. Goodbye."

It would take fifteen years before the hope that I spoke of would happen. How many times when my family and I were near poverty did I wonder if I had made the right choice. I hated a world run on money, and I didn't do well in it. I had so many doubtful moments wondering if God had forsaken me. But it was not God who had forsaken man, but people who had forsaken God and their brothers and sisters on this planet. Truly we are "thy brother's keeper," and every decision that one makes for selfishness and greed affects every human being upon this fallen planet. I would come to understand the depth of that truth in the years to come.

Betrayal

I had been forsaken by friends and my two wives, partly of course, my fault, but never had I experienced an outright preconceived plan by someone to betray me from the beginning of a relationship. I had seen it done by cheap con artists in Hollywood, lustful men promising parts in movies to pretty, hopeful actresses for a night in bed, or a producer who never produced anything but a scam, promising record contracts with phoney screen tests where

the musician paid to have his song recorded. I thought I had seen
it all until I met Miss X. I was selling women's shoes in Beverly
Hills, and she walked in one day. She was in her fifties but didn't
look it. She first came on to me sexually, and it worked. I was
lonely and needy in all areas. When she found out I was spiritually more mature than the average man and that I was a hopeful
singer/song-writer, she worked on both interests to feed me the bait
that would lead me to be used by her until she was tired of me and
found another sucker.

"I'm a spiritual advisor and a dream maker. I help make
dreams come true for people like yourself," she said.

She listened intently to my tales of woe about my Hollywood
experience and said she knew people in the business who could
help me. I had heard that before so I wasn't impressed, but she
was good at giving people false hopes, and I was very vulnerable
at the time. She acted as though she believed in me, so I talked
on. I told her the desires of my heart and secrets I usually didn't
tell strangers. The guides told me that after I had passed a test I
would soon be meeting a past Indian wife named Tenache who had
been with me in a previous life when I was an Apache. She looked
a little like an Indian that day and even had a headband on. So she
picked up on this one quickly.

"Oh I know that I've lived many Indian lives before."

That was all I needed to hear. I gave her my heart, hook, line
and sinker: she would send me cards signed "Tenache." I spent
most of my free time in bed with her and didn't bother to ask the
guides who came to me if she was Tenache or not. She even took
me to a psychic friend of hers who claimed to be able to tap into
the Akashic records (the heavenly book of life). She said that I
was her long lost twin flame* and that we had shared many lives.
Now, I wasn't that gullible, but the sex was good, and I had fallen
into the lust of the flesh. My spiritual eyes and heart were blind.
As it goes when one gets off the spiritual path for even a short
while, I fell deeply into her web. I didn't read *The URANTIA
Book* or attend meetings, thinking that in time I'd turn her on to the
Fifth Epochal Revelation, and we would spend the rest of our lives

together, I, a famous singer (thanks to her contacts) and an influential spiritual leader. Ha ha! We were a great "spiritual couple" under the sheets. We even prayed together on occasion, particularly about the oceanside apartment she wanted. I was the energy and catalyst she needed to get out of the city. She said we could live together and I could continue my music career and bring in some money by playing music around the area. So for weeks we looked and finally found a place. I had given up my apartment, planning to move in with her. She asked me to give her what little money I had left and my last paycheck from the shoe store. (I was fired because of the stock market drop that year) After I gave her everything I had and she put money down on the apartment, she told me I was no longer welcome to move in with her, but she wanted to stay friends, actually, to have an extra stud in her stable. I was heartsick. I had fallen in love with this woman and had never seen through her deception. She was the final blow to me in California, and I had no energy left to fight the Hollywood greed machine. My heart and mind turned to Arizona.

CHAPTER 7

THE SUPERSTITION MOUNTAINS—RECONTACT IS MADE

I had roamed the foothills of some of the mountains in Arizona before with an old acquaintance who had a studio in Apache Junction. He was a famous artist, Ted DeGrazia. He died a few years later. He had lived with the Pima Indians and loved riding on horseback through the mountains. As I thought about my time with him, I remembered one thing he had told me. "These Superstition mountains are magical and mysterious. Many who go in, never come back again." I felt these mountains drawing me.

I stopped over in Tempe, Arizona, to visit a group of *URANTIA Book* readers whom I had contacted when I was in California. A door was opened for me to stay a week or so. I needed time to figure out how I was going to exist in the mountains, as I was no mountain man. These new friends were far too intellectually oriented to believe my experiences with unseen celestial visitors. I wanted desperately to tell them, but I knew that I would only be ridiculed and considered a fool. Several years later, when I did go public with part of the experience, I was not believed by those intelligent, but closed-minded souls. It was strange that they read a book that talked about the millions of inhabited planets in our local universe, but they could not accept the fact that whatever is out there just might have wanted to communicate with little old us, you or me, or our next door neighbor. Even my dear friend and teacher of *The URANTIA Book* in California didn't believe in space craft from other worlds. In the years to come, I felt all alone, with the exception of my friend and mate, Niánn, who believed with me during the faith years before many of the earth changes that Celestial Overcontrol predicted came to pass. Their very doubts blocked the door to the reality and to the possible contact with these marvelous superhuman personalities; These unseen mentors only wanted human souls who were brave enough to venture away from the established thoughtforms, traditions, dogmas and religions of misinformed and confused humanity. The **Ashtar Command** of the Pleiades would call these contactees "eagles." The name was given by Paladin, the second in command of the space fleet, who had repersonalized on the earth plane and had lived several lives here; one as a Nez Percé Indian, in which his name was Sky Hawk. A hawk, like an eagle, can fly alone and doesn't need the flock. I had been told that we too must be able to fly alone with the new truth that our extraterrestrial friends were attempting to give us which would help bring about the changes our planet so desperately needed. I had so much to learn and so many changes to make myself. Soon Sky Hawk himself would tell me these very things.

I decided one day to go to the local food co-op in Tempe, and as I looked at the bulletin board, a flyer jumped out at me. It said that a community somewhere in the Arizona mountains wanted men and women to come and be part of a work/study program for at least three months. My heart danced. This was it. I contacted them and made arrangements to go there on Thanksgiving Day. Twenty of us met in a small country store to make connections with the community's leaders and some of the members, who drove us in their four-wheel-drive vehicles ten miles into the desert mountain region. I had left my car at a deserted ranch and didn't see it again for about two and a half months. The nearest town was about thirty miles away via the main road.

Apart from wilderness survival skills and learning to live off what the land had to offer, the community also taught metaphysical principles. It was my first experience living in a tepee during the middle of winter with only a wood stove to give heat. Waking up in the early morning was always an experience. After living in southern California, I had a hard time getting used to the cold. The afternoons warmed up, but the sun went down behind the mountain at about 3:30 p.m. and it got dark around 6:00. I had plenty of time to commune with nature and God, and I made the best of this time of solitude.

Those who lived in the community, and those students who came to learn, all prayed, ate and sang together daily. It was a beautiful experience, with people actually trying an alternative lifestyle and really working on loving each other. Yes, we had our personality conflicts, but it did seem that these people tried a little harder to be allowing and loving. Forgiving each other when we were hurt could be so difficult for our proud hearts. Contrary to the popular belief that "love means never having to say you're sorry," we found that sincere apology and asking for forgiveness was a necessity for harmonious living. At the time, I thought that I wanted to stay there for the rest of my life. I truly loved many of the people, but soon my plans were to change again.

My job was supplying wood to the individual tepees and other simple living quarters and helping to construct a deer fence. One snowy day I was alone, as usual, splitting wood at the far corner of the land when I felt a presence come near me. I heard a voice outside of myself say, "Hello Gabriel." I turned around to greet whoever was there, thinking it must be someone from the group or a hiker. It was a strong masculine voice, but I didn't see anyone. It was just too beautiful outside in the snow to be frightened, so I stopped and asked who was there. I first asked God to protect me and then waited, shutting my eyes and letting the snow fall upon my face. Once in awhile I would look up for one more glimpse of the snowflakes that were coming down. After a few moments of silent waiting, I heard a voice within me say, "We would like to use your body to speak to you. Would you give us permission?" I somehow felt that this was what God wanted me to do. So after asking how, they said to just move my mind back as far as possible and they would use my voice box. I did as I was instructed and felt the presence of more than one being around me. Soon I felt a strong essence in my mind and body, but I felt that I was also there, in control, so I had no fear, being on sacred Indian land of the Dineh—the People. I should have guessed at how they would introduce themselves, as I was interested in Indian spirituality at the time.

"My name is Sky Hawk, and I have had several Native American lives."

My voice was actually speaking. I was listening to my own voice, and I knew I was in some kind of trance; yet totally aware of what was happening.

"Is this called channeling?" I asked in my mind.

"That is a contemporary understanding of a very scientific interdimensional communication, based upon ancient beliefs of spiritualism and **mediumship**. We are not only spirits, we have bodies. Some in our administration, however, are more spirit than flesh; but we will teach you these things in the proper sequence and time-space frame."

I wondered what was meant by all that.

I decided to tell no one there about the incident; besides, I thought I might be flipping out. A few days went by and I was working on the deer fence again when I felt someone near me. I quickly prayed and shut my eyes as before and backed as far away from my body as I could. I then felt an urge to speak and out came another entity's communication. It did not give its name. "I am a finaliter, sent by Michael* of Nebadon to help the people of your fallen planet. You have much to learn. You must learn to become a clear vessel for our transmission to be one hundred percent accurate. You can interrupt us at any time or stop us. Some who will come will be much different than others. We are under orders not to allow you to see us until the proper time. I am the commander of a fleet of three thousand spacecraft that will participate in the evacuation of your planet when the change point comes. You are needed to help us prepare for this evacuation. It will not be an easy task. You will be called a fraud and a deceiver, and you will find few to follow you until the earth changes or chaos of some kind begins to touch the lives of your countrymen. You have the beginning data of the Fifth Epochal Revelation within your mind. We can use that and add to it to help change those who are willing to listen. We will make clear the concepts of the revelation and give you continuing revelation through experience.

As you begin to walk into the fourth dimension, you can teach others to do the same. I leave you now."

Sky Hawk began to come on a daily basis. He told me that I would be meeting a wife from a past Apache life in which my name had been Gentle Eagle. I was amazed.

"Your spirit has remained the same for many incarnations now, as a result of spiritual advancement. This woman will be a complementary polarity to you, and together you will be teachers of the Continuing Fifth Epochal Revelation."

"What is her name? What does she look like? How old is she?" I eagerly asked.

"All of these questions cannot be answered, for you must know her in a higher way."

I had read what some authors wrote about soul mates* and twin flames and was delighted that my time had come to meet mine. I did sense I had one. In the years to come, I would learn the cosmic reality of what would become known as **complementary polarities**. My female complement would become one of the world's leading authorities on the subject, which was part of the Fifth Epochal Revelatory truth that was to continually come to and through me from these higher beings of other worlds and dimensions.

I began checking out all of the available young women who came for the weekend retreats. I knew I would be meeting her soon. I also thought I knew how the dark forces worked against something good that was about to happen, but I had no idea how deceiving the evil unseen forces could be. And I too often forgot that we were all in such a battle.

The very next weekend, one of the most beautiful dark-haired women I had ever seen anywhere showed up for a weekend retreat. She was part Mexican and part Navajo. Needless to say, I thought this was the one Sky Hawk told me was coming. I was elated. I spent as much time with her as I could, for I knew she was only staying for a few days. Her name was Maria. One night we talked after dinner.

"Do you believe in past lives?" I quickly got to the point.

"Our group believes in Jesus Christ and the Bible. 'It is appointed for man and woman to be born, to die, and then the judgement'."

I knew that verse well, as I used to spout it all of the time, just like Maria. She continued,

"We are in the New-Age movement because we don't believe in the rapture or institutional Christianity, but we do not accept all that's in the New Age."

"Good," I responded, "neither do I."

She was so pretty. I didn't want to argue with her about reincarnation. I didn't believe in it either. I did know, however, that there were millions of souls who had been incarnated back to this planet several times. The celestial guides had given me a "video tape" of a few of mine. I would later learn directly from them that the words they used to explain such phenomena were: "reconstruction," **"repersonalization,"** and **"rematerialization."** Each method was much different from the other, and numerous variables of spiritual ascension of the soul would determine what method the universe administrators would order for a particular soul.

All I could think of at the time was making love to this beauty. So I changed the subject to the environment and we talked about how messed up the planet was. Like most people, we never really got down to the bottom line, whatever that might be for the individual at the time, avoiding any issue that might raise the other person's hair a little, particularly spiritual hairs. I played the game well with Maria. She was quite good too. I guess she also learned how not to step on toes. I couldn't have been more blind at the time, and more in lust.

When I got back to my tepee, I was ashamed of myself for not being sincere with her, leading her on, when all of the time I knew something was the matter with our communication on a very necessary spiritual level. But when I saw her again, I resorted to my beating-around-the-bush conversation: she looked so good! Even though she left without any physical contact between us, I knew that given the right circumstances and time, I could be making love to that beauty. I had made plans with her to visit her community in Phoenix at the first opportunity.

The very next weekend my true spiritual complement arrived with her three children. She was special and attractive, but not dark like I thought she should be. She seemed very Anglo and I was looking for a Native American. Besides, she had three children from a previous marriage and I wanted no part of that reality. That is, until her oldest daughter told me about her mother growing up on several Indian reservations and teaching on the San Carlos Apache reservation, where I had lived a past life according to Sky Hawk, and had spent many weekends in this life when I had lived in Tucson. I started a conversation and found her to be very spiritually mature. Her name was Nancy. She told me, and made an open announcement to the group, that she had resigned from her teaching position at Globe High School because she felt God was calling her to do some other kind of spiritual work. She had no idea how, where or with whom she was to do this work, but she planned on selling her home and moving from Globe, in search of God's will for her life. Since her family and financial security were there, I had great respect for her already; she had the courage to venture into the unknown. I knew that kind of call. "Many are called, but few [choose and] are chosen." After eighteen years of following that kind of call, I had to say that it wasn't getting any easier. I knew Nancy was in for growth and loneliness, for few of her family and friends would understand her, or the decisions that God would ask her to make in order to follow that call.

I visited her in Globe as soon as I could. Her home reflected her Indian life on the reservations, with a variety of baskets, pottery, rugs and paintings spread throughout. She was an intelligent and loving soul. If she had any faults at all, I thought that she was too trusting of people, too naive about the dark side of most of us. She could be easily used, and I found out soon that she had been. But she prayed for those who used her and tried to love them, even though they would still try to use and mistreat her. I thought that when God made her he must have thrown the mold away. Everyone loved her, except those few who hated her goodness. Those kind of people did the same to Jesus Christ when they crucified him. I found myself wanting to protect and teach her about the evil in man's heart. I guess from the very beginning I loved her because she loved all she met and only saw the good in them. I even told her all the negative things about me I could think of, but that didn't scare her off.

We communicated on a very high level, like we had known each other for years. Soon I forgot all about Maria, as I realized that I had been more in lust than in love. I felt a peace about continuing a relationship with Nancy, even though I knew intuitively that her children would not accept me. I just felt God somehow would work it out for the good of all. Their father had been talking to Nancy about taking the children because he wanted to be a full-time parent. This was difficult for her, letting her children go, but she also felt that this was God's will. As she was leaving her security for the unknown, the children would be better provided for financially with their father. I knew that it would be a lifelong commitment with her and so did she. Both of us wanted God's will above our own desires. I knew that she was the one spoken of by Sky Hawk and the other guides, and she felt that I was the one spoken of in a psychic reading she had received a few months before I met her. So our new adventure together began.

CHAPTER 8

MEETING THE MIDWAYERS

I told Nancy all about what had happened to me concerning Sky Hawk and the other celestial visitors. Gradually, over the years they gave back memories, depending on how well I could be trusted with the information and reality of what had happened to me in previous existences. It wasn't until later, that I remembered being on a spaceship, or what had happened in Mexico. But I couldn't deny the experience in the Arizona mountains and felt that the beings, whoever they were, were real. Because of them, Nancy and I had met. That, for me, was beginning proof of their reality. One evening in our meditation time together, I decided to try and reach these unseen beings. I asked for God's protection as usual and left it up to him as to whom he would send. Soon, both Nancy and I felt a different energy in the room. I listened for a voice and soon heard one say hello and give me two names.

"We are Gabron and Niánn, primary midwayers assigned to your watchcare. Usually secondary midwayers attend to these administrations, but your task is special and your planet is in grave danger."

I wondered if what I had just heard was real, as we did not hear audible voices. So I asked Nancy if she had heard the female midwayer's name.

"It sounded like Neon, like the light bulb."

I asked if that was all she had heard, and her answer was in the affirmative. Even though I had heard more, I was overjoyed that Nancy had picked up that much. I asked these particular entities to spell out their names.

"G-a-b-r-o-n and N-i-a-n-n, and it is I, the male of the two who speaks to you. Nancy's cosmic name is also Niánn and from now on she should be called by that. It means "cosmic woman of grace." We were given birth by your ancestors who were the staff of the **Caligastia one hundred**, who were here from other worlds many thousands of years ago."

"Do you live in a spacecraft?" I asked.

"No, we have never left this planet. We await the first stages of light and life on Urantia. Our job is to help teach you the solution to the world's various problems. We are in contact, and have been for thousands of years, with beings that have far surpassed your planet in its spiritual and social evolution; but we have not been allowed, until now, to contact humans like yourself in this manner because they did not have the mindal capacity to understand the answers. Because of the vocabulary you have of the beginning Fifth Epochal Revelation, and some understanding of its concepts, we and others can use you as a vessel of communication for true change on your planet."

"But why me? There are others who know the book better than I, and they also have the vocabulary," I inquired.

"There are many reasons why the Universe Directors chose you. The majority of readers have followed interpretations from the founding organization that are not completely correct. You are, and have been for many repersonalizations, a free spirit and open to hear from the Spirit of Truth* that our Universe Father* left here for all to understand cosmic reality. You are honest with yourself, with your neighbors and with your God. You are not likely to accept even our truth without deep introspection and soul searching with the Spirit of Truth. You have done this ever since you asked this Spirit to come into your present reality.

"You and Niánn are of the **Cosmic Reserve Corps of Destiny**. Your tasks will be to awaken others of the corps, Urantian and cosmic. Many of them will be called **starseed** by the New-Age teachers and channels of lower-plane communication; but in reality, in the universe of Nebadon,* even some first-time Urantians have starseed genetics. If you have been here before, you are not from this planet. Do you know the ascension plan of Michael for the system of Satania in his universe?"

I answered, "I do understand the seven mansion worlds and the inward journey through space toward Havona* and Paradise."*

"This is good, but there are many on your planet who are not originally from Nebadon. Many have repersonalized here for special assignments. Because they are not from your local universe they are not required to adhere to the ascension plan for Nebadon, Urantia (Earth) and most of its residents.

"This information is Continuing Fifth Epochal Revelation, and you must continue to study the Fifth Epochal Revelation that is now in print (*The URANTIA Book*) so that we and others who will speak to and through you can use that data to widen your understanding. We want to bring to Urantia new concepts of Continuing Fifth Epochal Revelation at the highest level. Eventually when you are at the level of the first psychic circle, we can complete what is already written. Your worst enemies will be those in the "spiritual" groups. You will not be accepted as a true Fifth Epochal Revelation channel until the mid-nineties. You and Niánn will have many years of being accused of fraud and deception. It will be very difficult and lonely. There will probably come a period when you yourselves even deny our reality."

"But why would I do that?" I asked.

"Because your path will not be easy. Many of your **cosmic children** will be brought to you, along with sisters and brothers of cosmic origin. You will even meet a past-life mother and father that you love very much, but it is doubtful that they will accept your work until the trials come to your country. Some will stay and work with you for awhile, but when the real tests come, they will deny you, us and the work. You will suffer much verbal abuse, and much of it will come from those to whom you have shown nothing but love. The majority of them will be cosmic family. You see, it is the will of the Universal Father[*] of Paradise that members of the same family units live, work and grow together. This is called the union of souls.[*] When this happens on planets in the third dimension, such as Urantia, and particularly on the thirty-seven planets which fell during the rebellion of Satania, then the planet is ready for the pre-stages of light and life."

"Do you mean the promised return of Jesus Christ?" I asked.

"First there will be the appointment of the new **Planetary Prince** of Urantia, whom we speculate will be **Machiventa Melchizedek**. The **Extension Schools** and government of Melchizedek, will be established using human personalities like yourself. You will have the **mandate of the Bright and Morning Star** of Salvington, * an overcontrol **mandate**; and another couple you will be meeting in the future will be the first of others to have the mandate of Machiventa Melchizedek as **Vicegerent First Ambassadors** to the Planetary Prince. Either Christ Michael will return as he promised or Trinity Teacher Sons* from Paradise will come. Michael will come, but we are not sure of the sequence."

"When do you think this will happen?"

"No more than ten years or around May of the year 2000 or 2001 AD," answered Gabron.

"That is the date that was told to a prophet of this century by the name of Richard Kreninger; he started the Stelle Community in Illinois and another in Texas," I replied excitedly.

"That is correct; the date is accurate according to cosmic alignment of the first seven planets of Satania to be settled in light and life. The earth will be totally cleansed of all negative **diotribes** within dark souls. The energies that will enter the physical earth as a result of this alignment will cause the plates to make their final shifts. There will be few survivors left on Urantia when this happens."

I drew a conclusion, "So, we must be taken away first."

The midwayer's answer was, "Correct, and as many as will harken to our words and the voices of many prophets of old in these last days of your present civilization."

For many months afterward Niánn and I developed a relationship with the midwayers. In the meantime, we were being guided to Prescott, Arizona, to live. We were told that we would probably be there for two years, no longer than three. I could have stayed a lifetime, as the area and the home we purchased were beautiful. But many factors would lead to our moving after two years, just as the guides had said. It was not so much my willingness to be in God's perfect will as it was more the unwillingness of others to be in God's perfect will. It is much easier to follow a Godless reality, an energy or force, for in this manner there is no rule to follow but your own; you plan your own life. Then there were those who believed in a personal God but just didn't seem to be able to hear from that God very well. They picked and chose their reality, just like those who claimed that God was an energy. When the real tests came so many failed, mostly because Urantia consists of billions of individuals trapped in wrong thinking and hidden agendas. Lucifer,* the fallen system ruler of Satania believed in his Creator Father; however, he didn't believe in God's program for him or for the other created beings of the grand universe.

"What does this all have to do with solving the problems of our planet?" you ask. "This is all so intangible and unseen. The existence of Lucifer cannot be proven. Even God remains a mystery to most." The midwayers had told us very clearly that one must come to the conclusion that there was evil in this world and thus, wrong actions. In his rebellion, Lucifer taught that there was no evil, all was relative, and there was no absolute truth; and so billions of beings of various orders fell into these lies. About 200,000 years ago self-assertion and unbridled liberty had also been presented by Lucifer and been accepted by these fallen ones, and these Luciferic teachings would be accepted by many up until the change point on Urantia. These falsehoods produced artists and heros who told the public, "I'll do it my way." Mr. and Mrs. America followed their example, and so did the children, resulting in an explosive situation on the planet during the change point in the late nineties.

I begged the midwayers to become visible, but they said that it was not time and that it would actually spoil my education and growth on this planet as an "agondonter" (one who follows God's will by faith). "Agon" were the first four letters to both agondonter and agony. I remember the word well because as the midwayers had taught us, agony is often the initial knowing of being in God's perfect will, moment to moment, as opposed to the memories of being out of His will. We discovered that soon after moving into his will the feeling of agony changed to emotions of joy and relief and a sense of deep peace. It made me think twice about decisions and slowed me down before I spoke like a fool. Most souls who were aware they had guides, had midwayers, but often these people thought these beings were deceased relatives or spirits of past souls who had lived on this planet. Midwayers are not human, nor are they pure spirit. The primary midwayers are the offspring of the one hundred superhuman mortals from other worlds who came with the Planetary Prince; the secondary midwayers originated much later from an offspring of **Adam and Eve** (Material Sons and Daughters*) and a descendent of the one hundred superhumans who had come thousands of years before. These midwayers remain on Earth until we humans get it together enough to bring our planet into the pre-stages of light and life. According to the midwayers, up until November of 1988 our planet could have taken a quantum leap or spiritual shift in consciousness. The change then would have come in a much gentler way, without so much catastrophe to individuals and to the planet. But not enough people could move out of their old ways of thinking, (thoughts create both pollution and healing) their antiquated religious institutions, or their dogmatic views of reality which were based upon politics or social conditions. The root of the problems on Urantia was not the poisoned environment, but the dirty and polluted minds of the inhabitants. And the ignorant millions of people who were God-conscious but could not break away from tradition, what about them? They were just as much a cause of the problems, for they unknowingly were a part of the evil that keeps millions of souls in bondage to false beliefs perpetuated by leaders who enjoy their seats of power and prestige. Do all roads lead to the same God, as many have said? What many of these roads lead to is war, poverty, injustice of all sorts, environmental pollution and spiritual confusion. Should all Catholics become Protestants or all Christians, Buddhists? Or vice versa? None of these systems of religious thought had really made a dent in the real problems of our planet. So, our question to the midwayers and other higher intelligences was, "Where do we go from here?"

"The Fifth Epochal Revelation," was their answer, "that which is already in print and that which will continue to come to Urantia for the next forty years. It contains all of the truths of the previous evolutionary religions and points out their non-truths. It gives the pure teachings of our Creator Son,* Christ Michael, who is Jesus to you Urantians;* and it speaks of the cosmology of his universe and his Father's grand universe. It reveals some of the worlds in the grand universe and some of the beings that exist on them. It explains the vast administration of the grand universe so that you humans on Urantia can feel secure in a friendly and ordered universe, even though the majority of the occupants on your planet are presently in rebellion. Getting the writings into your hands is hard enough, making the proper changes in your life according to the concepts of cosmic truth and reality is the real problem. Putting that spoken statement into practical service with the one you love is another thing altogether," said Gabron in one transmission. "We have found that humans say one thing and show in their actions something else. All of you are your brother's keeper; and when the majority of you can learn what this means on the highest level, your planet will change for the better, but not before. Many who do practice love to the degree that it is real, are stuck within a framework of religious dogmas that have other wrong realities which cause just as much damage to the one you are loving and giving to and usually negates the good you may have done for that person. It is like giving hungry people food without knowing that the food contains a bacteria that will slowly poison them."

Over the months and years to come, I would learn the problems in their specifics from the guides and from actual experiences with cosmic family members and others who would be sent to us by Providence. Learning to trust the guides was not easy, even for Niánn and me, for they very often pointed out flaws in our characters that we did not want to deal with, or they would have us do things that our lower natures interpreted as unpleasant.

I became a private channel (actually I was an Audio Fusion Material Complement) for these beings to speak with the humans under their watchcare. I did this reluctantly because people would say that they wanted to hear the truth, but when it was given to them, they had a million and one reasons for rejecting it. I too made my own excuses when these celestial counselors told me where I had to change things in my life. I learned in my early days in metaphysical groups that the phony psychics or the ones with little spiritual understanding would either tell people what they wanted to hear (by picking up the vibrations of their desires and thoughts) or they would simply lie. But these particular psychics were very popular. Everyone wanted to come into some financial windfall and most, both single and married alike, were still looking for their soul mate or twin flame, their Prince Charming or Cinderella. The guides who came through me told these people that their proper mates and complements were there for them in the future, but that tremendous changes had to be made in their individual lives in order for the Universe Supervisors* to have them meet each other. Very few of those people were willing to make those changes. Also, many couples were already in relationships that they did not belong in, some with children. The problems were vast. Much of the planet's confusion could have been healed in the proper relationship of the family unit, each member knowing his or her appropriate place. With complementary-polarity unions between husband and wife and soul-mate unions between friends and co-workers, all can be of like mind and purpose, working, playing and growing together, but each still being individualistic. This was missing on our planet. With the help of our unseen but much felt friends, Niánn and I committed ourselves to educate individuals with these truths and realities in a world on the brink of destruction: truth and answers that very few wanted to hear.

CHAPTER 9

THE PLEIADIAN CONNECTION

The Ashtar Command

One evening about six months after making contact with the midwayers in 1987, Gabron said that another entity wanted to speak to Niánn and me. I agreed, having complete trust in them by now. Soon a very powerful personality, much different from the midwayers, entered my body. I felt safe, however, before he ever spoke and told me that he was a Father-circuited being of the light.

"My name is Ashtar and I am originally from the Pleiades. I am a mortal who has become a finaliter from Paradise. I am in command of a vast space fleet of thousands of vessels called the Ashtar Command. I am under the authority of Michael of Salvington (capital of the universe of Nebadon) and his first administrator, Gabriel, the Bright and Morning Star. I take orders only from them or their direct superiors. My function is to help bring Continuing Fifth Epochal Revelation to Urantia and to help the angelic forces in the evacuation of humans during the earth changes to come."

The memory of my close encounter in Mexico had been erased from my mind at that time, and this was harder for me to believe than the reality of the midwayers. I had been familiar with the Billy Meier sightings and encounters in Switzerland from reading about them; they were also Pleiadian visitors. Spaceships! This I didn't expect. I cut Ashtar off and prayed to God for guidance. For many hours Niánn and I talked about the experience. Since my memory banks were devoid of the encounter in Mexico, I had never told Niánn about it; but I did remember the distant sighting of a vessel that changed directions in the Arizona mountains.

Niánn also told me about the sighting she had seen on Mingus Mountain one summer, and I recalled reading about many other people's encounters with UFOs. So I asked the midwayers to come and explain. They told me that they work directly with the Ashtar Command, which includes mortals on various levels of ascension status, as well as with other superhuman and angelic personalities. The leaders of this command, Ashtar, Zoltec and Paladin, were finaliters, presently in seventh stage morontia bodies* so that they could exist in physical surroundings, like spacecrafts.

"The Ashtar Command is, you might say, in Christian terminology like the hand of Christ ready to rapture the church at the time of the great tribulation," explained Gabron.

The midwayers said there were other methods that could be used to evacuate a planet's inhabitants, but because of our fallen state, and our evolution in body and spirit we could not utilize these methods. Urantia was several hundred thousand years behind in development. When the higher or spiritual body is fully developed, the physical follows suit. To spell it out more simply, we were walking around in "degenerate mechanisms." (The midwayers have quite a sense of humor)

After several days of soul searching, I decided to allow Ashtar to speak to me again. So I asked Michael to send Ashtar, if he was of God.

"I appreciate your sense of loyalty to your God and the forces of light. This is why we allow you to cut us off. We have no real control over you. If what we say is not truly agreed upon with the Fragment of the Father* and Spirit of Truth within, then we are not of the light. But beings of the light can also be misunderstood by a channel or person who is not ready to die to self and get off the cosmic fence. This is why the highest and purest messages from the Universe Supervisors can come only to tried and tested vessels, and so you have much pain to go through."

I didn't like that message at all. I thought that I had experienced enough pain in my life, and so I shut him off again, for several weeks this time. I also turned off the midwayers who I felt would tell me the same thing. Why me? Why didn't they pick on someone else? How about some master in India or Tibet or somewhere "sacred"? We in America had become so comfortable and complacent. So what if people were starving in other countries and dying off from diseases that we in Western Civilization had long since cured? So what if twenty-five thousand people died in an earthquake in China? That night we could have a barbecue. In our fat country of American materialism the Haves controlled the Have Nots. The Haves allowed the Have Nots to work in unfulfilling jobs in order to buy the things they didn't really need. But once the Have Nots tried to get in on a piece of the pie, to get a position of influence, the Haves closed the doors. If the Haves thought they could own an individual, then that person might get in, but if they thought they could not control the person, that person became their enemy. So few dared to dream of great things, or dared to think they could make a difference in the world. After I had gone through these thoughts of realization, I decided to get back into the battle and stop feeling sorry for myself. I decided to accept the challenge of being a Audio Fusion Material Complement of the light and allow these beings to give the answers that few wanted to hear.

Global Sovereignty Will Prevent Global Wars

"Good evening, my friend. My name is Paladin and I am second in command to Ashtar.[5] I come to speak to you this evening on law, liberty and sovereignty. It is written:

"If one man craves freedom—liberty—he must remember that *all* other men long for the same freedom. Groups of such liberty-loving mortals cannot live together in peace without becoming subservient to such laws, rules, and regulations as will grant each person the same degree of freedom while at the same time safeguarding an equal degree of freedom for all of his fellow

---

[5]Paladin was made Chief of Finaliters on Urantia in January 1992, basically because of the ascension of Gabriel of Sedona and other of his seed. This is technically explained in Paper 226 of *The Cosmic Family, Volume I*.

mortals. If one man is to be absolutely free, then another must become an absolute slave. And the relative nature of freedom is true socially, economically, and politically. Freedom is the gift of civilization made possible by the enforcement of LAW." (*The URANTIA Book,* page 1490:4)

When men who make the laws divorce themselves, from their Creator and the will of the Universal Father, unjust laws are created. And these men gain office because they are voted in by the majority of people who have also disconnected themselves from universe sovereignty.

"Christ said concerning these times, 'There shall be wars and rumors of wars—nation will rise against nation—just as long as the world's political sovereignty is divided and unjustly held by a group of nation-states.... But global wars will go on until the government of mankind is created. Global sovereignty will prevent global wars—nothing else can.... all notions of the supposed rights of self-determination [must be abandoned].'"
(*The URANTIA Book,* page 1490:6, 7, 8)

I interrupted Paladin here and said, "But what about Nelson Mandela and his movement; is he not a great leader?"

"He should be trying to free the people of the planet, not just South Africa. It has to be a global movement, not just a national one. The context has to become planetary. All of you humans on Urantia are citizens of the planet and must begin to see yourselves as such. The supposed rights of self-determination must be abandoned by individual peoples. War is not man's great and terrible disease; war is a symptom, a result. The real disease is the virus of national sovereignty. World law must come into being and must be enforced by world government, the sovereignty of all the people on this planet. Under global administration the national parties will be afforded a real opportunity to realize and enjoy the personal liberties of genuine democracy. The fallacy of self-determination will be ended. With global regulation of money and trade will come the new era of worldwide peace. Soon a global language may evolve and the hope of a global religion, or at least a religion with a global perspective. Collective security will never afford a lasting peace until all humankind is included. The political sovereignty of representative human government will bring rest to troubled Earth. The spiritual brotherhood of man will forever insure good will among all people. This is the way of the Universal Father of All; there is no other way."

The Cosmic Family
Getting Over The Basic Problems

Over the months we found Paladin to be a very strong-speaking grandfather type with a great sense of humor. He said that his job was not to placate us humans with soft words and untrue hopes about our planet. He said that strong words were needed to awaken people, so that they could change by coming out of their complacency and false pride. This, he stated, included me.

"Most of the people of your planet believe in God, but in that belief they murder each other in God's name, lie, cheat and steal, all feeling that they are right with their individual God. Those of you who have existed on other planets and are here now have forgotten that you are of one family. Those many billions here for the first time have never known what a family truly is and how wonderful it is to be surrounded by loved ones: grandfathers, grandmothers, uncles, aunts, cousins, brothers, sisters, and children, who care about you and would help you when needed," explained Paladin.

I knew what it was like to grow up around my family back in Pittsburgh, Pennsylvania. I had known both my great-grandparents, and also my grandparents on my mother's side. I realized they all loved me and all of their grandchildren, and they made us feel special. When I grew older and needed my car repaired, I called my cousin Vince; if we needed a plumber, we called another relative. Families could live a lot cheaper when love and cooperation were working within the extended family community.

Paladin continued, "Today in your planet's hour of need, the Universe Father is trying to bring cosmic family back together again to work and serve each other and humanity. If you seek the Father's perfect will, those of you now on Urantia who are originally from another universe or from other superhuman origins, will be brought together to meet your first parents, brothers and sisters. You parents will meet your first sons and daughters, and those of you who have grown spiritually together in the past on Earth and on other planets, will be reunited to live in communities and to teach the principles of the Divine New Order on Urantia. Many of these teachings have to do with proper relationships between family members, which lead to right tribal government and global rule. Many of the great civilizations of the past functioned in this forgotten order. The Dalamatians* understood the cosmic family and the divine authority of the universe. A family needs a head and a body with arms and feet. When people come together today for environmental or other humanitarian concerns, most want to be the head; and those who do assume leadership are not the ones chosen by God to lead. Your Urantia governments attest to this truth, as do the majority of your religious and economic institutions. As the Native Americans say, 'the grandfathers will return to the tribes to rule them again.'

"And so thousands of souls are repersonalizing this century to become communities first and then the cities of the future. But it will not be easy even for them, for they must find their God first, over and above all the false teaching in both the New Age and all religions. Then they must die to their selfishness. For many reasons such as self-will and misplaced loyalties, many will fail to find themselves or the perfect will of the Universal Father. Humans have a hard time discovering God's path in life, for they do not override their desires, usually based on lust (not necessarily sexual) of some sort. Even though a desire or motive is good, that may not mean it is of God. Many good works have been done in the name of God, when greater things could have been accomplished if God's plan had been followed. Many who achieve financial success are failures in the eyes of the Universe Directors, who have been trying to lead them into the simplicity of God's will. In Western Civilization millions of souls seek careers for financial security and fail to learn the true security of being in God's perfect will. Many who try to walk the true path for awhile, give up because of impatience. God's timetable is usually a lot longer than your own. In America where one may be more able to seek one's true destiny because of more freedoms, the enemy becomes sin. Americans as a whole do not want to deal with or believe in the reality of evil, sin and iniquity.

"So millions of Catholics believe that they can go on being their dark 'normal' selves, as long as they confess their sins once in awhile to a priest or receive last rites before they die. Protestants feel that because they have been saved, born again or baptized, that this event has earned for them entrance into eternity or Heaven. Go to church on Sundays, and on Monday it's okay to act like the son of the devil. The world is full of conformists, people who play the game well within the framework of what is accepted. What your planet needs are eagles, those who fly alone without pleasing the crowd. Those few brave souls can bring about change on your planet of clones and robots."

There was that word again, "eagles." Why was it for the past year I had felt a fixation for the eagle? I didn't remember at the time, but when I was taken by Overcontrol they told me that the coming evacuation of our planet was called "The Evacuation of the Eagles." Paladin had lived several Indian repersonalizations (he had introduced himself to me at first as "Sky Hawk") and had chosen the name eagles for those who would be called and be taken into the ships, then brought back after the cataclysms were over. These eagle souls would be the ones to build a new Earth, a new Urantia. What I didn't know at the time was that it would be Niánn's and my job to help gather the eagles together from all over the planet. Others would be chosen to do similar things on different levels.

"Your level is the highest and most important work on the planet today," yelled Paladin one day when I was not believing the reality of what was happening to me.

"I'm just a guy from Pittsburgh; my father was a steelworker. I've always felt just one step away from being homeless and on the streets, like so many thousands of other poor souls," I moaned.

Paladin responded, "The world tries to make you fit in, to conform, to get degrees from its universities of madness, to accept the Hollywood delusion, and to buy into the materialistic bondage of its false reality. If you don't, you are considered a failure or an oddball. Few are able to exist comfortably outside of this system; and if you succeed enough to make any kind of living in an alternative way, those still trapped in the system will tell you to get a real job. If you somehow become rich by becoming a "star" Hollywood puppet, you will become their hero, oddball or not. Is this not the reality of your country, and the reality your country sells to the rest of the planet?"

I had to agree one hundred percent with Paladin.

"Many in your country don't see the problems, not the real ones. They can't even ask the right questions to begin to find the solutions. They see everybody else as the problem, but not themselves. If they, as individuals, would accept just a little responsibility for the mess this planet is in, change, true change would come. The best way for people to see their faults is for a loved one to point them out. Even then the individual may not accept what is observed about them by people who are closest and know them best. This is why community living is the highest ideal for the evolutionary worlds of time and space, like Urantia. If your pastor tells you what is wrong with you and you don't like it, you can go down the street and join another church without dealing with the problem. In a family or community situation it's not always that easy to leave. But many families do split up and move away from each other and very little growth takes place. True leadership is missing in many families on the planet, and there is tremendous imbalance between the male role and female role in the home. Many parents do not want to accept the responsibility of raising their children in the highest way, and many are just ignorant about what they as parents should do. Admitting error is not easy."

"You spoke of the imbalance between male and female in the home; what do you mean?" I asked.

"In America, many women want to be the boss and they do not want to hear of submission to their husbands. They want authority both in the home and in the workplace. So they lose their female-ness and become like men. There is a good reason for this; there has been a terrible abuse of authority by males. But there is a very high truth in the concept of appropriate submission of a woman in the home to a spiritually balanced male. If this truth is not applied in the home, you have two men in daily combat, one in pants and the other in a dress. The children become very confused in this disharmony and misunderstanding of roles. You will see many women leading their men by the nose because the men have not grown into the spiritual leaders in the home and community that God has ordained for them. All suffer when this happens. For centuries women have taken the burden of spiritual leadership, as well as child-care and other tasks, and it has caused much im-balance and unhappiness within each family member. The home, the neighborhood, the city, the nation and the planet all feel the effects of the unalignment of the male and female in their proper roles with each other and with their God."

Throughout the many years to come, Niánn and I would discover the truth of those statements by Paladin as we tried to teach proper male and female roles in the home and community. It would take the collapse of our culture, economy and war in our land to really change the obstinate minds of men and women in America. Before the national tragedies, a high percentage of the couples who left our community did so because the women would not allow the men to take their proper roles in the home. They wanted to keep control and that was that. All were attracted to the truths of the Fifth Epochal Revelation, and many were aware of the danger our planet was in environmentally, economically and politically; but they could not see themselves as part of the real problem—the spiritual problem. After all, they all believed in a Higher Power. Some were teachers themselves of metaphysical principles that they believed to be truths; but most of them did not really understand the simple living reality of the teachings of our Creator Son, Jesus Christ, as applied to their daily lives.

The midwayers one evening quoted from *The URANTIA Book*

Some day a reformation in the Christian church may strike deep enough to get back to the unadulterated religious teachings of Jesus, the author and finisher of our faith.

The Apostle Paul later on transformed this new gospel into Christianity, a religion embodying his own theological views and portraying his own *personal experience* with the Jesus of the Damascus road. The gospel of the kingdom is founded on the personal religious experience of the Jesus of Galilee. Christianity is founded almost exclusively on the personal religious experience of the Apostle Paul.
(*The URANTIA Book*, page 2091:4)

Jesus founded the religion of personal experience in doing the will of God and serving the human brotherhood. Paul founded a religion in which the glorified Jesus became the object of worship and the brotherhood consisted of fellow believers in the divine Christ.
(*The URANTIA Book*, page 2092:4)

No matter how high an ideal or advanced an achievement society attains, it can never transcend Jesus' teachings. The ideal of all social attainment can only be realized in the appropriation of Jesus' kingdom of the brotherhood of man and the fatherhood of God.

We humans do not have to be jealous or envious of one another if we realize that each of us has a special place in this world according to our Universal Father's master plan. But how many on this planet really ask our Father his will concerning even the simplest of things, let alone the most important? Many pray, "Thy will be done," and then do their own thing, just as society has taught them. Few understand the moment-to-moment walk with the Father that is necessary to bring peace to Urantia. There cannot be a religion by rote; it has to be a daily revelation with a

living, real and personal God. Only then will humankind understand brotherhood with one another.

"We are all in this together," a female musician friend once
said to me. We certainly do not escape the law of cause and effect.
What goes around comes around. If we had made the right
decisions in the past, the right results would have returned to us.
When decisions based on greed and selfishness are made, that is
what is reaped. Give and it will come back to you, take and you
will continue to lose. Many souls are energy drainers and take
from the very essence of other souls. They draw the energy from
others and control them with their minds. These takers feed their
egos with the trouble they cause others and the rest of the planet.
They become so good at it that they appear as the good guys, doing
others a favor. If a loud bell would have rung every time a wrong
motive was the intent in someone's heart who seemed to be good,
it would have been a very noisy planet indeed. Our unseen
friends, who know human nature better than most, gave us good
lessons on the true heart of humankind. I thought I understood the
human heart, but the midwayers said I had a lot to learn in that
area; and soon they arranged for my education, as they did for
many on the planet. God was trying to bring cosmic family
together all over the planet, and these people experienced interpersonal relationships as never before.

I had met people whom I liked or disliked immediately upon
meeting them, but never with the intensity and in such numbers as
began to come into our lives in Prescott, Arizona. In the past forty
years there had been perhaps three really close friends in my life,
but in just a few months there were a dozen or more people we had
met who we actually wanted to move in with us, to become a part
of our extended family. We met mother figures, father figures,
sisters and brothers, sons and daughters. I loved Niánn with all
my heart, but suddenly several women came into my life that I felt
in love with and desired. One woman I particularly loved with a
deep, almost supernatural feeling. The guides called her Setta and
told me that she and I were past third-dimensional complementary

polarities and that we had spent several lives together as husband and wife. They said it was my job to bring these women into fourth-dimensional reality, but at the time it seemed impossible. The communication, even between Setta and I, was poor, and we ended up in an argument in most conversations. I never once was unfaithful to Niánn, and she knew on a higher level what was happening. Many of us starseed had come from planets in another universe where pluralistic marriages were the norm.[6] These interuniversal cultures were very different from Western civilization on Urantia. These realities and memories were deep within the genes of our molecular being. Some of us would be the cosmic pioneers to bring interuniversal culture to Urantia, which would become the norm in many **sector** regions of the Divine New Order and part of the laws of the Machiventa Government after the change point.

Niánn loved these people too, particularly Setta. They all would be very attracted to us and then they would leave for one reason or another, many not even understanding their own feelings or our past-life relationships. Niánn and I had a slight advantage, as the guides would tell us our past connections with these people; but we could not tell them, as they were not yet ready. We prayed for them as though they were part of our family, even though many of them could not have cared less if we lived or died. It was little consolation from the guides when they would remind us that this same reality would happen all over the planet to other people of the future Divine New Order communities. Cosmic parents would feel the joy of meeting their past children and other relatives and loved ones, then suffer the pain of losing them to the world system, their own selfishness and the chains that Caligastia, * the fallen Planetary Prince of Urantia, still had on them. I would get all of the blame.

---

[6]Pluralistic marriages of interuniversal cultures can only work when all involved are highly spiritual and emotionally mature. All would have to be aligned to the Divine Government to learn the divine reality principles of pluralistic marriages. These interuniversal realities can presently only be learned and lived at Planetary Headquarters.

Those years were very difficult for me, as I had the gift and calling that very few wanted or even believed in at the time. I began to hate the word "channel," and calling me a contact personality or interplanetary receiver didn't help things, nor did it put food on the table for my children. People were just so blind to the real problems and were so right in their own eyes. They could not see with the real love of Christ and with cosmic truth. True reality was far from them. I felt so helpless in this world and so often wanted to give up myself. To join the rat race just to be accepted would have been so easy. You know the game. Get a 9 to 5 job. Don't rock the boat (even if it is sinking). Don't talk about politics or religion. Maybe even become a musician for the environment, like all of the other do-gooders. Or maybe just preach the love message. It doesn't change the planet but it rakes in the bucks. People liked to hear of a loving God who forgave them for being unloving and unforgiving with their neighbors, but they just hated hearing of a God of judgement and justice. They didn't want to stand before that God one day. That's right, a truth that nobody wanted to hear.

CHAPTER 10

SOUL MATES BEGIN TO COME

When Niánn and I were just about ready to give up the belief that cosmic family really existed, or that if they existed they would ever know their relationship to us, some came to join the community. Their legal names were not as important as were the names the guides gave to them. These new names would reflect the future person this soul was called by God to become. It was a cosmic name given before they ever entered this plane. All over the planet, we were told, were thousands of souls like these beings called to transformation, but few would really heed the call. Even in our small group in Prescott, these people would deny their own reality and fall back into the world system before they finally gave their hearts to us and our work. It would take the great tragedies that struck our nation for them to rejoin us, but they came back one by one. How Niánn and I suffered in the interim period. How we missed them, for in the brief six months they had been with us we had grown to love them as family.

In the beginning, before the tragedies, Mikal joined us. He didn't live with us at first but remained loyal to us and the guides for many months, while others who we knew were of the cosmic family fell by the wayside. When he came to stay with us, he had a hard time living in close contact with others and in many ways was unbending. This was his downfall the guides said, and would cause him much grief in the future. He was divorced and had grown children. He had a business degree, but was working in a job far below his potential. According to the guides, he had the capacity to become a great administrator one day, and they urged him to quit his job and work with us full time. But he declined and eventually was the first of the original community to leave us, doubting the reality of the guides.

Paladin said one day, "People on your planet, and particularly in Western Civilization, think that by putting on different clothes, changing their hair style or changing their foods, they have made a major transformation. Some even change their names and jobs and geographic location, but the root problem is always there. It is the spirit of the person that must change, all else will follow. The turtles must become the eagles. No outside transformation will grow wings on a timid soul."

Jonathan and Evening Star were the first to live with us. They realized that they were supernaturally led to us, but later would forget that and even deny it. Evening Star was from California and Jonathan was from West Germany, but was an American citizen. Evening Star was a clinical therapist and Jonathan was a carpenter. We were told of the many lives that we had shared together in the past on this planet and others. All of us felt this to be true and grew to love each other. Niánn felt closest to Mikal and I to Jonathan. All three were our cosmic children. It was difficult at first to accept the role of father to Mikal who was a few years older than I in this life, but I made the transition inwardly and loved him as a son. He never knew how deeply I felt about him, at least, not until I would share that with him one evening, when we were lifted by our space friends and we were about two solar systems away from Urantia. Mikal rejoined the community after the earth changes began to happen, but remained a skeptic about the spaceships until one day he found himself in one. This was an unfortunate reality for Mikal; his doubts prevented many of his loved ones from joining our community and being spared physical death, as they too could have been taken in the ships.

In this life, Jonathan was first sent to be my brother through the womb of my mother but had died when he was three days old. Another similar couple had to be found as parents halfway around the world, and thirty-five years later Jonathan and I met for the first time. I loved him as both my brother and cosmic son. We really felt that with Jonathan we had a true friend and one who would be loyal to us and the work through the change point and after. Evening Star had the tendency to be insincere with her words. We never knew when to believe her, but Jonathan invariably meant what he said. He seemed to understand the teachings of the need for a union of souls better than the others, and with this one loyal soul we felt we had the foundation for a future Divine New Order community. The guides said that one loyal member of the cosmic family would draw another. That was a universal law; when souls of like mind came together for a common purpose, the power of heaven would be available to them on the highest levels. We would not only meet and become friends with these people, but their unseen guides would also become a part of our lives and reality. Angels, midwayers and other superhuman beings assigned to the human watchcare could now speak to me and all of us about cosmic truth and the future Divine New Order.

We all ate together, prayed together, laughed and cried together. But most of all, we had a common purpose: to inform the people of the planet about the future earth changes, the need for community life and the necessary evacuation by spaceships or light body* for those who would respond.

One evening an angel called Destin spoke. "There will be sacred/protected areas all over the planet that will be supernaturally protected during the earth changes and possible final war. At a point in time even these areas will no longer be safe. It is hoped that thousands of people will be living in these protected and Divine New Order areas and that you will have the organization on an international scale to mobilize millions of others when the final evacuation will be necessary. Your group will be responsible for seven locations around the planet. It will seem like an impossible job in the beginning, and you will probably want to give up."

Little did I realize just how hard it would be, and I almost gave up when Jonathan left. He was persuaded by a pretty ex-girlfriend who came to supposedly be part of our community. She wanted to travel and he had itchy feet, being a traveling man all of his life, so she played up to another young man, and Jonathan became jealous. She won Jonathan's lust for her and maybe his heart; and the next thing we knew they left together, taking Evening Star with them. Before Jonathan left town with the confused triangle, he spread the rumor that I was a fraud and God knows what else. We were left with all of the bills and high mortgage payments.

Months earlier, we had been directed by the guides to sell the house (they knew what was coming) and move to Sedona, Arizona, which would become the key protected area and Planetary Headquarters. Because the community members left so suddenly, we had to take a twenty thousand dollar loss on the home. We also had to deal with the hatefulness of Niánn's ex-husband who had put an unjust judgement against the proceeds of the sale. By the time we were finished with lawyers' fees and closing fees, we didn't have enough left to even dream of obtaining land for a community. We needed a miracle.

Evening Star was a very gentle female spirit, and our two babies, Alcyone and Sonta-An had loved her. For several weeks after the group left, the children, who had grown accustomed to them as family, were very upset and cried a lot. It was as if they knew on a higher level that some of the family was missing. Evening Star just could not face up to her own lack of self-esteem and self-motivation. When we or her guides would try to share her precious potential with her and how to use her gifts, she would pretend enough to let us believe she understood, but inwardly she resented our instruction. After these family members left, the guides shared with us that our community breakdown was a small example of the Lucifer rebellion. Only God the Father and Michael the Son and a few other Universe Supervisors knew what was in the heart of Lucifer, and his potential to fall.

Niánn and I were in a state of shock for several months because we felt that despite any differences or hurts to one another, they would not leave us or the work we felt they were called to. We had much to learn about the human heart and its weaknesses.

It was our continued learning that eased the pain over the years when many of the soul-mate family members we had met would go their own way, and because of this we were being educated about the true problems of the entire planet.

We became wiser about the complexities of the human psyche when Terra and Sastar met in our home. I had first met Terra in California and immediately loved him. I didn't know until years later, when the guides told me, that he was my cosmic son and had been in my human family as a brother in several past repersonalizations. He was a tall, dark and handsome man, with a sensitive, kind soul. He had just received distribution on his New-Age instrumental album from a major company in Hollywood, and he was at a high point in life. He left L.A. searching for another city in which to relocate. We had been told in advance by the guides that God wanted Terra to join our community. Terra didn't agree with that at all. Hollywood was still a bug within him, which he didn't realize. He thought he just needed a bigger city than Prescott to reach the success level he desired. We prayed that he would at least not go back to L.A. He did for awhile, but temporarily ended up in Tucson.

Sastar had been aware of the Ashtar Command when she lived in California and was directed by the Command through a lower-level channel to come to Prescott. She came to several private channelings and was instructed by Celestial Overcontrol to become part of our community. The moment Niánn and I had seen her, we loved her. We spent the first Christmas in Prescott with Sastar and had many nights of high-level spiritual conversations. She was intelligent and well-read, divorced, with five grown children. Celestial Overcontrol was very forceful in telling the people of Prescott about the upcoming earth changes, a message the conservative mindset did not want to hear and so many of the New-Age community there rejected our work. Sastar could not stand with us in this area and eventually denied the validity of our work and that I was a true Ashtar channel. We loved her very much, and she was Niánn's cosmic daughter; I was not her cosmic father, but in past lives on this planet I had been her older brother. She was told of my brother relationship with her by the guides, but they never revealed Niánn's true cosmic relationship with her.

Terra was staying with us and we invited Sastar over for dinner one evening. Sastar was immediately attracted to Terra; as a matter of fact, she was beside herself with adoration for him. When they started talking, it turned out that they both were from the same midwestern town and had attended the same high school. Although they both lived in L.A. at the same time, they had not met until in our home. It was a definite providential meeting. We were told much about their past lives together, but could only tell them bits and pieces because of their unalignment with our work and with Celestial Overcontrol.

Years later, after the first big earthquake hit L.A. and San Francisco killing thousands, they found out where we were and joined us. By this time we were in Sedona and had several hundred in our community. Terra was instrumental in helping to produce several motion pictures of high consciousness, saving thousands of lives and reaching millions with higher truths, as the people of the planet were then ready to hear the answers few had wanted to hear before. Within the body of the community we were able to accomplish great things in many areas, because we had so many minds working together for a common purpose. It was too bad it took the deaths of many of their loved ones before others could accept the answers themselves. So many of us, including myself, would have had the desires of our hearts answered if the alignment of cosmic family could have come years before the cataclysms and economic upheavals. The joy and fulfillment we did experience was mixed with great sadness because of the death and destruction all over the planet and in our own backyard of America.

CHAPTER 11

DIVING IN

More of the cosmic family began to come to us in ways which we realized at the time were divinely directed. One day a gentleman came to look at our antique furniture and spent several hours talking about spiritual things; he immediately liked both of us. We even talked about community living and purchasing land, and he said that this was also an idea of his. His name in past repersonalizations was Woman's Eye because he was easily led astray by women; his wife's name in a past repersonalization was Kala, meaning cautious one. In that past life, Woman's Eye also had married Kala who had led him many times to do other than what God's will was for him, for she was fearful and cautious. Because of this, Woman's Eye never became a leader among his tribe, as he was always busy trying to please Kala. In this present life we saw the same circumstances being the reality. Woman's Eye loved learning and growing spiritually, and although he said his wife did, she was actually more interested in other things that pulled her away from spiritual growth; and she would not commit herself to any study that would take time away from her other involvements. Woman's Eye was not enough of a leader to lead the way, thus both of them never aligned themselves with our work.

We saw this same scenario take place with so many other couples who came to us. A question was posed by the midwayers, "Does God ask us to come to a cliff in life and just jump over, leaving all behind with no guarantee of landing safely except the faith that one is in the perfect will of the Creator?"

The answer to this is an unquestionable yes. But we found few who were willing to take the dive. Usually the men were the first willing to jump, but misplaced loyalties to their women and their own lack of courage kept them from their destinies and held them in their own smallness. We saw the reality of what could have transpired if they had stayed with us.

Urell and Anignea came to us; he was an intellectual and she was an intuitive, sensitive controller. She was willing to allow him freedom as long as the freedom that he pursued aligned with her own wishes. Whenever it did not, she would assume authority over him. This same spirit was in the souls of many women in Western Civilization and was one of the greatest imbalances in the family prior to the change point and Divine New Order in May of 2000 or 2001. The love shown between us was felt not only by Urell and Anignea but also by Urell's two **star children** who were cosmic children to Niánn and I. These children even said that they really wanted to live with us. They sensed a higher reality and past association with us. But all of the love experienced was denied by Urell and Anignea when Anignea began to lose control of Urell.

Apo and Apoleaha came to us knowing that God was calling them to a new way of life, particularly the husband, Apo, who knew that he was being called into a life of spiritual destiny. The first plans were for them to move into our new cottage, in which they would have had to invest a few thousand dollars. Apo was more willing to do this. They were also told that an opening would come up for them which would be a metaphysical bookstore and spiritual outreach for the community and would be a sufficient source of income for them. Apo was willing to dive in, and at first made the necessary steps, but Apoleaha was reluctant to go the distance and persuaded Apo not to join our work and our hearts. One week after they left, the next door neighbor told us that they were moving and would be renting their home and asked if we knew of anyone who would be interested in renting. Also there appeared in the local newspaper an ad for a metaphysical book-store. We saw that the destiny of this family had been missed. We also felt we had lost something, as we loved them very much.

As each person we met left us, we felt much pain and grief because we could see a little of the future and believed in the actualization and fulfillment that would come with our union, but this new future was being held back because of their obstinacy and misplaced loyalties. I particularly had a love-hate relationship in my heart for those whom I knew had erred in their judgement, not only hurting themselves but those who loved them. In their unalignment to the perfect will of God, fulfillment of destiny could not be realized. When one soul is out of divine will, out of the eternal purpose, it affects the whole planet starting at the level of the family unit.

Zordon and Zella came to us with much pain and brokenness of past repersonalizations, and both in need of counseling. We immediately loved Zordon and felt in this gentle but manly human being a courageous loyalty that needed direction. When Zella saw his affection toward us, she became overly protective and eventually caused the breakup of our relationship, using a number of accusations, as people will do who do not want to look at the real problem. Both had tremendous potential to become counselors for the afflicted and addicted. Had they remained with us, within five years they could have been authors and leaders in this field.

In all of these cases, the men were not spiritually strong enough to follow the will of God and allow the women to follow their example. All of them were kept on a leash by their women until the tragedies of the late nineties and the deaths of many of their loved ones. Some of the men were then courageous enough to leave these women when they realized that they not only held them back but held back the consciousness of the planet and their own children's future growth.

CHAPTER 12

INAPPROPRIATE RELATIONSHIPS

Judas and Magna came to us and entered our classes. We had from the very beginning a great love for Magna and were told by the guides that her relationship with Judas was a mismatch and that she had a Native American complement who would be led to her as she aligned herself more perfectly with her God. This we could not tell her until the proper time, and when we did, she was angry with us, as she was still with Judas. His name, given to us by Celestial Overcontrol, we believed at the time, was an indication of the type of person he was. Although we showed him love and respect, he denied us the same, gossiped about us and saw problems in my character, where perhaps there were none. All this because he subconsciously knew that we were aware that they did not belong together. Physically, Magna was a tremendously beautiful woman with a sensitive heart and giving nature. Judas was a selfish individual and an opportunist.

From time eternal there was in the mind of God a plan for a union of souls, male and female, on all evolutionary worlds where the birth of the children and the spiritual growth of the planet was the primal order. This perfect plan, a masterpiece, was upset by the Lucifer rebellion, the subsequent fall of the Planetary Prince, Caligastia, and the later default of the Material Son and Daughter, Adam and Eve. Because of the spiritual decadence and genetic imbalance, Urantia became a planet where marriages and mating between the opposite sexes were not marriages of cosmic origin and spiritual attunement, but marriages of animalistic origin and materialistic expediency. That was true of twentieth-century civilization, especially America. The teachings of complementary polarities and soul mates go far beyond the scope of my sharing in this orientation. I will briefly state that it became quite evident that there were few males and females who were united in true fourth-dimensional complementary polarity unions. Even those who wrote books on the subject of twin flames and soul mates and who were initiators in the field, were not united with their true complementary polarities and in fact had divorced the wives with whom they co-authored their first books. Most individuals, having married the prince or princess of their dreams, soon discovered that they did not get all that they had hoped or bargained for in their mate. The reasons for this were numerous. The spiritual growth of the individual, or lack of it, is the foremost reason for either obtaining a high-stage soul mate or complement, or a low-stage or non soul mate. Since the various cultures of the planet and the existing realities within them were far from fourth-dimensional cosmic reality, on an international level, souls had to be educated with new concepts and new ways of looking at reality, particularly interpersonal relationships.

It was the belief of certain individuals, that those who looked good, were in good health and were financially successful, would be able to find their perfect mate. A good look into that Hollywood delusion should have shown Western Civilization that this was not a true reality. The universe is consistent in that it gives the motive of the heart the answer it deserves. Most of us found that life did not go exactly as we had planned. Many of those who succeeded in certain career choices were spiritual failures. Character faults were present in their personalities to the extent that those individuals were only a shell of what they could have been. Better to be a happy plumber in the perfect will of the Creator than a miserable surgeon out of the Father's will. Many females who had become imbalanced in their energy, dominated their men and chose men who had become feminine in their character. Many men chose the successful businesswoman with a similar career, thinking that this would be a common denominator in their relationship and discovered that they had only obtained a combatant and competitor.

Many couples who came to us simply did not belong together, and those who had personal transmissions were told this. These people had become trapped in their own circumstances, and truth was something they said they wanted to hear but in reality were not willing to accept when it was given to them. Until these people as individual ascending sons and daughters had chosen to take the first steps of dying to their own wills and seeking the Father's will for their ascension to Paradise, they would never be ready to accept the truth. This search for the Father's will begins on the evolutionary worlds in the lowest stages, such as Urantia.

Inappropriate relationships and friendships of any kind between male and female begin at an early age and continue in the peer group, education, business and recreational activities. Some close friends are selected simply because of their ability to do something that the other can not do or because of their accomplishment in a particular field. An example of this would be the teenage boy who hangs around with those who play sports well and becomes a close friend with the best athlete because he is the most highly respected, and possibly some of that respect will rub off on the nonathletic boy. It does not matter that the athlete is an angry person with a character disorder. As long as he is accepted by the peer group, it doesn't matter that he might be a thief. If the nonathletic boy could see the future, he might see himself accosted in the store along with the athletic thief and being accused of shoplifting because of his association with his hero. Had his parents directed him to choose his friends based on other values, firstly spiritual, then the universe would have drawn these friends to him; because his thoughts and desires would have created the energy that the unseen guides of these other souls could have used to bring them his way. But great truths still have to be learned by the people of Urantia, who will not be ready for them until the near collapse of what we know as civilization. Sometimes the very longings within the heart can draw the object of that longing into our sphere. The degree of alignment with God is the degree that the object of your desire will come to you. It is hard to give an example, but many people who are sitting on the cosmic fence of choice between total surrender and partial surrender to God, draw energy to them in varying degrees. For instance, a woman who is in 75% alignment with her God might draw a mate from one corner of the world into the very city where she lives, but never meet that man until the other 25% of her will is aligned with God; and of course the man would have to be properly aligned.

One summer evening Niánn and I were drawn to an Indian pow-wow. While we were there watching the dancing and enjoying the drums, I felt in the very essence of my being the reality of my past complementary polarity relationship with Setta. She was in many ways at that moment the very essence of the music I was hearing and the heartbeat of the drums. Niánn pointed out to me that Setta was sitting in the corner of the bleachers. A strange coincidence, as at this time she was living in another city. It was Niánn who first felt the urge to go to the pow-wow, for Setta was not only longing for her complementary polarity, but also for her sister relationship, and Niánn was her highest. The motives of her heart may have been good, but in third-dimensional reality her thoughts were quite confused by what people thought and said she needed and what society said she should do. The universe will always do what is most correct, perfect and loving for the motive of the soul that sends out these longings to God; but few there are who, when longings are answered by God to some degree, recognize the answer within the cosmic family souls that God sends.

Personal Audience/Office Transmission.
Giving Souls Their Point Of Origin.
(A Major Part Of My Mandate)

It would be our job to teach the people of Urantia. Both the souls born here and those from planets of other universes, needed to know their reality of existence, and all to be brought together in a planetary consciousness based upon individual origin and divine destiny. Paladin and the midwayers told me to request a full-face picture from those wanting to know their point of origin, whether you were from this universe or another. Gradually I began to know the difference in soul age. Paladin came through and gave specifics. My opinion was, and still is, never final. Celestial Overcontrol wanted me to learn the discernment on my own by looking at a picture if the person was not present. Later I would do many transmissions by mail. It became impossible to see each person who wanted a personal transmission and have a private audience and bring Paladin through. They wanted to eventually speak to only the most humble and those who really wanted to follow the will of God. For several years, however, Paladin would confront many proud souls who considered themselves "spiritual teachers and leaders" about their own darkness. They didn't only receive information about their point of origin, they were also shown their areas of evil, sin, or iniquity that they didn't want to see. No one else loved them enough or was brave enough to tell them, or perhaps no one saw. They were told about their immediate destiny and what they needed to do to reach their highest destiny. The majority of them were in inappropriate relationships. However, many dear souls knew Paladin was right and did what was needed to join the Divine Government in which many of them had important roles to play. In many ways the community was quite diversified. We had no formal worship service or dress codes. Where meat eating would be wrong for one person, it would be totally correct for another. Where one wife might have been the highest ideal for one Nebadon pair, it could have been inadequate for another. In some universes there may be several husbands for one wife, not the highest interuniversal ideal, but nevertheless an interuniversal fact, to which some on Urantia are genetically linked. For many years these indeed were the answers that few accepted. Because they did not want to hear, they didn't want anyone else to consider them either.

CHAPTER 13

UNIVERSAL ORIGIN

Our unseen mentors began to share with us the vastness of the grand universe, its administration and its inhabitants. One day Paladin came through and said, in his normal and humorous way, "All humans are mortals in the universe of Nebadon, but not all mortals are human. You humans with penises and vaginas will find this reality quite different in the Orion system. What may be quite common in lovemaking on Urantia may be quite uncommon on planets of another universe where the physical reality may be quite different. Along with the Urantian Adam and Eve progeny on this planet is the life plasm in the progeny of the Adams and Eves from planets in other universes. Material Sons and Daughters from other universes are quite different from Material Sons and Daughters from Nebadon. Where the ideal of monogamy may be the highest ideal of Nebadon, it may not be the ideal of **Avalon**. Not all humans present on Urantia are from Urantia; some have been here for centuries but are not originally from Urantia. They have been mixed with humans of Urantian origin or humans from any of the other planets in Nebadon and then expected to function normally, accepting not only the social and planetary norms, but the local universe norms. In all of these areas you have an alien trying to function by the standards of what is to him an alien world. On planets that have not fallen, there can be an amalgamation of not only interplanetary but interuniversal relationships, marriages and administrative functions, because the natures of these individuals are understood and allowed. On these worlds of unfallen reality where no rebellion has occurred, circuits have not been cut off between them and other planets in their universe and outside of it. But on the thirty-seven fallen planets of the system of Satania in Nebadon, cosmic chaos exists in all manner of socialization, integration and actualization of its planetary citizenry."

At that moment in time Paladin asked me to remember when I had visited some Mexican prisons, all of the prisoners, no matter what their crime, were thrown together in one social structure. In the same cell may have been a murderer and a shoplifter, a rapist with a tax evader, a gentle sensitive soul with a violent one. In this kind of environment it was like the animalistic societies of primitive man. The strongest control. The most sensitive and gentle ones found themselves either dying or changing into a character harder than who they really were and having to accept the norms of that particular deranged, cruel and uncivilized prison.

Having to accept and live by the norms of the majority, over the years I began to feel like a prisoner on Urantia, and I saw others who also felt like prisoners to those norms. The difference was that I had realized it to the degree that I wanted to no longer be in prison. I was not happy there and tried to awaken those, at whatever level I could, to their own imprisonment. It was an impossible task. When they began to realize that what I was saying just might be true, their family, friends and societal structure would all draw them back into the Luciferic thought pattern and the Caligastia timetable. Once back into that "reality" individuals denied their cosmic identity, earning their living in unfulfilling jobs, looking for sex partners (because the appetites needed feeding), eating the wrong foods, drinking impure water and associating with souls far below their highest potential that they themselves had not realized to the fullest. Those souls, like the majority in the world, either needed a major tragedy to awaken them, or for the universe to arrange a slow series of constant disappointments and trials, with the hope that they would be enlightened to true fourth-dimensional reality.

One day Paladin again spoke: "Since Caligastia's staff of one hundred came to Urantia, and after the fall 200,000 years ago, their progeny have had instincts, talents, abilities and genetic inheritance far different from humans of Urantian origin. It was hoped by the Universe Supervisors, even up to the twentieth century, that these descendents would be able to flow into, not only the norms of the planet, but the norms of the other planets of the universe of Nebadon, the universal code and law in which their ancestors had learned to function while they actively served and administered. They were also those that were only on an assignment and would have to go back to their own universe and super-universe[*] for completion and total actualization of reality. It was determined after approximately the mid-sixties of the twentieth century that these descendents could not function under the Nebadon code. They could come to the highest spiritual attainment, far surpassing their Urantian brothers in many areas, but could not be totally fulfilled or complete within the norms and morality of Urantia and its social structure. So it was determined by the Universe Supervisors and mandated by Michael of Salvington that those who could be used as contact personalities would be given Continuing Fifth Epochal Revelation at various levels that would complement that which was already given in the 1934-35 papers (*The URANTIA Book*).

"We all live in an evolving universe; and in an evolving universe no one book can contain the total truth of the cosmic reality of any one planet, let alone a system, universe, super-universe, or master universe.[*] This is what the schools of ascension are for, to supplement the answers to questions that could only be partially understood in the previous plane, to synthesize the omnipresent reality of the Absolute and the Ultimate God of Paradise who has reached out of his reality to teach his creation in a continuing process, the secrets of eternity. No one lesson, no one text, no one life upon a planet or plane can encompass that lesson, that total truth, for it is a gift and a process of growth.

"In the larger cities of America there is ethnocentrism in one's neighborhood, and some can tell what neighborhood a person is from simply by conversation. Others may not be able to do this outside of the city, but those within the city who know the various neighborhoods are adept in this discernment. We, with an objective view, not only of a system of planets, but a constellation of planets, a universe of planets, a minor and major sector of planets, a superuniverse of planets and a grand universe of planets can tell what universe and neighborhood you are from and can totally, with one hundred percent accuracy, recognize your talents, abilities, how you think and react to reality, and your quest or nonquest for God."

CHAPTER 14

LEAVING THE OLD BEHIND, CHANGING YOUR NAME OR WHAT WILL MY FRIENDS SAY?

I remember that back in Pittsburgh, 1985, the transition in changing my name to Gabriel was not easy. I found out very quickly that few of my old friends would call me Gabriel, and definitely not my parents or close relatives. The reasons varied. I didn't even realize at the time that I was beginning to shift from the third to the fourth dimension. All of the **apostles** of Jesus were given a new name to make their transition. Simon became Peter, and Saul became Paul, but as long as I stayed in Pittsburgh I would be Tony. Actually, the name given at confirmation in the Catholic Church is a name symbolic of a spiritual rebirth. At twelve years old, when most Catholics of my generation supposedly made their commitment to God, the only things on their minds were looking pretty or handsome in their white outfits, and what gifts they might get. It had become just rote for the adults also.

There is a cosmic reality that remains the same. A cosmic name is our inheritance from the Universe Father, not only for the mortals of the evolutionary worlds like Urantia, but for all the ascending sons and daughters of God and all orders of beings in the grand universe, in which we of Urantia were like a grain of sand on a seashore.

Some of the reasons why people wouldn't call me Gabriel was plain old sin. To be more specific, they had envy, jealousy, greed and false pride. I began to find this out while in Pittsburgh. I met a record producer of New-Age music from San Francisco; let's call him Mr. Lost. He had all of the previously mentioned faults. He would not admit that my album was good and picked on the bad timing of the drummer in some of the parts of a couple of songs. When I asked him to pinpoint exactly where, it turned out to be a drum machine part, and not the drummer. I did use both, but drum machines don't lose time. He called me Gabriel until he found out my birth name was Tony. Strange, I thought. I realized that in Hollywood jealous hearts would not recognize another's struggle to become a success. If they couldn't make the meta-morphosis themselves, they didn't want you to either; but if you became rich or famous, they wanted to be your best friend. "I knew you would make it" or "I believed in you all of the time," were their comments when you succeeded. I met many Mr. and Mrs. Losts all over the country, and they could be very painful for any soul trying to evolve spiritually. Yes, I wanted to have my music heard by the masses; yes, I wanted to be influential in music and films so that I could help our planet and other struggling artists, but I could not have cared less about being famous. As a matter of fact, the Hollywood persona that colored the world with materialistic and sexual lust, nauseated me. I think it would have sickened any spiritually healthy person.

Other people would have liked to have made a change in them-selves, but because of misplaced loyalties to a spouse, job, religion or career, they subconsciously would not accept the eagle's courage. I began wearing an earring in my left ear, a long hanging one, to show my desire to be different. The earring was an outward sign of an already inner decision. A lot of men I met, who had jobs where this would not be accepted, and macho men who claimed it was not manly, snickered at me. The reality was they didn't have the courage to quit the jobs they were unhappy in, or leave friends who kept them on a lower level. Christ said that old wine skins were no good for new wine. New thinking brings about many changes in life and one must look forward to each challenge of newness. In Pittsburgh, for about a year, new friends were calling me Gabriel and old friends stuck to calling me Tony. I had to leave my hometown for good to complete the metamor-phosis, and it took several years before I actually knew I was the Gabriel that God wanted me to be.

The Cloak of Respectability

Try to buck the system in any way and see what happens. When terrible things happen to the innocent, people would say, "What a pity, what a shame." Like the respectable lawyer who overcharged his clients, or his secretary who knew she was working for a legal thief but didn't see herself as part of the problem. How about the people who worked for title companies that took a good part of people's hard earned dollars, all in the name of service? Did they quit their jobs in protest of their company's policies? How about those who worked for war weapon corporations or liquor industries? Why did they stay? "For the money," they said. "I have a wife and children to support; I have to survive," said Mr. and Mrs. America. Would God have wanted you to survive by placing a gun to someone's head and taking their food if you had none? The moral complacency of Americans helped to destroy the modern world. When greed was allowed to rule in the hearts of neighbors, peers and business associates without confrontation by ethics, civilizations were destroyed. How many had died in the latter half of the twentieth century because they could not afford proper medical care? The answer is millions. Even those assistants who worked for so-called men of healing could not afford their employers' services themselves.

All of these formerly complacent ones were called, "voices crying in the wilderness," bums and radicals when they left their jobs or careers in the establishment. The true artist who had helped bring souls to God-consciousness was a dying breed in the twentieth century, and in the name of art, so-called artists with materialistic values helped to choke the life force out of billions of souls around the planet. When you become a material girl or boy, man or woman, you don't become the true you, the astral or spiritual you; and you don't become a candidate for a higher plane of existence as an ascending son or daughter, but you do have to spend another lifetime on a planet much like Urantia or worse. If you're lucky, maybe you get to choose your next hell.

CHAPTER 15

THE PROTECTED AREAS

We had been told by the Ashtar Command and by various celestial intelligences that all throughout the planet there would be interlocking grid systems and **ley lines** of supernatural origin that would create a web that only a few of our modern scientists were beginning to recognize. Protected mountains and valleys on the planet were interconnected to others in different geographic locations on various continents. These interdimensional portals, these sonic tunnels, these tunnels of cosmic energy, unknown to man, served as passageways for extraterrestrial and interdimensional travel on Urantia. At the very center of each transport area was a surrounding circular area that put out energy. This depended upon the kinds of beings that entered the vortex* or energy reflective circuit. We on our planet had named these places of incomprehensible energy, vortexes; but the finaliter, Paladin, gave us the new term of energy reflective circuits, and this is the term I will use to describe an area under the divine supervision of intergalactic and interdimensional authority and protection. It may be as small as an acre or as large as a thousand acres, with tributaries shooting out in all directions connecting with complementary energy reflective circuits in other geographic areas, perhaps on the same continent or on another. We were told that the consciousness of the people in that area, the mass consciousness in relationship to their link with their Creator God, would determine what representatives of the cosmic family would be sent to that area and what supernatural forces would be working there. Just because an energy reflective circuit had been so in the past, did not mean that it would remain one; it could function in the present only if the humans in that area recognized the Cosmic Father of All, his authority, and the authority of those he had mandated in human form. These leaders were yet to be recognized, but in the days of crisis that lay ahead they would become manifest and known.

We were moving from Prescott, an area that had lost its chance of becoming divinely protected, and for the next several months it seemed that all the forces of evil were bent on keeping us from entering the protected area in Sedona where we were told to go. Let us call it Secret Valley. For two and a half months Niánn and I, with our twenty-three-month-old twins and two-month-old son lived in a tent while forces of good and evil battled through the red tape of obtaining a loan approval. The home that was selected in an affordable price range, was near a protected mountain in Sedona, linked to Salvington, the capital of our universe. The energies manifested in this area were of a balanced female circuit, even more so than the nearby male circuit that was also of cosmic balance. Hundreds of interdimensional beings who had mastered the female aspect of God had entered through this area. The very soil itself was being artificially injected, by the Life Carriers* to produce food under subnormal conditions. The area would also receive rain when other areas in Arizona would experience drought. Great gusts of wind would come from time to time to clear away the pollution in the air, and this was all taking place before we ever lived in the area. Finally we acquired the home and moved in. The forces of evil were still fighting very hard to keep us in financial despair and fear, for they did not want our work to succeed. We had no idea as to how other members of the cosmic family and our human family would come to live in a safe area with us, as we hardly had enough income to sustain our basic needs, let alone purchase more land. Yet we were told that this would happen, and we began to see the reality of it in the months and years ahead.

Certain communities who were led by extraterrestrial guidance were asked to go to specific geographic areas. Some of those areas had already experienced earthquakes, volcanic eruptions and tidal waves. When they arrived, the people living there were in chaos and fear; many had no hope of survival and didn't care because their loved ones had already been killed. The true spiritual ones of the planet were guided by the extraterrestrials to explain what was really happening to our planet and to prepare those who would listen, for evacuation by alien space craft, so they could be brought back to a new world, a new earth. Some were able to transcend by light body transference rather than by spacecraft evacuation. Those who would listen would indeed survive and give hope to all who had to be awakened. The tragedies were not happening due to God's wrath, but through the cause-and-effect pattern of negative thoughtforms with which man had disfigured this planet for 200,000 years, since the fall of its Planetary Prince. Man's inhumanity to his brother, his greed and pride and lust for false power, his lack of understanding of cosmic truth was now making Mother Earth explode within and without.

These special areas would serve as a shield of divine protection for all who were committed to come out of the old ways and into the Divine New Order and Government of the Planetary Prince. When they began to commit themselves to higher truths and higher teachers, they were able to put aside their false pride and intellectual nuances and accommodate within themselves the humility to become students with questions to ask rather than with answers to give. Unfortunately, until many of them found that they had no food for their stomachs or no roof over their heads, they hung onto their illusions of the great American dream which was influencing the whole planet. Materialism and mechanistic technology had totally replaced the extended family, and the values of mankind deteriorated as those in control of governments desired even more power and material gain. Cancer of the soul is much worse than cancer of the body, for it causes the possible everlasting separation from its Creator, while death of the body can actually bring the soul closer to its Creator.

We began to see our neighbors moving away as soon as we moved in, especially those with fundamentalist ideas that could not be easily changed. Still, we were very discouraged when we would meet members of the cosmic family who yet did not understand the necessity of commitment and adherence to our counsel, which was always the counsel of the higher intelligences who spoke through me. As they proceeded in their own way, we saw much turmoil take place in their lives, all of which could have been avoided.

While living in the tent, we met people from all over the world and found them to be pretty much the same; materialistically oriented with misplaced loyalties to human family members and careers that promised security, misplaced loyalties to spouses and dreams based upon the same Babylonian principles that had destroyed civilization after civilization. Many heard the truth when they had private transmission sessions with Paladin. But since he told people what they needed to hear, not always what they wanted to hear, many of these souls did not accept the higher teachings until tragedy struck Earth. It was amazing to see the condition of a lost soul. To the higher intelligences a lost soul is defined as "any soul who is not totally experiencing the divine fulfillment and total actualization of all of his or her dreams, talents and abilities and who is not in a right relationship with the Creator." It would be safe to say that most souls on the planet were lost souls. During the beginning days of the purification, dozens of families and single people, were beginning to be moved from the area by unseen forces.

Many homes in Secret Valley were repossessed by banks and left empty; the occupants of many others just moved. The energies of truth and love within the five-mile radius, and in particular the one-mile radius of the Planetary Prince in Sedona, was so powerful that those less loving, nonbelievers in absolutes, could not resonate there. Slowly these vacant homes were occupied by cosmic family members who were awakened and were still allowed by the Universe Supervisors to come into the area of safety. It was common during the later years, before the change point, to see smaller spacecraft land, bringing representatives of Christ Michael in human form who walked about the land with me, discussing the organization and administration needed in governing the community and in the future evacuation that would take place. With some of the unseen friends becoming visible, the role of leader became much easier. Actually, as more souls loyal to Christ Michael arrived (those who truly loved him more than anyone or anything else) the ministry began to prosper financially as well, enabling us to acquire land and facilities. It was not the most loyal who arrived first, but souls that tested Niánn's and my faith time and time again. Some were mandated for their potential loyalty to God, and their mindal ability to comprehend Continuing Fifth Epochal Revelation. In many cases their virtue did not match their mindal ability.

The first two older cosmic family souls to arrive, came six months after they contacted us by letter in November of 1990. They had been with us in past lives. One was my cosmic half-brother. He would provide Niánn and me with much education as to discerning the soul and our responsibility to love unconditionally. The Bright and Morning Star said that my cosmic half-brother had great capacity for both good and evil. We unfortunately have had to deal with the unstabilized spirituality of this soul and others. We have found that in dealing with cosmic relatives there has been a certain agony and ecstasy of experiences in interactions with more experienced and powerful souls.[7] I began to truly learn the mercy of God.

---

[7]See Chapter 22, par. 2

CHAPTER 16

THE ADJUDICATION BY THE BRIGHT AND MORNING STAR VERSUS LUCIFER, THE ESTABLISHMENT OF THE GOVERNMENT OF THE PLANETARY PRINCE USING HUMAN PERSONALITIES AND THE ANNOUNCE-MENT OF MACHIVENTA MELCHIZEDEK AS THAT PLANETARY PRINCE OF URANTIA

Against all odds, Niánn and I and the children finally moved into our new home in November of 1990. The house was situated facing dead center of the energy reflective circuit and mountain. It was one of the most beautiful sites on the planet and people from all over the world came to see this mountain. Although some will find out its name, I choose to not yet reveal its exact location. It was so good to be in a home again after living in a tent with the three children for almost three months. After having used all of our savings to make the down payment on the home, we had only $25.00 to our name to provide for all our necessities, but I had faith that since the guides said we should be there, it would all work out. We started meeting neighbors, some of which were cosmic family, but they were not at first responding to our work. By December of 1990 I had become very depressed. Now that we were here in this protected area I felt so lost. Where were the higher souls that were promised? Where were our cosmic family members? We had to continue to sell many of our sentimental items in order to exist. Finally, Niánn obtained a position as a teacher in a Montessori school. The midwayers helped us by hiding our mortgage transaction from the loan company for three months until we were able to make the payments; the lending institution did not even know we existed. If those beginning cosmic family members would have aligned themselves there, would have been no need for some of the actions taken behind the scenes by the midwayers.

In November of 1990 we received our first letter from the two older souls mentioned. We hardly believed what we read; they were actually *URANTIA Book* readers and teachers and were interested in Continuing Fifth Epochal Revelation and wanted to talk to us further! We began the correspondence, and I felt that sooner or later we would disagree on something major, but to my surprise our relationship only got better. We began having long telephone conversations, which we always looked forward to; and it soon became quite obvious that somehow we would all have to be together. Paladin made it clear that these two men would indeed come to Sedona, and began to tell me of our cosmic connection. It didn't take long to realize that this was the couple that, three years before, the midwayers had mentioned we would be meeting in the future. In May of 1991 they joined us in Sedona, Arizona, and were living within walking distance from us in a central location of the energy reflective circuit, compliments of the Midwayer Commission* (a location by human methods not so easy to obtain). We all saw the hand of God begin to work with us. They recognized that I had the mandate of the Bright and Morning Star, and I recognized that they had the mandate as the first of the Vicegerent First Ambassadors to Machiventa Melchizedek. Neither one of us really understood exactly what that meant; *we are still learning.* With our joining in the union of souls, the four of us created our own energy reflective circuit which enabled other representatives of the Machiventa Government, including Machiventa, to speak to us. Soon, other cosmic family members from around the world began corresponding and had a desire to join us and become part of the Extension Schools of Melchizedek. Soon to be with us from Australia, was the former editor of *Six-O-Six*, Delphius, who is a cosmic daughter of Niánn and I. We awaited with great expectation her arrival and the arrival of others at her level of spiritual ascension. In September of 1991, Desmond and Lexia came from Santa Fe. In Sedona, several others aligned after the coming together of the first four elders. When Delphius arrived, the energy reflective circuit created by the union of souls became stronger and drew others from various parts of the planet who resonated with that vibration.

At this time on October 9, 1991, I am being asked to interrupt this narrative to present a transmission by the Bright and Morning Star, Gabriel of Salvington.* (This transmission became Paper 213 of *The Cosmic Family, Volume I*)

"My adjudication began in approximately 1911, Earth time. This occurrence had been prophesied through other prophets. It began with the early Papers of the Fifth Epochal Revelation and slowly, throughout the years, with representatives of my government, under the mandate of Christ Michael, our Universe Sovereign, rematerializing on Urantia. In 1934 and 1935 a higher vibratory frequency was established. In 1955 an even higher vibratory frequency was established. In 1967, quite unknown to the Urantia movement,* another vibratory frequency was established. By this time the Urantia movement had fallen from the clear reception of their Thought Adjusters* and the Spirit of Truth within them. Had they been open to the voice of God, many of them, and so many other millions, would have received the baptism of the Holy Spirit of my Divine Mother, the Universe Mother Spirit,* and would have manifested the gifts of her spirit. It would have enabled them to receive and understand the Continuing Fifth Epochal Revelation now being given through the mandated personality, Gabriel of Sedona. Many Protestants and Catholics alike received these gifts. If the obstinate *URANTIA Book* readers had asked for it, they too would have received the manifestations of the Mother circuits and could have been an aid to those Protestants and Catholics to help them in the understanding of the Fifth Epochal Revelation. I call upon all *URANTIA Book* readers to receive the baptism of the Universe Mother Spirit and humble themselves and seek learning from God and Continuing Fifth Epochal Revelation which the Spirit of God is pouring out upon this planet for all who have ears to hear. It is her last gift before her rebirth. It is a complement to the Thought Adjuster and the Spirit of Truth within. It is the dance of the renaissance. It is the fruit of the tree of life. It is the cleansing water of the soul. It is the mirror of complacency and pride. It is the fire for the slothful. It is milk from the breast of the Mother for the obstinate, and the final covering by the divine hand from our Paradise Father. It is the awakening light in the eyes of all souls who receive her; the essence of true respect and submission to the Father and all personalities who are elders within the Father circuits of time and space, particularly to those who are mandated within the Government of Machiventa Melchizedek, the present Planetary Prince of Urantia.

"It is not within the text of this transmission to define the mandate of the Bright and Morning Star given to Gabriel of Sedona or the mandate of Machiventa Melchizedek given to other future Ambassadors. However, what I do give is so that you, who are chosen to read this transmission, can activate that which is within you as reservists and awaken you to your proper destinies and soul urges. It is the mandate of the Bright and Morning Star given to Gabriel of Sedona, to manifest to all the vast cosmic family quite real physical blessings, to change circumstances and to come against any of the evil forces on behalf of any of those cosmic family members who wish to align themselves with the **First Cosmic Family** and the establishment of the Machiventa Government upon this planet. It is a mandate that brings the highest love mates together: their highest spiritual complements. It is a mandate of fulfillment to individual personalities and souls. It is a mandate of perfection which comes from the overcontrol of thousands of unseen celestials on this planet. It is a mandate of universe administration unified on a third-dimensional plane entering the fourth dimension. It is a mandate of interdimensional and interplanetary communication. It is the reopening of the circuits of Nebadon and Orvonton* with your world, Urantia. There is only one personality on any one planet who can have my mandate, co-shared by his highest spiritual complement. It is a mandate of healing of the soul, **astral body**, and all other bodies which you will come to learn about, including the physical. It is a time and space-warp mandate that knows no boundaries within its universe of existence, that being Nebadon. The past, present and future are coexistent within this mandate.

"You will come to learn of these things since you have this personality with you and I am with you, Gabriel of Sedona being the Audio Fusion Material Complement for me. Until your planet has entered the first stages of light and life, a process that is being greatly accelerated by this adjudication and within the government of Machiventa Melchizedek, I, the Bright and Morning Star, take personal representation and overcontrol. All those within the First Cosmic Family who align themselves perfectly with their God, first-time Urantians and those from other universes and particularly those of Avalon, to some degree can manifest the power, harmony and love of this mandate. I bid you all, who are to be part of this great work and manifest destiny, to come from the four corners of this planet. The harvest is ripe but the harvesters are few.

"In servitude and eternal loyalty and love to my Father Christ Michael of Nebadon, the Bright and Morning Star of Salvington; as transmitted through the Audio Fusion Material Complement, Gabriel of Sedona."

A transmission from Machiventa Melchizedek, Paper 214 from *The Cosmic Family, Volume I.*

HOLOGRAM APPEARANCE OF MACHIVENTA MEL-
CHIZEDEK TO ONE OF HIS POTENTIAL MATERIAL
COMPLEMENTS AND POTENTIAL VICEGERENT FIRST
AMBASSADORS, WITH THE ANNOUNCEMENT OF HIS
ELEVATION TO THE OFFICE OF PLANETARY PRINCE
OF URANTIA; CLARIFICATION OF THE TITLE OF THE
PLANETARY PRINCE; AND WARNING TO CALIGASTIA
REGARDING PROTECTION AND SAFE PASSAGE FOR
ALL THOSE CALLED TO THE EXTENSION SCHOOLS
OF MELCHIZEDEK AT PLANETARY HEADQUARTERS IN
SEDONA, ARIZONA, U.S.A.

"It was decided by Christ Michael, the Bright and Morning Star, the Acting **Governor General of Urantia**, and the Chief of Seraphim[*] that it was time that I announce to human personalities the reestablishment of the seat of the Planetary Prince on Urantia. It happened on December 9, 1989, in Santa Fe, New Mexico, U.S.A., an area very close to several energy reflective circuits near Four Corners in which hundreds of celestial visitations had been made by physical spacecraft and seraphic transport[*] alike, an area that had slowly deteriorated in mass consciousness from the spiritual position it had been designated to obtain. We had previously found our audio receiver in 1987, and he was given the complete mandate of the Bright and Morning Star and all that went with it. Now it was time to appoint the first two of the potential hologram receivers, who would act as a representative of myself after 2040 - 2050 AD. Other celestial personalities would form images of themselves through the light body of all future Vicegerent First Ambassadors. They were appointed to be the first two to serve Gabriel of Sedona and Niánn, with the mandate of the Bright and Morning Star. These two potential Vicegerent Ambassadors were apostles of Jesus in the first century. Far from saints, they still had much spiritual growth to obtain. It was decided that my announcement would first be made to these two[8] as they had the higher mindal ability to comprehend and follow up with an announcement of my appointment to the rest of the world. Now in this century the virtue of their heart would have to match their mind. They would be given the opportunity to complement the virtue of Gabriel and Niánn and the mandate of the Bright and Morning Star. Several others[9] had been contacted but failed to step completely out of the Caligastia system and make my announcement public.

"Caligastia was told many things that I cannot give in this transmission, but what I can say is, that he was not allowed to try to take their lives or cause any physical accidents to the first two potential Vicegerent First Ambassadors, or any others in the future; also upon their leaving, neither he nor any of his representatives would be allowed within a five-mile radius of their physical bodies. A half dozen angelic beings were assigned to protect this radius until these two would eventually come to the protected area at Planetary Headquarters in Sedona, Arizona. The reason I give this information is because those who read this transmission and know you are also supposed to be in Sedona, Arizona, might wonder if Caligastia

---

[8]Note: Because there will eventually be other Vicegerent First Ambassadors, we prefer not to use the names of the first two, as all future stabilized First Ambassadors will share this mandate. For approximately 40 years they will be tried and tested before they become actual full stabilized third-to-first-circle First Ambassadors. When the mandate of the Bright and Morning Star leaves the planet, the ambassadors and all mandated personalities of the 12 World Councils will still have to be accountable to the overcontrol of the Bright and Morning Star mandate and the then Gabriel of Satania, which Gabriel of Sedona will become. Their individual godly authority will depend upon their loyalty to Christ Michael and the Universal Father and the love of God in their hearts.

[9]Before December 1989 certain prospective reservists and Vicegerent First Ambassadors were contacted by the Midwayer Commission and Machiventa in Toronto, Ont., Vancouver, B.C., Canada, and other energy reflective circuits.

could try to do the same thing to you. Fear not, for if your alignment is in the will of the Father, you will have that same protection until you reach your destination within the Aquarian Concepts Community at Planetary Headquarters in Sedona, Arizona, U.S.A. What these two did not know then, is that my government would be established in Sedona, and I physically would live there, although unseen at this time, but ever present within the same five-mile radius of Gabriel, Niánn, and other family members. This first community will be the prototype for the first cities of the Divine New Order. It is not just a government of human beings, but a government with divine overcontrol and design, using mortals to exemplify the administration of divine projections within a lower world framework.

"The signature of any mandated elder to the mandate of the Bright and Morning Star carries with it a warning to those who assume to be spiritual teachers, but whose motives are far from divine. To those who call themselves messengers of the brotherhood of light, channellers of **archangels** or even of Michael or whomever they claim to be contacting, it is a warning that they must humble themselves and become students at the Extension Schools of Melchizedek. They first must find their true God and the Creator Son of that God, the ruler of their universe of Nebadon, Christ Michael, and then submit to his appointed and mandated human personalities. The first of these is Gabriel of Sedona and Niánn, and second, the **Liaison Ministers** and all other elders, men and women alike, who have first aligned themselves with their complementary polarities and cosmic ancestors at Planetary Headquarters. If they refuse to heed the request of these mandated elders then they have refused me, for their signature carries the complete authority of the Office of the Planetary Prince of Urantia, just as Gabriel's name carries the complete authority of the Office of the Bright and Morning Star of Salvington. Each of them will come to learn of the complexities of their own mandates in the years ahead, and so will all of Urantia. We suggest to those who are interested in the healing of their physical bodies that you request PAPER 205 of *The Cosmic Family, Vol. I.* Gabriel works within the astral, **Tron therapists** and stabilized third-**circle** Vicegerent First Ambassadors will work with the etheric[10].

"**Sananda**" was the title of Christ Michael on another planet when he took the office of Planetary Prince in one of his bestowals. It is not the name of Christ Michael and never has been, not on this planet or any other. If you receive a personal letter of request from either Gabriel or other personalities of the Divine Government, I pray that you treat it with the utmost respect, for any reason they would have to contact you is in accordance with the true spiritual government of this universe and the lines of communication therein, starting with Christ Michael and proceeding from the Bright and Morning Star to myself, Machiventa Melchizedek, on Urantia. We have at our fingertips thousands of supermortal and celestial personalities to see to it that you begin to respect their requests, for this indeed is the adjudication of Urantia. Truly, let the love of God brighten your horizons. Let the discipline of God guide your thoughts and let godlike humility direct your decisions.

"Machiventa Melchizedek, Planetary Prince of Urantia; in cooperation with the Bright and Morning Star of Salvington; as transmitted through the Audio Fusion Material Complement, Gabriel of Sedona."

---

[10]At the time of editing this second edition, May, 1995, no potential Vicegerent First Ambassador had stabilized on the third psychic circle. Four former apostles of the first century, James, John, Matthew, Luke, and Paul, which include the two mentioned on page 103, have been unable to so far. James is the closest candidate. *Santeen who has a higher mandate as a Liaison Minister is the only example of the office of Vicegerent First Ambassador functioning the way it should under the mandate of the Bright and Morning Star.*

CHAPTER 17

THE CHAOS BEGINS

When thousands of American troops were being sent into Saudi Arabia, it was hard to believe that the majority of Americans were still waving flags and wanting war. Little did they know that thousands of lives would be lost (mostly Iraqis, but that was okay because they were the new bad people) and all because a few families in control of the world's third-dimensional structure wished to keep that control. The rest of the voices that cried out for God and country were as puppets on the strings of those in power, and these voices willingly sent their sons and daughters off to die so that the rich could stay rich, while they themselves wondered where the next meal was coming from and could not even afford proper medical care. The majority of those sent to war could not afford a proper education, and that's why the military had been an option; they had few other choices. This was the way that "Big Brother" decided things for those who had voted them into power and kept them there. The powerful ones' sons and daughters went to the exclusive colleges and were able to choose a career of their hearts' desire, they lived in the grandest of mansions and wore the finest clothes. It was unpatriotic to talk against one's country and some said it was even ungodly, for surely God was with America. What America did not know was that their sons and daughters were being drawn into an immense trap by those who hated them and all that they supposedly stood for. The game was being played. In their palms were the sons and daughters of the patriotic puppets, not only in America but in all of the countries in the world where nationalistic tendencies led people to believe that their nation was God's country. The whole concept of being a planetary citizen was lost except to just a few so-called idealists who sang a song called "Planetary Brotherhood and Fatherhood of God", but the music of this song was only silence to the deaf ears of the proud, arrogant and spiritually blind. The

106

stage was set for the almost final destruction of mankind; it did not matter who fired the first shot, the shooting began. More and more troops were required to go to the Middle East; and in the beginning, since nuclear weapons were decided against by the United Nations, it was conventional war. Although the war ended in a few months, over the following years the Arab countries one by one began to turn against the United States, and wars escalated. It was an unbelievable mess. The nation of Israel, that so many fundamentalists said would not be destroyed, was overtaken by the united Arab powers and genocide took place in the millions. It was a long war, lasting into the late nineties. American men in their forties were being drafted and so were many women. Children were being left parentless as a result of this long war.

By the late nineties our community was growing all of our own food and supplying all our own energy by solar power and another technique which I won't mention here. This technique was given to us by Celestial Overcontrol. Hundreds of cosmic family members were now living in Secret Valley. Many who came, got in by the skin of their teeth and many of them did not last long as there was much discipline and sacrifice required. The only ticket into the fourth dimension, which our planet was about to enter, was the study of Fifth Epochal Revelation, and **CFER**. The dying of the self that God demands of each individual was a prerequisite to the continual stay in Secret Valley. We do not quite know how our unseen protectors kept away the lawless and criminal element from our valley. All I can say is that throughout the years the only problems we had were with those we allowed in to become a part of us and who were not sincere and had to be removed.

When the Chinese saw that the U.S. was finally weakened to the point of almost helplessness on the home front, they attacked our country. First they allied with the united Arab nations and marched into the Arab lands and attacked the Americans there. It was the Chinese who also led the attack against the *nation* of Israel; but by this time "the true Israel" was safe in the protected areas around the planet under the human leadership who were, in turn, in submission to their supermortal leaders.

It took a certain amount of faith for the cosmic family members to remain in the protected areas when the food supply was low and when at times it seemed that there was some stability in our country; at least that was what the news media reported. Those who were not in one hundred percent compliance with the will of God would fall back into wanting the desires of Babylon and of the flesh. It was these who had to be discovered before the final evacuation.

Little did we know that our planet was a great testing ground and that our communities were the final laboratories for those entering the fourth dimension. Many came to me during these times and said that they could better serve the community back in the world by making money and therefore being able to buy the things that we needed. Others said that they would be able to become influential in getting the things we needed. Some even said that they could go out there and outright steal the things. Many were impatient in waiting for their proper complementary polarity to come and some were envious of those who had their complements or even two complements, and they had none. It took awhile for me to see that life within the community would not yet be heaven, that I could not trust the human heart. I gave the benefit of the doubt to all who claimed they wanted to walk into the fourth dimension, but sooner or later would show their true selves. As I did not want to become callous in my heart or cold in the handling of those I loved, I allowed myself to be vulnerable, choosing to be hurt by those who would betray me, rather than be a brother and leader who could not love or trust. I knew that one day I would be able to have total trust in those with us who had been tried and tested by God. I longed for that day when not one Judas would be left among our company. As I have mentioned, faith was necessary for those of the community. It became increasingly obvious that it would be advantageous to identify those souls who lacked the faith needed to grow into a fourth-dimensional person.

When the Chinese attacked our country, most of the communication lines were down and we received very few, and later, no channels on the television. So we really had no idea of what was happening. We would see overhead, hundreds of aircrafts and had no idea whose they were, but we took our guesses in the beginning. Later we knew, for they were pointed out by our celestial friends who were not allowed at that time to interfere in any physical manner. In the end they would intervene to stop complete nuclear destruction, but only then would they take part; by that time, however, one third of mankind had already annihilated themselves.

Nevertheless, on some occasions, the unseen forces did protect us from intruders in a very visible way. On one occasion several thousand Chinese troops were about to come over the mountains into our valley. We climbed the mountain and watched them as they came closer and closer to our protected area and we prayed for intervention. I had contacted the midwayers upon hearing of the Chinese arrival, but did not receive an answer. We had very few weapons and were not prepared for physical battle and certainly not with an army of trained soldiers. It was early morning and the Chinese began to awaken from their slumber and to break camp when we spotted on the horizon three vessels that crisscrossed the skyline and became visible to our eyes and to the Chinese. These ships were approximately as long as a football field, and as they came closer to the earth we could hear the hum that their mighty energies caused. The elements of the earth, the trees and rocks shook with the winds of the force, similar to the effect of a landing helicopter, but with much greater power; and these ships were about a mile above us. They lined themselves up between the invaders and us, and shots were first fired by the Chinese. We even saw what looked like nuclear rockets being fired at these vessels, but nothing seemed to penetrate the energy field around them. The next thing we saw was a light coming out from these ships and extending to the earth. The light grew brighter and brighter until it became almost like red energy and seemed very hot. We did not know what it felt like to the Chinese, but I can tell you that in a matter of a few minutes of being in this red energy the Chinese abandoned their weapons, turned and fled. Thousands of them ran, taking off their clothes which soon burst into flames. The next day we went down into the field where the Chinese had been. All we found was abandoned equipment, weapons and clothing, but no bodies. It seemed that no one had lost their lives. They knew as we did, that a superhuman intelligence did not want them to go any farther into our valley. They also saw the three magnificent ships take off and disappear into the sky in a matter of seconds. Whatever this force was, the Chinese did not want to mess with it again.

On another occasion it was winter and very cold. Our wood supply had dwindled down to nothing; but we did not feel that it was safe to go out of our protected area, for by this time everyone in the community felt it was insane to venture into the world. After we had come to this conclusion, for the next several summers we stocked up on our wood supply and thought it would last till the turn of the century. But we underestimated, and there had been much abuse by those who were used to living in gas and electrically heated environments. Many were beginning to doubt the sacredness of this area, and I prayed for an answer. About nine one evening, it was quite dark with a quarter moon, we saw lights coming across the sky. A huge ship appeared and then a smaller one came out of her and landed where we were. Out came Paladin; after receiving some instructions I was given two metallic items that looked like briefcases; inside of them were pellets which Paladin called Velecian pellets from a planet called Velecia in a distant solar system. These pellets burned for weeks at a time without being recharged. They could be lit by a match and recharged by putting them into sunlight. There were enough in the cases to last for the next five years and wood to burn for heat would no longer be necessary.

On another occasion we had heard from a distant source that there was a band of looters and rapists coming our way. These gangs were led by those criminals who had escaped from the prisons and formed armies of thieves bent upon attacking anyone who had any semblance of goodness and morality. Police were rarely available, being more concerned with the imposing Chinese forces and the protection of the inner cities and wealthier areas within them. Many militia groups were formed by the so-called honest citizens and many little battles occurred between such groups. We had heard various rumors about this band of cutthroats taking young women and killing everyone else. The men of this band prided themselves on their physical prowess and often gave captured men a chance to live if, in physical combat with one of them, the captured man won. As this renegade band drew nearer to our valley, we wondered if God had abandoned us, the Machiventa Government included. We prayed to the Father of All for divine intervention. When the band got to the pass that led into our valley and began coming down, the men in our community decided to fight them with whatever we had, so we were positioned behind rocks and trees.

As our community did not believe in storing fire arms for protection, we had very few weapons, particularly the kind of heavy artillery that the mob coming against us had. We had only a few rifles and shotguns that we would use for hunting if, for whatever reasons, the necessity arose. Up to that point necessity for hunting had never arisen, as we grew our own organic fruit, vegetables and meat. Unfortunately, the word got out, and they were coming to take it.

We fired a few shots in the air hoping that up in the canyon top they would hear it and be scared away. Our scouts came back and told us that they were still coming, that they were not intimidated by what they heard. They knew they had us outgunned. After a long session of prayer, trying to determine the will of God, the men in the community gathered up what few fire arms and weaponry we possessed, and moved forward up the hill to meet them. The women hid in protective cover on our land before we left.

Going up the hill, I had many thoughts. I remembered a situation, long before we had the land, when a community member, whose property we had used for gardening, got angry with me because I and Overcontrol told him that neither he nor his wife were to help themselves to the vegetables or fruits. Even if it was their own land, it was a community garden and the community member that had been appointed at the time to be head of garden produce distribution, was the one to make that decision. We found out that when there was no food in the markets, even members within our own community, who weren't closely aligned to the principles of the Divine Government and my mandate, would sneak into the garden and steal food. Many of the decisions that I had to make several years before the hard times came, were not understood by those at lower levels of understanding. I knew that if we didn't implement those necessary rules from the beginning, that when the terrible times came there would not be enough aligned to stop the unaligned from stealing and eating all the community garden food and either giving it to their unaligned loved ones in Sedona or taking it and storing it for their families in other states.

We were on our way up the hill, not knowing what we were going to face. We saw them coming from a distance once we got to a certain point. We were greatly out-numbered and out-weaponed. I knew that our only chance for victory was to surprise and ambush them. I asked the men to climb to higher elevations, which they did. We got above them and waited. The plan was first to start a rock slide, and to run down the hill at full strength in a surprise attack. As we waited, we all prayed for a miracle, as the hungry, angry band of men came right beneath us.

I was about ready to give the order to start the rock slide when I noticed they'd stopped in their tracks and were looking straight ahead. I looked through my binoculars and noticed their eyes and faces showed fright. I could not imagine what they saw. Many dropped their weapons and ran back up the hill. Others scrambled in various directions. A few came toward us, but realized it was a hard climb and began running down the hill and up another. They were completely frightened by what they saw. It took all of ten minutes for them to disappear behind the hill.

All of us quickly ran down to the point where they had stood. We stopped, and began to move more slowly, as we tried to see what they had seen. We looked straight ahead and saw absolutely nothing but the beautiful forest mountainside and our wonderful secret valley. I was shocked. I went down on my knees at that point and prayed. I asked Paladin to come in, which he did. He told me that thousands of midwayers had materialized, enough for these oncoming robbers to see them. I was ecstatic. We all were. Once the word got around, we were like a bunch of silly little boys, jumping up and down, shouting and yelling, making jokes. We knew from that point on, that we were as safe as a baby in its mother's arms, but we had to be tested. The tests God puts us through! In the end he always supports us if we do the right thing. "The act is ours, the consequence is God's," *The URANTIA Book* says. We are to take action, as protectors and leaders of our women and children. And when we do, God takes the next step.

Many of us old warriors, at least the majority, were relieved as we knew for sure, that we would never again have to pick up the sword, and that our days fighting with weapons were over. We knew God's invisible army would protect us from then on.

I remembered the war of 1967, when Israel defeated the Egyptian army in six days. It was reported that hundreds of Egyptians got out of their tanks in the same kind of fear. They too thought they had seen a larger army of tall, mighty men. The truth was they outnumbered the Israelis, had more guns, and from their position could not even have seen the Israeli army.

I recalled a verse in Exodus which said, "The Lord thy God will be an enemy to thy enemy and an adversary to thy adversaries." It is so good to be in the will of God. We heard reports that many of those who did not align with our community were dying of starvation. Many of them robbed and murdered attempting to get food. Some were too proud to come and ask us for help. Many were too weak to even attempt the trip. The only sanity left in the world seemed to be at Planetary Headquarters and the other safety areas where we had set up the other six communities.

What had happened that day was the talk of the community for many months to come. We all needed that physical event, for despair was great among us. The lawlessness of the land and the death around us was unimaginable. Many of our relatives, friends and acquaintances were not allowed in the protected areas and had to face all of that by themselves. There were few survivors. Had they only listened years ago! Had they gotten their priorities right in the previous years, they too would be experiencing the fourth-dimensional reality of God's other children from distant planets and dimensions. They too would have been fed, like the Israelites of old, with manna from the sky and would have been led by a pillar of fire by night.

CHAPTER 18

A NEW GARDEN OF EDEN

It was very evident to me, during the seventies, eighties and nineties, that the vegetables and fruits of the planet were losing their taste and nutritional values. Only in certain locations where communities had learned to get in touch with the Mother essence of the earth and her helpers, the elementals and Life Carriers, were fruit and vegetables produced that could give the nutritional value and medicinal usage they were designed for by the Universe Supervisors and the Creator Son, Michael, so many hundreds of thousands of years before. When the Material Son and Daughter, Adam and Eve, came here, they and their children lived in a environment conducive not only to physical growth and health but also to spiritual development. After the fall of Adam and Eve a second garden was started, but it never had the tree of life nor the aid of the Celestial Overseers. Because of the Caligastia rebellion the circuits were cut off from this Material Son and Daughter, as they were to the rest of the planet. Perhaps the *fountain of youth* that so many tales have been written about could have been realized if the superhuman complementary polarities, Adam and Eve, had not defaulted. Eating food that was vibrant and full of unique potentialities, would bring life and healing to those who partook of its nourishment and our planet would not have developed all of the various diseases that have caused so many untold deaths and suffering. As the Father of All cut Urantia's circuits, which made available cosmic knowledge, wisdom and interplanetary communication to the inhabitants, so had the Universe Mother cut off the essence of the healing properties within her garden. As the evil, sin and iniquity increased in the twentieth century, that which people ate became worse, and that which people drank polluted. Only in the protected areas would food be grown and water drunk that was not poisoned with the greed of man's impurities which manifested into the very soil of the earth itself.

We didn't know much about gardening when we first began to plant our little garden, and this was before we had acquired many acres surrounding us and also before we were talking to interplanetary botanists. But what we found was that whatever we planted seemed to grow twice as big and yield twice as much. We usually had enough left over to serve many other mouths besides our own. We began community gardens with people in the area in the early nineties. Little did we then know how important this garden would be to so many. When food shortages became common in America and gasoline so expensive that it was difficult to travel to buy food, the garden became a very sacred and protected place. We found out that many who came by to investigate, actually needed food and secretly hoped that we would offer them some. We began to see that if any real trouble broke out, many would come by and not ask, but just take. So we became more secretive about who we told. Those who came by were given food, and some purchased it by donation. We asked these to keep our gardens a secret as we did not have enough for the outside world. We also asked them if they were interested in joining our community with its spiritual emphasis. Those who were not interested in spiritual things did not come back. Those who were interested in spirituality joined, because they saw, by the growth of our plants that God was blessing our work.

One day, as Niánn and I were busy working in our garden, we noticed a wet area that was unusually damp for a hot sunny day. We asked each other who had turned on the water, but all denied doing it. We thought someone had secretly done it, or perhaps one of the children had, and did not tell. Several hours later we went back to the same spot and it was still very wet, so we took a shovel and began digging. We could not have dug more than a foot or two when water began shooting up. We had discovered a high water level coming from one of the tributaries of the nearby creek, an underground spring. We later found out from our unseen mentors that this spring was a gift from them to us. We used it for irrigation and our area became an oasis within a matter of months, with running water at all times and all of it drinkable. We were told that if the people all over the planet had been in alignment with their Creator, as individuals and nations are supposed to be, this would be their reality: every thorn a flower and every thistle a blade of grass, as the earth would be in harmony with herself. She would not want to spit up volcanic rock and so would be soft to walk upon and gentle to the bare foot. We began cleansing the area of all little stones, pebbles, rocks and thorns. At first just an acre was cleared and one could walk without shoes and not be harmed. Even the weeds seemed to obey the Divine New Order and were replaced by new plant life that developed at the rate the earth wanted it to. We had no names for these new plants, so the Universe Supervisors told me to name them. It became a hobby of mine to understand all of the plants, fruits and vegetables and I became extremely interested in botany. By the end of the twentieth century I enjoyed all aspects of agriculture and farming, particularly getting out and working with the soil and watching it respond in the harvests of the divine hand. Some of the foods that were new had a consistency and a taste very much like steak or other meat. It was most amazing. One could swear that we were eating meat. The only plant that came close to this before was eggplant.

We began to discover that certain fruits would do things to certain people, for the foods that one eats can also aid in the spiritual development. Medical science began discovering this in nutrition and diet studies many years before, but never to the degree that we discovered it from eating pure foods. In the organic growing of foods from the sixties through the nineties people were being cured of various diseases caused by eating foods that were produced from soil far below the standards of the Creator's original design. When our foods began to come near that original design, a whole new world opened up for us; and it was a unique and wonderful experience. Some people who ate the red foods, such as beets and watermelons, became full of energy and physically stronger. We began to see near superhuman feats take place. People slept less and arose early with vigor. Hard labor became no problem, even for people who were physically lazy; once their bodies became pure and they ate of these garden-original fruits and vegetables, they manifested the properties thereof. So the universe guides told us to feed red foods to certain of the slow moving people who had been reluctant to pick up a shovel and dig. When they ate these foods they became like a machine, working physically all day long, whereas before, they just wanted to use their brain power. When we fed the green fruits and vegetables to the hyper and physical people, they became more mentally oriented and wanted to do more creative, artistic work and administrative functions. It took quite some time to learn which diet should be given to what people. We learned a lot about natural ability as opposed to learned skill. The one thing we did not have to worry about any longer was motivation, for all one had to do was eat a magic piece of food and presto we had a volunteer for whatever the project was. We tried with older people, and sure enough, even those in their sixties and seventies and eighties wanted to do a young man's labor. If they had not grown old in a dying body on this dying planet, they would have been able what their light body was telling them to do. So we had to be careful with these foods and have supervision over what and how much was eaten. If mistakes were made in the food distribution, more careful supervision was needed in assigning work duties by the leaders and supervisors and I had the greatest responsibility. I did not want a 70-year-old having a heart attack trying to do a 20-year-old man's physical task. Nor did I want a skilled laborer trying to paint a masterpiece on canvas when something had to be built in a hurry. It was quite a lesson for all of us to learn what these foods brought out in the latent potentiality of both mind ability and physical prowess.

We had quite a few comical things happen. For example, we ate a certain yellow berry and as it was a new plant, no one but Celestial Overcontrol knew what it was. They wanted us to try it with the assurance that it was safe. So I was the first to partake and a few moments after eating the berries, I began to laugh for no reason. I felt euphoric and no matter what was said to me, it seemed like a laughing matter. So you can guess what I named this berry: the *laughing berry*. I passed these around and people ate them. I could hardly control my mirth, anticipating the first laugh out of them, particularly the ones who walked around with their droopy faces every day. I would even make the experience funnier by telling them stupid jokes that cracked them up. They thought it was the joke that made them laugh rather than the berry. When I wanted to hand these out to some others in the community, I would say, "Come on, I'm going to tell a joke." The droopy ones began to tell these stupid jokes, thinking they were funny. The other people who knew that these people never told a joke in their life, let alone a stupid one, asked, "What got into them?"

Other food seemed to break down certain inhibitions in people such as exaggerated concern with how one looks. We found that many began running around half naked or completely nude, where before they were very modest. This of course led to the desire for physical intimacy among certain members, and this was okay in itself, but it seemed, that was all they wanted to do for days at a time. We also saw what could be taken as infidelity occur among many members who normally would not have those thoughts. This resulted in both good and bad endings. We discovered that the food that led to this particular breakdown would be scientifically researched for the next several years in its spiritual and psychological implications on the human race, and would take a volume to explain. Let me say that many old maids ended up with husbands, and many bachelors ended up with wives. Dozens of inappropriate relationships ended and better ones began. It was not really the food that caused these problems; it was the fallen state of man and his concepts of reality that the fruits allowed to break down.

It was found in the twentieth century and even before, that certain foods could not be eaten by some people for they were in some way allergic to these. The pure foods of a **"Garden of Eden"** would definitely cause reactions in the spiritual and psychological realities of mankind. Thus food to us became very sacred and we began to eat accordingly. We grew food and raised livestock, both chemical-free. Flesh eating continued to be the reality for millions whose genetics were from flesh-eating worlds of other universes, like Avalon, Fanoving and Wolvering.

In the Divine New Order that will be set up on the planet, those who distribute these foods to the world in the agricultural sectors will be overseen by the oldest and most trusted souls of constellation status and above. In those early days I, as an Audio Fusion Material Complement, relied heavily upon my connection and communication with Universe Supervisors.

CHAPTER 19

THE CLOSING OF THE DOOR OF THE ARK

Up until the times of the final wars and continued deterioration of the food supply and other basic needs in our country, many of those whom we spoke about our work responded negatively. Some even stated that they were not at all interested in our work. When hard times came, many became our "best friends," and those we hadn't heard from for years began communicating with us by letter and phone, until telephone communication was no longer available. Dozens from all over the world came without notifying us and ended up on our doorstep. I found that those community members who had questioned my leadership and wanted to be leaders in situations and circumstances before this time, now did not want to take the responsibility of helping make a decision as what to do with these people and their children. Many of those who came were the biological and cosmic sons, daughters, brothers, sisters and friends of those already here; and so with each person who came uninvited, I had to connect with celestial intelligences to aid me in knowing what to do, for each circumstance was different and each person unique. Some of them I automatically knew I should turn away without giving them the opportunity to stay even one night. For these decisions I always was judged by those in the community with misplaced compassion and unclear discernment. Many community members came to me, expecting me to feel a sense of obligation because of their relationship to me or their relationship to God, and wanted me to allow some of their relatives to stay. I wondered why the democratic process of voting and going with majority rule could not be implemented in these situations. The guides told me to try it with one situation, and so I did.

At that time there were 150 adults over the age of 21 in the community. First of all, trying to get 150 adults together to have a vote was not as easy as it sounds, even when we were within walking distance of one another. The person in question had to come in to stay for at least a night and day, and so I automatically lost the option of not allowing the person, in the first place. Accepting that, the community was open to whatever negativity that person might bring. Even though it was top priority for the adults to come together, it took three days to get the majority of the people together, but only 55 turned up. Some of the women had to care for their small children. We then realized that baby-sitting by the older children had to be implemented so that more women could in the future attend important meetings, and this brought up more problems. But for that first time, we voted with the 55. It was decided by the majority of mostly men that this person, who just happened to be a male himself, would be asked to leave after being fed and counseled. I also had made that decision, but I never would have allowed the person entrance in the first place, but had agreed to it for the sake of the experiment. The person showered, was given a healthy meal, and was counseled by one of our elders. Even so, he was noticeably bitter, and when he left, he set fire to a corner of our land. Luckily it was noticed in time and almost no damage was done, but the intent was there. We also discovered that the decision of his staying or going was a much talked about topic of many of the members for days afterwards, taking them away from their other duties and tasks, especially since he was the biological son of one of the men in the community. Years ago he had been notified by us to join our community; this was done time and time again. So this one intrusion seemed to create a disturbance among us for at least a week after the incident. I asked the Midwayer Commission if I should continue with the democratic process. They said why not leave the decision up to the community members, and so a regular meeting was held, for which a week's notice was always given.

In the meantime, would you believe that there were other uninvited guests who came to the community, and I had to go through the democratic process again? An emergency meeting was called with proper child-care and other community functions covered. All 150 adults showed up within a two-hour time period. Things were looking up. This time it was about a young couple who obviously did not belong together. No one in the community knew them, but they had heard of us. After talking with this couple for just a short while, my immediate response was that if they agreed to have no further sexual relationship together and abide by the community rules, they could be given a trial period to stay. I then contacted my unseen mentors, and they told me something that the young couple did not tell me, that she was pregnant by her true complementary polarity of a third-dimensional seventh stage alignment and needed to return to him or for him to come to our community. So I was correct in my analysis. I did not mention this to the group. Both of them were quite charming. All of the women liked the couple, and everyone invited them to stay. She confessed openly that she was pregnant, and the couple was congratulated by all in the community. Of course the facilities for married couples was offered by some of the members, for it was taken for granted that they belonged to one another and that he was the father of her unborn child. I at this time wished that everyone in the community had that "relationship with their God moment to moment" like they said they did so that their guidance could tell them what was actually happening. I quietly prayed for an answer, hoping that I could come to some quick decision of what to do, knowing all the facts. I tested the waters of the community members' open channel to their Thought Adjuster and guides. I asked that we all be in prayer for a few moments to make sure that this majority decision was a correct one. I personally thought that surely now some of them would be told by their guidance that this woman was pregnant by another man, her higher complement. After five minutes of silence, no one spoke up. So I said, "Has anyone anything else to say about this couple staying in the married quarters?" No one responded. Some of them began to clap, welcoming the couple; soon all were applauding in agreement. I became silent for a few moments and connected with the midwayers. They told me to ask the young woman if she had anything to say to the community. She just thanked everyone and said that she and her husband would be assets to our community. The midwayers then told me to ask her which husband she was talking about, this one or the true father of her child? She looked at me in shock, and so I openly asked her who the father of her child was. She then broke down and admitted to all of us that her husband was a *URANTIA Book* reader and that was how she had heard about us in the first place. He also read our Continuing Fifth Epochal Revelation literature and wanted to come join our community, but she had not truly been interested in studying the Fifth Epochal Revelation. Of course I realized then that she had come to us only for food and shelter and not for spiritual reasons. She was personally ready to come into a fourth-dimensional relationship with her absent higher mate, but could not do it without her mindal willingness to become a student of the Fifth Epochal Revelation.

It was then easy for all of us to see that the whole process of screening these applicants would take time; and only those who were highly clairvoyant, mandated, connected material complements would be able to save the community much time and needless heartache. That was the last time that a democratic process took place. I made the motion to vote on whether this should take place again. I spoke out strongly against it and pointed out that the extent of my authority needed to be fully understood at the gates of our community when our lost friends, family and acquaintances were knocking at the door of our compassion. The vote was a unanimous 150 against the democratic process.

During the months and years ahead many were allowed to enter the gates of our community and stay with us. When I was in doubt, I always accepted the guidance of my unseen superiors; and many times I questioned the mercy of their decisions, for it was quite clear that it was these who caused the community the most problems and were themselves damaged physically and spiritually by the obstinacy of their thinking. Some of them physically transcended while with us, for they could not be healed, as the diseases progressed rapidly in their bodies and could not be corrected or reversed in time to save them. We also saw many miraculous healings.   When some who had physical illnesses changed their inappropriate thinking and false views of reality, their bodies began to respond, and their diseases to be cured.

I thanked God that finally all understood my mandate.[11] Soon our first community would grow into the hundreds, then with satellite communities worldwide.   By the turn of the century, millions were aware of our work and our communities.   The understanding of the authority of the mandate by Christ Michael, at whatever level, was absolutely essential.   Initially, before mail services were no longer available, our mailing list had been in the thousands, and it had become impossible for me to read all of the literature sent from people wanting to enter our community.   We simply did not have the time to respond to them personally; at first we tried responding with advice as to where they and their families could go for some supernatural protection.   But after a while, I was told not to send information to people, as that particular door was closed, because those communities that were set up around the planet were beginning to be overburdened with the entrance of newcomers.   The exodus from the cities of newly awakened souls were now in the thousands, and in the near future it would be in the millions.   But by then, new communities would be out of the question as chaos and confusion would rule.

One of the communities that we helped set up in England decided that they wanted out from under my and Celestial Overcontrol's supervision.   They had decided that in their community, in all decisions the democratic process would be the rule over and above the authority of the designated leader I had sent there.   You might say that this was a repeat of history: parliament and Oliver Cromwell versus the king.   That England was the country where

---

[11]It should be understood by readers that before the printing of this book, all responsible mandated personalities, from Liaison Ministers to Second Assistants and all permanent community members, knew that the democratic vote was not the best way or divine way.   The trust that they had in Gabriel and Niánn was well earned.

this kind of rebellion was to take place in one of our communities should have been anticipated, because the people still had an earthly queen and well-developed parliament. The reality is, that if certain monarchs are not in contact with their God, parliament should indeed rule. That is why Divine New Order communities are set up with the board of six as parliament, in cooperation with the **watcher** or director of the community; and in areas where the leader feels he needs counsel, he does not have to go to the angelic realms and above, he can simply go to his parliament. But if the parliament all feel one way and the leader feels another, that leader who is chosen of God to be in that position should be able to have full authority to act upon his inner and outer guidance. A leader who is an active and functioning administrator simply cannot come before a parliament of six, sixty, six hundred, six thousand, six million, every time certain decisions need to be made. It is understood by the six and the six million that the decisions made by the leader are made in the best interests of all concerned. The leaders of God will be put into those positions by the hand of God. It is up to God to decide the ways and means, and for all to recognize the mandate God has given that individual. The leaders men put into authority, men can oust. Their authority lasts as long as the men who put them there want them there. The governments of men get away from them because they become too large, bureaucratic, and impersonal. Eventually a strong leader can indeed become very powerful. Unfortunately, if these men are not moment to moment in contact with their heavenly Father and the heavenly Father's Universe Supervisors, these men create dictatorships and impersonal rule over underprivileged, undereducated and underemployed people. Divine government must be set up, and those humans appointed to be leaders in this divine government, must have a relationship with their Creator and be an appointed vessel of the Creator for that administrative position. The appointment by man alone will not and cannot guarantee good leadership. Men who have been appointed by God, at whatever level they know their God, and appointed by man, have the cohesion to some extent to bring harmony, justice and peace to the peoples of their country. Imagine governmental leaders who understand the vast cosmology of the grand universe with all its various beings created to aid in administrating a local planet and are able to call upon these celestial beings for aid and advice. I was told that this would be the case very soon. These leaders would be working with Machiventa Melchizedek, the Planetary Prince of Urantia, and be overcontrolled by the Bright and Morning Star himself. All of those who had gotten into the ark before the door was closed were able to help Urantia set up this government.

As we were returning to Urantia and looking through the portholes of the spaceship, we realized many millions had died and gone to the mansion worlds, which we had an opportunity to visit before we returned to the earth. It was an unusual experience, of course, since they had died to get there and we had been transported there in a ship and in light body. They had received new bodies, but we had our old ones still functioning on a higher frequency, premorontia or light body, with the anticipation of receiving new ones when we returned home to Urantia. The amazing thing was that we would not have to die to get one. We were told that we would walk into a very highly advanced technological device in the resurrection hall and somehow drop our old bodies and receive a new one. The complete technological process is only known by certain **seraphim** who were entrusted with this divine administration. I looked forward to receiving my new body and put in my order, so to speak, for one of at least six feet, for I was tired of being 5'6" and having a metabolism that seemed to gain weight just by smelling food. What seemed to be in only the minds of science fiction writers was happening before my very eyes. Humans being humans, there were many jokes among the women about what size and shape of breasts they would obtain; and men, of course, joked about their future penises. But we all, with great expectation, desired these bodies that would need less sleep, less food and would be lighter. These bodies would complement our new ascension to the fourth dimension and the first psychic circle, with the addition of two extra higher circuits (chakras), so that we would be able to communicate with some of the higher intelligences who would administer the government of our planet.

CHAPTER 20

"THE HEAVENLY COURT"

It was an awesome sight in August (Urantia time) of the year 2000 when billions of souls were brought before the Ancients of Days* on Uversa, our superuniverse capital. You might say everybody was there. Mortals and beings from millions of inhabited worlds came, some by seraphic transport, some rematerialized and some by spacecraft. I can not describe in human vocabulary the majesty of grandeur our eyes beheld. The court consisted of the three Ancients of Days and millions of their assistants, from angels to Mighty Messengers* to finaliters of all stages and planets. Midwayers were also there, all visible to the mortal eye. Indeed every knee did bow before the representatives of the Universal Father, the Ancients of Days. They were the most beautiful beings I had ever seen. When they entered the arena, the natural colors emitted from the already beautiful surroundings and beings became totally white. It seemed as bright as the Earth's sun, and all had to adjust their vision to look again. But it wasn't sunlight, it was the Sons' Light; the Sons of God lit up not only the outward but the inward. I saw every sin that I ever committed in the next hour of total quiet before these judges of superuniverse justice.

Since this was a judgement concerning the rebellious planets in the universe of Nebadon, including Urantia, the next divine personality to arrive was Michael of Nebadon, the Creator Son, who Earth knew as Jesus Christ, along with Immanuel, the Union of Days* from Paradise, and Gabriel, the Bright and Morning Star, the head administrator of the universe. We could not determine the mode of transportation, but it seemed as though one moment they were not there and the next minute they were. Once they were seen and their divine presence felt, billions of beings of all orders fell to their knees. From this position I gazed and saw three

128

distinct colors: white, yet different from the Ancients of Days', a violet, and what is considered an ultraviolet. When the colors of these beings began to combine with the already brilliant colors of the supermortal beings, it was like looking into a kaleidoscope. No words were spoken by these beings, nothing needed to be said, for all present knew that for all practical purposes they had met their God and that every secret within their hearts was known to them. As I began to clear my vision, I saw hundreds of thousands of mortals getting up at once and moving to the center of the arena. I felt internally that these were some of the millions of fallen starseed, that partook in the Lucifer rebellion and now they had been called in their hearts to answer for particular sins in their lives. For what seemed about half an hour of Urantia time, all stood in front of these beings, bowed and then I heard very distinctly an archangel make a proclamation and read the ruling of the Ancients of Days that all of these souls be sent to planet 609 of Satania, a planet in the primitive stage of development, and that these souls would enter as primitive mortals with the hope of learning particular things they did not learn as more civilized beings on Urantia. I was so glad that I was not among them. The next thing I saw was some sort of gigantic craft hover above them; I could not tell, when I looked closely, if it was mechanical or not. It made a musical sound and was beautiful. Within twenty to thirty seconds several hundreds of thousands of mortals kneeling before Michael disappeared. I said a silent prayer to God, "Dear Father, forgive me again for anything I have ever done." Before I continued, I felt the voice of God within me say, "Be still and know that I am God, faithful one, for you know that you are to return to Urantia." So I quieted myself and felt greatly relieved. Again I saw several hundred thousand from this vast array of billions come to the center. The same scenario took place. I heard another proclamation from the archangel who said, "You will be sent to planet 617 of Satania, the planet of warlike tribes, hatred and cannibalism. It is hoped that during your lifetime there you will realize the things you did not realize on Urantia and change your own cannibalistic attitudes that not only killed the flesh of your brothers and sisters, but their souls as well." Then I saw a red flame coming from the archangel, engulfing every one of the several hundred thousand in the center of the arena. Again I saw a great ship gather all these souls and in a matter of seconds they were gone. This same sequence continued. Several million were sent to fallen planets. The sons and daughters remaining were those who would ascend to a higher plane.

When all of the rebellious souls who should have been ascending were gone, the magnificence of the moment became even greater. I cannot put it into words. There was present a feeling of eternity. All my fear was gone. I knew that every wicked soul from that vast array of billions was gone. Next I saw millions of angels of all orders coming into the center and dancing, you might say, in the spirit. I wondered what they were dancing to, and as soon as I had the thought, I began to hear music: music like I had never heard before. I and others started dancing, and like a domino effect, when each began to wonder about it, they heard the music too, and began dancing. I saw Christ Michael, Immanuel and Gabriel dancing, holding each other's arms going round and round. They seemed to be above anything material, as were many of the other superhuman beings. But all mortals were confined to the material ground and matter. This went on for what seemed like over an hour of Earth time, all laughing with joy unspeakable. Then the music stopped and there was quiet. Hundreds of thousands were again called to the center of the arena, but there was a different feeling as those in the center began dancing again, for they had no fear of the proclamation from the Sons of God, whose angel then proclaimed that these souls would advance to the first mansion world. At that moment I looked with superhuman vision and saw many I knew, those who did not make it into the ship with us. I wanted to go to them, but I knew that I could not at that moment, yet I somehow knew that I would soon visit them on the first mansion world. I could not explain my knowing, I just knew. Then the great mother ship came above, sang its song, and in an instant all these souls were gone into the arms of Morontia Companions.* For several hours, billions of souls were sent to the seven mansion worlds. All temporarily visited mansonia #1.

According to their spiritual attainment they were then assigned to a specific world.

After those who were assigned to the mansion worlds had departed, I felt it was my turn to go to the center with several hundred thousand, not only from my ship but from others. We got up and walked toward the center with no fear, knowing we had been forgiven. This was not a judgement of descension but of ascension. We heard the proclamation, "Go back to Urantia, fulfill your dreams and the dreams of your children, and make manifest the kingdom of God. Power will be given to you. You will be put into positions of authority, rightly earned. Because you have been scorned as latter-day prophets for my namesake, you shall be justified. Well done my good and faithful servants. Your planet is no longer the planet of the fallen, but of the righteous. You will be instructed by your superiors and you will be the superiors of others. The chain of command will be a chain of cooperation, love and understanding based on wanting the best for each of your comrades and respecting each individual soul for his or her unique abilities and talents. What one cannot do, another can. See your brothers and sisters as extensions of yourselves, for there is only one mind, that of the Universal Father, the Absolute and Ultimate of All. Join in that mind and teach others about the mind of harmony and joint effort in goodness, kindness, humility and unselfishness. Let this be the new portrait of Urantia. Allow yourselves to be the brush of God, your words to one another to be the paint. Return to your planet and create the masterpiece."

It felt as if I moved in slow motion away from the divine Sons to the ship, the Star of Bethlehem. Awaiting us were beings who had received their judgements before in other universes and other superuniverses. I somehow would know them better. Whereas they could not speak to us before on certain matters, I felt there would now be more of a sharing, for truly the veil was lifted. The present reality I was experiencing was worth every ounce of pain, suffering and tribulation I had ever gone through; I would have gladly gone through it again to arrive at this place.

CHAPTER 21

COMING BACK—THE LANDING AND THE DIVINE
GOVERNMENT
(Speculated date 2004 - 2008 AD)

$\mathbf{A}$s our craft drew nearer to Urantia, I felt certain feelings, memories and pains of all kinds lifting. We had been briefed by the Universe Supervisors that this would happen as our third-dimensional bodies began to lose the lower circuits and we moved into the first psychic circle, as Urantia was now on a fourth-dimensional plane. Lucifer had always tried to make the body more than what it really was; that was why we had tried to dress it so well in all shades of color. If man would have been more concerned about feeding the soul, the spiritual food necessary for its ascension survival, the terrible tragedies that took place on our planet, particularly in its climax during the tribulation period, would not have had to occur. Wasn't it Solomon who said, "Vanity of vanities, all is vanity"? I could hardly wait to set foot on Urantia again, which had been realigned with the basic cosmic concepts of absolute truths that would be the foundation for all of the human race living upon it. As I pondered on these things, many hundreds of thousands of mortals were being prepared to land.

All of the humans who had been evacuated from Urantia several years before were being prepared to descend in smaller vessels from the mother ships. The beings of higher morontia[*] and spirit bodies would be beamed down, and still others would go by seraphic transport and other methods of light-body transference. As I watched from the portals of my vessel, I saw descend in a mighty armada, thousands of crafts of different shapes, each representing the planet from which it came. We were told that Gabriel, the Bright and Morning Star, and Christ Michael would be coming in their own way of transport and to prepare ourselves for a most magnificent spectacle. But there was no way that I could ever have imagined just how magnificent this sight would be. An array of colors, hundreds of which I had never seen before; began coming from a distant point in our system, traveling many times the speed of light. As it came into our local system of Satania, it began to slow down, and when it approached our proximity, we could see that it was so large that it looked like a planet or a satellite world. It seemed to dance in the sky, and it was evident that the gods rode in this vessel. Indeed they did, for accompanying the Creator Son, Christ Michael, were Immanuel, the Union of Days, the Constellation Fathers,* the Bright and Morning Star, hundreds of finaliters, thousands of angels of all orders, and many others too numerous to name. This tremendous craft took the lead and began to descend over the old United States of America, which now would be the United States of Urantia, with one planetary government. When the craft landed it became a permanent structure, a city within itself that would not ascend again. I estimated that it was the size of New Mexico, Arizona, Colorado and Utah put together. We were all told right then and there, if we had any doubts, that its name was New Jerusalem. All of the thousands of vessels landed in close proximity.

After celebrating, thousands were organized and sent to different parts of the planet. I was glad that I would be one to help administer the new government,[12] along with those of higher intelligence who would head the leadership in a higher ascension. I was so happy to have been chosen because of my choice to be in the perfect will of God. Also, for several years I had studied the Fifth Epochal Revelation and Continuing Fifth Epochal Revelation and learned about these beings. Soon the official inauguration of previously mandated human personalities would begin, along with

---

[12]On this side of the Celestial Divine Government, as human mortals with the mandate of the Bright and Morning Star of Salvington, we had to grow into the reality that we were to become, the Planetary Prince and Princess of Urantia, a function of responsibility we were being trained for over a period of thousands of years, as will be explained in the next chapter.

mortals from other planets and former Urantians who chose to come back from the sixth and seventh mansion worlds as part of their ascension to help upstep the process. This new government would be ruled by the precepts of cosmic absolutes and law, which I had come to understand many years ago on Urantia. Now, some basic cosmic rules would govern our planet: the fatherhood of God and the brotherhood of man; the continued knowledge of the existence of an ascension plan for ascending sons and daughters of various systems and universes; the training and sacrifices needed from these souls; the recognition of Christ Michael as the Universe Sovereign and God of Nebadon; the understanding of submission to higher authority and elder wisdom, and knowledge and reverence for such, not only for the higher intelligences who have such attributes, but also for those mortals who had attained such spiritual virtues; an awareness that immortality was not inherent in the master universe and that all beings had to earn that immortality by their love for God and their neighbor, whether that neighbor be of this planet or another. We could no longer think of ourselves as nationalistic citizens or even as planetary citizens, but as universal citizens, all living together on the decimal and **experimental planet** called Urantia with one goal: to reach the Paradise center, the home of all those who choose with their free will to ascend to this divine womb, where we were once in the mind of God and then became a living, thinking reality.

As I began to see the hundreds of orders and thousands of beings from other worlds that I had never seen walk around Urantia before, even though I had talked with some of them as an Audio Fusion Material Complement, I knew that this was indeed a new beginning, an Orvonton celebration. I knew that the master plan of the Divine Father for this little planet called Urantia was beginning to take shape and that some kind of marriage was taking place. As soon as I had that thought, I saw falling from the heavens what seemed like rice, but in reality it was the tears of the Universe Mother Spirit drenching her new planet with her cries of complete and total joy, for she now had given birth to the new seed for her Divine New Order.

THE CONTINUING STORY

The following chapters were written after this book was first published in July, 1992. All of these chapters deal with recent events that have happened.

CHAPTER 22

WHAT WILL MY FRIENDS SAY THIS TIME:
WHEN THE SAINTS COME MARCHING IN?

I don't know if I could have written this chapter before this date July 21, 1993. I still feel it will be very difficult for me. Yet I feel it is what God wants me to do. Our humility can be an enemy to us as well as a friend. It was easier for me to accept that I was an unbalanced chief called Samba,[13] in Arizona, 6000 years ago, because I see all the imperfections in my character. I work on them daily. I have come a long way, but know I still have a way to go. I have asked God often why I was given the human mandate of the Bright and Morning Star and why God invested me with such great responsibilities. I had a very difficult time when the celestial guides told me that I was someone who had been labeled a saint in the past. At first I was not able to share this with anyone. So many people in the New Age go about claiming to be saints, kings, queens, pharaohs and Indian chiefs that I did not and do not want to be associated with this company. On the negative side of humility, if we are an **ovan soul**, we can never really tune into the now-opening memory circuits as long as we see ourselves as just a farm boy or girl from Iowa, or just a steel worker's son from Pittsburgh. We cannot come into our cosmic mind if we are rooted in insecurity. I still am not ready to share with the world all of my past existences, but I know that God wants me to share some of them at this time. as well as some of the past lives of other elders in our community of the First Cosmic Family.

The Catholic church and other facets of Christendom have made saints out of very ordinary men and women who had many

---

[13]Gabriel was told he had been Samba in 1989. In 1995 a restaurant, called "Sambas" was opened in Sedona. Coincidence or cosmic humor?

faults in their character, but through legends they have become bigger than life and more perfect in character than they actually were. Many miracles ascribed to them have been made up or exaggerated.

I must start with the first personality Paladin said I had been, one that I had a hard time believing to be true. I must say at this point that this chapter is a lot easier because of another book that came into my possession through a cosmic brother, in February, 1993, called *Secret Places of the Lion*. The book spoke of a "Goodly Company" who have come into earth existences time and time again to assist mankind for thousands of years, and the author correctly linked several of my lives that Paladin had told me I had lived. I just love it when God confirms information about anything with another source that resonates with every atom of my body. He correctly linked Akhenaten (or Ikhnaton), Pharaoh of Egypt, who tried to bring the One God, Aten, to his people, with Peter the apostle. Niánn, Paladin said, was Nefertiti, Akhenaten's wife and Hanna (or Perpetua as *The URANTIA Book* calls her), Peter's wife. Anyone who has seen the bust of the beautiful queen, Nefertiti, should certainly recognize the same bone structure in Niánn's face. In the beginning of our experience in Prescott, Paladin and other celestial entities had "dangled the carrot" often as to who Niánn and I and others, then with us, were. Now I realize that the reason they do that is that they want us, if possible, to come to con-clusions by self-discovery. It should have been quite clear to me who I was, but Peter was too awesome a character for me to walk in his footsteps. I actually looked forward to meeting him one day and I was quite willing to believe that he was someone else on the planet. When I lived in Tucson I played one of the apostles in a play called *Simon Peter*. At the time I felt I should have played Peter and that I could have portrayed him better than the actor who did. Now I know why I felt like that. However, the actor who played Peter was a classical singer and gave an outstanding performance. Since I wasn't much of a fisherman in this life, this fact also bothered me. Paladin told us that many of the talents and gifts many destiny reservists once had are kept from them, or else they would be doing something other than what God wanted them to do. Of course Peter went out in a boat and threw out a net. That I can see myself doing, laying back, feet up, reading a good book, waiting for the fish to bite. Yup, that's me all right. I certainly identify with his impulsiveness. I have asked our Lord for forgiveness so often in this area. I can see a tremendous improvement in my forties as compared to my twenties and thirties. Since Jesus forgave Peter for denying him three times, I have always found it easy to forgive others. I am disappointed when they think I haven't forgiven them, mostly because I realize they haven't forgiven themselves.

One former apostle was told he was Menes, the first dynasty Pharaoh of Egypt and Ramses I, the founder of the 19th dynasty. I had no problem believing this. On Easter, April, 1992, the Bright and Morning Star, who fused with me, gave this apostle's identity as John the Revelator of the first century. Shortly after that an elder and teacher in our community, was told he was the apostle James of the first century. In that life they were brothers. In this life they have been friends for over thirty years, and together teaching about the Kingdom for twenty-three of them. Peter, James and John were aides to Jesus. We, who were the inner circle with Jesus in the first century are now back together. Our lives touched bases in many repersonalizations. We had much to work out from our astral past. *The URANTIA Book* makes it quite clear that the apostles were imperfect men. I think the details of their imperfections were written in the Fifth Epochal Revelation, so that we now in the twentieth century can understand the interrelationships between one another in a higher spiritualized mind. Character growth can be quite slow, sometimes taking up to the seventh mansion world of Satania. I found that as a song-writer/lyricist/singer, it is easier to write and sing the words than to live up to them. It could take lifetimes. I sometimes began to doubt the whole reality, because I saw imperfections in myself and the other apostles and disciples, but I could not deny so many wonderful serendipities that have happened with the Bright and Morning Star, Paladin and others. I began to forgive myself and prayed to be able to love others unconditionally, despite their faults. One of our community prayers was and still is that: *community members be more conscious of past-life interactions with each other, so that present interactions with each other can be more highly understood.*

Now to top it off, Paladin one day confirmed, after dangling the carrot for four years, that I was also Francis of Assisi. Here we go again. I saw Franco Zeffirellis' film *Brother Sun Sister Moon*, and the famous director had Francis far too female for me. Peter the Apostle, Francis the Wimp?

Niánn was told she was Sister Clare. That I could see for sure. Community members, particularly the females, still come to Mother Clare and confess their most hidden secrets and perhaps what they consider sins. Niánn, of course, has never encouraged this. When I read that Francis was a warrior before his conversion and was in prison for a year, I began to realize that most accounts of him left out his male strength. Trying to find the balance between the male and female circuits can take many lifetimes, both in other universes and on the higher mansion worlds of Satania. For some ovan souls it has taken ten lifetimes or more to reach a balance or stabilization. Francis had to incarnate as an African warrior, who was taken to North Carolina to become a slave. Earlier in this book I spoke of being picked to sing lead in a 100-voice black gospel choir in Los Angeles and how hard it was to leave and become a serious student of *The URANTIA Book*. The soul of my astral, past black life was very much a part of me in this life. Francis also incarnated as Gentle Eagle, an Apache warrior. I identified with Gentle Eagle easily. I feel at home in Arizona, the home of the Apaches, and still feel very much the warrior. Peter was ready to draw the sword at any moment. In several lifetimes after Akhenaten and before Peter, (which I'm not ready to reveal to the world as yet) I settled disputes by the sword. Jesus' words to Peter, I believe, began a real change in him: "Those that live by the sword die by the sword. Put your sword away."

In this life I have tried to learn the way of the peaceful warrior. Perhaps Peter, repersonalized as Francis, should have connected more with the Father circuits to bring about the Renaissance that God wanted, in a much larger way. As it happened, the soul of Peter, in trying to become more **Mother-circuited** in that life, became too effeminate. Francis later realized that he did not have to go to the Pope for permission to do God's will. He realized that his movement did not have to be endorsed by the Catholic church, that he should have left the Catholic church with its many false doctrines. He was already sick from his travels in Africa when he tried to share these thoughts with his closest friends. They believed that he was delirious; some thought he was losing his mind. "Leave the Catholic church? Why that is heresy," they told him. He realized that God had tried to reach him when he first started his ministry, but he shut that part of God off. Just like in this life, when a young man tried to share *The URANTIA Book* with the then Rev. Tony, I defended the Bible with the same misplaced loyalty. As mentioned earlier in this book, I considered becoming a Catholic priest and lived in two Benedictine monasteries, one in Arizona and one in New Mexico, and a third order Franciscan community in Montrose, Colorado. In this life the Catholic church still had quite a hold on me.

In Prescott in 1989, an entity came through me as a walk-in and introduced himself as Francis of Assisi. I did not know at that time that this was a part of my astral self. He indeed was a past part of me that was much more at peace with himself than I was at that time. Francis never had to live in 20th century America. Francis of Assisi's movement spread rapidly in the 13th century; the time was ripe and there was not much competition. Today in the religious arena, there are thousands of self-proclaimed prophets, healers etc. The equation: marketing + fame = avatarness ($M + F = A$), seems to be the unfortunate rule. After twenty years of ministry I had only a handful of students and didn't feel successful by my standards. One day a wonderful thing happened that Niánn witnessed. Our parakeet escaped from the cage and was wildly flying into windows and walls. He never came to anyone

before when this occasionally happened. Francis called him and
the little bird flew immediately to his finger, just like you see on so
many pictures of Francis. What an experience that was for me,
somewhere in between dimensions observing this. It wasn't until
several days later that I was told that I was Francis. I am so
blessed when others say they see that kind of gentleness in me.
Many men with various levels of gentleness think they have to
suppress it because our society has distorted views of what a man
is. I still feel that I went too far into an imbalance of the Father
circuits in later repersonalizations and am now trying hard to
balance myself out. Our planet needs balanced men, balanced
fathers and husbands. Our community is trying to understand from
a cosmic perspective the uniqueness of what it is to be a male or a
female, an ascending son or daughter. I began to see that my
success as the balanced human being with godly virtue I was
becoming, even if it is not recognized by others, is more valuable
than gold. I would prefer to have a few students with the highest
understanding of God, who are actively trying to deal with their
lower natures, than 10,000 who really don't want to deal with their
own baggage.

In November, 1993, I became aware of another repersonalization. What Francis was not able to do in the 13th century, this
same soul was able to do in the 16th century. This time as a
Catholic priest, he started the reformation in the church, which led
to the Protestant movement. Luther, like Francis, was a musician
and wrote many songs of worship that are still sung today. In this
life he had a greater balance between the Father/Mother circuits
and was able to take the courageous step away from the Catholic
Church and lead others to do the same. He regained his Father
circuits without too much of an imbalance and recaptured the
essence of his ancient name. Martin means "ancient warrior." I
had many lives as a warrior swinging the sword, that's why Jesus
told Peter to put down the sword. He was talking about Peter's
past lives. Of course he was also talking to all of the future
generations of warrior souls on this planet. I am not ready at this
time to share publicly the identity of the two most well-known

warrior souls.[14] I can say that both tried to unify the then-known world. One almost accomplished it, but died young. Many in the community know who I was as these warriors. I still am trying to unify the world and conquer it, now with the sword of truth: the fatherhood of God and the brotherhood of man. Luther was asked by Christ Michael to translate the Bible of the Catholic Church. This took tremendous courage and reflected Luther's confidence in his relationship with God. Today I am asked to bring through Continuing Fifth Epochal Revelation of which *The URANTIA Book* is the first one tenth! Many believe *The URANTIA Book* to be all there is—complete. Even though the book itself (p. 1109) refutes that claim. I have felt this calling to make the world a better place since I was a little boy. I don't feel it is important to share a past life unless something constructive can be communicated to benefit you. If you are a starseed, it may help you to tune into a possibly noble past aspect of yourself. It doesn't matter if you were a saint or a great person in the past, it's today that's important. However, it is time for starseed to find their past noble selves. I'm sure many of you have similar feelings of something you need to accomplish to aid our planet. We must also recognize other, negative traits, that perhaps we had in the past, so we can under-stand ourselves better in the present. Luther was prone to bouts of depression, like I was in my former lives as Ikhnaton and Francis. Like them he was often sick. Trying to change oneself is not easy, but it is a must before you can begin to help others change them-selves, or try to help change the world. Ikhnaton, Peter, Francis of Assisi, Martin Luther, and the two warrior souls, all were leaders of men and women because they first dealt with themselves. Each soul was like a Bright and Morning Star in their time. With each life the same soul became brighter and brighter in the reflective image of God. Remember, it's not ego to "know

---

[14]Since this chapter was written, the identity of one of these warrior souls was revealed by Machiventa Melchizedek in Paper 291, which was published in the Nov/Dec, 1993, issue of *The Salvington Circuit* and is included in Chapter 24 of this book.

thyself," it's ego to think too highly of one's self. I know I've still got a long, long way to go.

There have been a few interesting "coincidences" in my life. I was named Anthony Joseph at baptism. Anthony of Padua was Francis' closest friend. I am also the Joseph of Jacob. In the book *The Secret Places of the Lion* the author, George Hunt Williamson, has Francis and a half-brother of Joseph linked. My real name in Italian is "Dell Erba" which means "of the earth or grass." Amadon, my 3-year-old son, was given my original Italian name. This is the Amadon of *The URANTIA Book* and he is certainly of the Earth.

> *What of Amadon of Urantia, does he still stand unmoved?* [emphasis mine]
> (*The URANTIA Book*, page 762:2)

The Catholic church that I was baptized in as a child was St Peters. It was on Fernando Street which is a derivative of Francesco (Francis). My confirmation name is Thomas. In Prescott a son of the apostle Thomas, Mikal, was with us. Mikal is my cosmic son. Overcontrol led me to believe that Mikal was Thomas the Apostle, I feel, because Peter and Thomas were very close friends. I think Thomas may be with us now, but Overcontrol will not confirm it yet.

In this life I almost died of grief when I lost my beloved second wife. Now I know she was a cosmic complement. Akhenaten and Francis both died in a state of grief. Akhenaten felt rejection from his loved ones and the people of Egypt because they would not accept his God—the one God—Aten. You can read what *The URANTIA Book* says about him on page 1047. I still have a tendency to be depressed with life in general. It always seems that I should be somewhere else, no doubt on a distant planet. People can be so cruel to one another. This saddens me deeply. It's much easier to love than to hate, to give than to take, to be an instrument of peace rather than an instrument of war.

One of the greatest proofs of the reality of what is happening here at Planetary Headquarters is the high quality of people in the Aquarian Concepts Community. This indeed is a blessing for me and all of us. Niánn, who shares the mandate of the Bright and Morning Star with me, is one of the most generous persons I know, and brings clarity to most interpersonal conflicts. She has been a professional tour guide for Spirit Steps/Dorian Tours, a touring company in Sedona, and is able to incorporate our spiritual teachings in her work. She is quite suited for this, as on her biological father's side she is a descendent of Meriwether Lewis of the Lewis and Clark expedition. Figuratively, we have both climbed many mountains together. She is the educational director of The Extension Schools of Melchizedek for adults, teens and children. I have watched her spend 4 to 6 hours each Sunday writing up curriculum for each child; that is dedication.

Santeen, my right arm and cosmic son, and a student of *The URANTIA Book* for 29 years, is discussed in a following chapter. He is an elder, teacher, and Liaison Minister of the Bright and Morning Star mandate to the general public. The Liaison Ministers' mandate is the second highest on the planet. (Paper 273 of *The Cosmic Family, Volume III*, published in the May/June 1994 issue of *The Salvington Circuit*) He also is our representative on the business side of the ministry.

Marayeh, elder and Vicegerent Liaison Minister, is head of the counselors.[15] With a Ph.D in psychology and many years of living in a community, she fills this position, not because of her Ph.D, but because of her spiritual maturity. She has been able to add education to experience, because of her willingness to become a student of CFER. She is also a member of the editing team. Marayeh was a reader of *The URANTIA Book* for 15 years. She is

---

[15]It should be understood that Gabriel and Niánn are the highest counselors on the planet and that Marayeh is of course under their authority in this area and in training to become a Morontia Counselor. It is hoped that many at Planetary Headquarters can become morontia counselors.

truly humble. We are blessed to have her here.

Delphius, elder, teacher, editor of our biannual publication *The Salvington Circuit*, and head of the editing team, is also a Vicegerent Liaison Minister of the Bright and Morning Star mandate. She is Niánn's and my cosmic daughter. She was my mother, Queen Tiye, in Egypt when I was Akhenaten, and in fact the person who introduced me to the one-God concept in that life. She also was Mary Magdalene, which *The URANTIA Book* describes as the most aggressive of the women's corps and their main spokesperson. In this life she was baptized as Magdalena Johanna Maria and became editor of *Six-O-Six*, an Australian Urantia movement publication with an international readership. Anyone who has read some of her articles in various publications realizes she can still be aggressive when she needs to be. In the first century, Jesus used her to be his messenger to the apostles with the glad tidings of his resurrection. In this century Christ Michael is still using her to be his messenger as a Liaison Minister to the general public. In the last century she was Niánn's mother when as Lydia Jackson she became the wife of Ralph Waldo Emerson. Niánn was their eldest daughter, Ellen, and in this life Niánn is a direct descendant of Ralph Waldo Emerson, her name being Emerson Chase. The Emerson family in the last century hosted many people at their home, including groups of philosophers and writers. In this life, both Niánn and Delphius still open their doors to many people. Delphius has been a reader of *The URANTIA Book* for over 15 years.

Katrina, a Vicegerent Liaison Minister, elder, and teacher is the educational coordinator of *The Starseed Extension Schools for Teens and Children*, and Niánn's assistant. She has a Ed.D. in education. She was Katharina von Bora in the sixteenth century, the wife of Martin Luther. In this life she is from a long linage of Lutherans; her grandfather was a Lutheran minister. Her spiritual journey had taken her to India twice before she found *The URANTIA Book*. Katrina also plays flute in the Bright and Morning Star Band. Her cosmic name is Len'mana, meaning "Flute Maiden".

Kamon, an elder, Vicegerent Liaison Minister and teacher, my and Niánn's cosmic son, is a warrior of the light. He has stood by me in many battles of past centuries. Now, as a peaceful warrior, he is truly a kind, generous and humble man who loves Jesus, Christ Michael. He has been a student of *The URANTIA Book* for 17 years. Kamon is the head of food production and distribution for the community.

Rafeel (James), an elder with a MA in library science, works with the editing team and is a brilliant teacher and gentle soul. When he speaks, he commands attention because of the strong vocal chords God gave him, fused with sincerity of purpose. He has been a reader of *The URANTIA Book* for over 25 years.

Two of our **First Assistants** to the mandate of the Bright and Morning Star are Desmond and Lexia. They bring a high degree of loyalty and steadiness. They answer all questions on procedure in the community. Both are willing to do what needs to be done, from working in the gardens to running errands, printing tasks, bookkeeping, or construction. You name it, and one of them has probably done it. Much of their hard work goes unnoticed to many in the community. Their dedication has made life easier for many. Desmond is a member of the healing team as a massage therapist and a drummer in the Bright and Morning Star Band.

Celinas is my and Niánn's executive secretary, an attorney, and most efficient administrative First Assistant. She is a generous soul who has served with me in many spiritual renaissances.

Tarenta is a First Assistant and tour guide with *Spirit Steps*. He has had several past lives as a Native American.

Centria is a First Assistant and tour guide with *Spirit Steps* and also has had several lives as a Native American.

Blue Evening Star, a Vicegerent First Assistant, was formerly known as Kathleen Blue Corn and was deeply involved with Native

American spirituality. She has lived a simple life outside of society for many years and presently builds tepees and yurts through her ministry called *Living Shelter Crafts*. She now has incorporated this background with the Fifth Epochal Revelation and Continuing Fifth Epochal Revelation, to write a book *Tipis & Yurts, Authentic Designs for Circular Shelters*. Published by Lark Books. She is also a teacher in the children's schools of Melchizedek. In the first century she was in the women's corps.

Taleon and Saline are Vicegerent First Assistants and head gardeners. They are in charge of the artistic design of the Third Garden or Avalon Gardens.

Landau is a Vicegerent First Assistant. He is a M.D. who is learning a higher way to heal. He has been a reader of *The URANTIA Book* for 8 years. This brilliant native first-time Urantian should be an inspiration to all Urantians.

Talias was a Catholic nun for 16 years and worked as a social worker in the Sisters of St. Joseph Order. She is my and Niánn's cosmic daughter and a Second Assistant. She has done what so many need to do: she has stepped out of a lower reality into a higher one. She has been a URANTIA Book reader for 12 years.

Anton is a Second Assistant. He is a second-time Urantian who was Barnabas of the first century. He is a brilliant stone mason whose walls resemble first-century construction, which adds to the past/future motif of community living environment.

Martha is Martha, the sister of Lazarus and Mary, of the first century. She is just as warm and loving as you read about in the New Testament and *The URANTIA Book*. She is a second-time Urantian and in this life from a long line of apostolic ministers.

John, first-century apostle and self-proclaimed "Beloved of Jesus", still is dealing with his self-importance, but we love him anyway. He loves the teachings of *The URANTIA Book* and sacrificed personal luxury when he lived out of a car for six years in order to take the teachings to many others. Through radio broadcasts, he was willing to speak out against injustices by those in positions of power, which almost cost him his life. He has been a reader of *The URANTIA Book* for over 25 years.

Matthew is a student and **second-time Urantian**. He is gifted in the financial aspects of the ministry like he was in the first century, and is continually learning the higher ways of doing fourth-dimensional business.

All of the aforementioned and just about all of the members here at this time have had past lives together. Many of the old unsettled disputes still surface. All of these souls are here because they have connected with God's will enough to find us at Planetary Headquarters. Here the real struggles between good and evil begin, the struggles of the lower self with the higher self. Most believed they had lived past lives before they came here. Many of us have recognized each other on some level when we first met. I felt God wanted me to write this chapter for many reasons. One of them is that you who read this may open memory circuits to your own past if you are an ovan soul. Perhaps you have an inkling of some past-life experience. It is within my mandate to help you open those circuits. The beings who speak through me, mainly Paladin, want to tell you about your destiny, now. Perhaps you are a destiny reservist or a cosmic reservist. A profound experience happened to all of us when Isis, a woman in her seventies from California, visited us. Although not a URANTIA Book reader, she had for a long time thought she was Joanna of the first century. Her presence among us brought out old patterns of behavior between us apostles of the first century. It seems she was a buffer in the first century between the apostles. Paladin confirmed she was the Joanna of the first century. If you stay around people who think you're nuts for even slightly suggesting you may be picking up on feelings of a past life, you will not find your destiny purpose in this lifetime. You need to be around others who are discussing their past lives as well as working hard to fulfill

God's will in this one. What's really important is who you are now. We don't realize our past and who we were or what we did just to brag about it. Much of the past can be used to help us understand ourselves in the present. If what we learn about the past helps us to become more Christlike and function in a more spiritual mind, then that is what knowing past lives is about. The light or darkness of a person's past should add to the light of a person's present.

I used to think that when you died and woke up, you were like the highest angel—perfect. Now I know that ascension is just that, ascension. You wake up just like you were and start from there. For us starseed and second-time Urantians, we are not consciously aware that we have been here before. We have no memories of our former life; we are not yet eternalized. With the opening of our memory circuits, we are just beginning to find out about our past life experiences. The circuits are just beginning to open since the upstepping of the adjudication. It is a very slow process. Even slower is growth in virtue. The mind can actually develop intellectually and you can still be a very ungodlike person. For centuries you may hang onto various forms of pride and other evil ways. In *The Cosmic Family* volumes this is explained by the Finaliter, Paladin, very scientifically. I speak now and all through this book from my heart, bringing what wisdom I can in layman's terms. I also used to think that when the apostles returned, they would perform many great miracles and bring many people to God. Now I know that they were and still are very human, and that the greatest miracle they could perform would be to change themselves. The apostles are back on Urantia. Some by choice, some because they had to. Believe me, none are perfect as the Master they once followed. Some have fulfilled part of their destiny being in the Urantia movement, but have not yet accepted the Continuing Fifth Epochal Revelation. Some may not make it to Planetary Headquarters and others will. Many come, stay for a while, leave and default. It is so painful for us to see this happen. When we confront certain individuals who have been seared in their consciousness about their iniquity, they behave like the criminal in prison: sorry they got caught, but not sorry they did the crime.

Soul Diagnosis And Soul Surgery—My Hard-earned Ability

True clairvoyance comes from being like God. Greater virtue, fused with mindal ability, seasoned with experience over hundreds and thousands of years, gives an ascending soul clairvoyance. An aspect of this "seeing" is soul discernment. The New Testament calls it "discerning the spirits." In the Christian interpretation many see this as the ability to discern an evil spirit of some kind, when you could not before. They teach that this "gift" came at Pentecost with the reception of the Spirit of Truth; others teach it comes with the additional baptism of the Holy Spirit. I feel both interpretations are correct. But it is an evolving ability, not a complete gift upon reception. It continues, I'm sure, to finality. The understanding of the soul is a cosmic science, and few have the ability to truly recognize good from evil, and error from iniquity at the level necessary to become a good counselor of the soul. Many of us can sense a very iniquitous or a very good person to some degree, as there are indeed many levels of good and evil. Many beautiful people die of various diseases because of incorrect thinking. Others are very iniquitous. Many are quite obvious in their evil; others have become skilled at deception, so skilled they even deceive themselves in their wrongdoing. They are hard to detect. Many appear to be angels of light. They know the right words of the metaphysical/spiritual/religious circles. They can deceive the very elect of God. They are in the circles of the good seed and consider themselves teachers and leaders of those more humble and not sophisticated in mind and manipulation. These are the millions of starseed and some of the two thousand second-time Urantians. The older the starseed, the better they are able to deceive others. When the problem is self-deception and they feel they are in the right, they will go to their graves with their own self-righteousness and various forms of pride. Some souls who have been called saints by the Catholic church fit this description. Some souls who reached a higher spiritual ascension in virtue at some point in their past on this planet, have fallen backward, and never really stabilized.

The first apostles of Christ are not exempt from having to stabilize on the psychic circles mentioned in *The URANTIA Book*. Many have the tendency to see only the good in others, and perhaps that's all they want to see. I too have been fooled by cosmic brothers and sons. I did not want to see the other parts of them that the Spirit of Truth was trying to show me. I didn't even want to hear it directly from the beings I was in contact with. That's what most of us do: we cut off what is unpleasant to look at. I had to learn to listen. Usually we love them too much to see the wrong in them. Unfortunately, if they are not as evolved as we are spiritually, they end up hurting us by turning against our higher truths and virtues. The souls who have the greatest ability for good, but have not stabilized, can also cause the most problems and have the highest potential to go either way, toward evil or toward good. Sometimes the more virtuous venture into error for a few days, weeks, months, years or decades, sometimes even for lifetimes. A second-time Urantian with the highest genetics can ascend to levels of mind superior to that of a two-hundred-thou-sand-year-old starseed who has continually fallen backwards. This was the hope of Overcontrol for second-time Urantians who were allowed to return to their native planet during the adjudication. Urantia is a planet of either rapid spiritual growth or deterioration. When I see into the soul of a certain individual and know that they possibly are months away from changing in some areas and years in others, I have to practice unconditional love when they say that they have changed, but do the same inappropriate thing a few days later. Some of the most iniquitous will spend many more lifetimes on fallen worlds, perhaps worlds worse than this one. The same judgement can happen to those who are so right in their own eyes and are not intentionally harmful. Pride results in blindness to many forms of error. Pride is worse than any drug addiction. Many heroin and cocaine addicts or alcoholics will go to the higher mansion worlds, long before a prideful soul. The prideful and arrogant will be quite lucky if they make the first mansion world.

So many claim to be spiritual. They may claim to be healers and shamans and priests. I get nauseated when I read most "New Age" literature. There is so much plagiarism. There are catchwords that everyone "in the metaphysical know" uses. They expound on a bunch of garbage they don't even believe or understand. They distort new revelation and real truth that they read or hear from a higher teacher. I have already seen my work plagiarized, and books published that became major sellers with lower level and distorted information from the concepts of Continuing Fifth Epochal revelation, (*The Cosmic Family, Volume I*) etc. which we had published in *The Salvington Circuit* and other public mailings, before we even released the book. There's no credibility. The majority have no fear of God because they don't truly know him. They teach instant healing and sell themselves as those who walk and talk with the angels. I could understand why many would think that I'm just another kook, without having properly investigated my work and our community. There are very few real spiritual teachers and healers on the planet. At this time I feel it would be very appropriate to insert part of a transmission on spirituality from *The Cosmic Family, Volume I*.

WHAT IS SPIRITUALITY?

"First of all, we will tell you what it isn't. It isn't a dress code. No form of dress makes a man holy or wise or indeed spiritual, not robes, not collars, not turbans. It is not the way a person walks. It is not their height or their weight. It is not in their ability to speak, nor their intellectual acquirements. No degree given to man or woman can make them spiritual. No university on this planet can proclaim in their schools of theology that a person is now spiritual. No fast or sacrifice can make a person spiritual. Neither can the diet of certain foods or vegetarianism as opposed to meat eating make a person spiritual. No substance found in the earth and ingested can make a person spiritual. No chemical injected by modern science can produce a spiritual personality. No amount of wealth, fame or prestige can bring spirituality to a person. No appointment of position by man to man in any capacity can make a person spiritual. No self-sacrifice, no matter how great, alone can make a person spiritual; not the giving of a son or daughter or their rightful husband or wife to God, nor the giving of one's income, nor the continued public announcement to others that you are God's chosen. No amount of adulation of man for man can make another spiritual.

"True spirituality or virtue is a process that begins based upon certain universe laws and procedures. True spirituality cannot be defined so simply. For example, even those who appear to present the fruits of the spirit may not be spiritual at all. The virtues said to bring about the fruits of the spirit can be disguised at various levels of deception in the third dimension. True spirituality is not so simple, and many factors have to be taken into consideration. Virtue for an ascending son or daughter is an acquired thing. It is learned over a period of time and that time may be hundreds, thousands and indeed, millions of years. It does not come upon you as the Baptists and Pentecostals say, in a moment of time, upon the reception of the Spirit of Truth, making you perfect. It is an eternal process. When you reach finality you can begin to say that you are spiritual. Throughout the grand universe the degree to which you are truly spiritual is the degree of your own individual blessedness. Blessedness is the beginning of individual happiness; but blessedness is higher than happiness, for one can be happy in sin. For too long on Urantia Lucifer has tried to replace spirituality with other things, thereby decreasing happiness for so many millions at whatever level they could acquire happiness. Whatever your level of spirituality, it creates the reality in which you find yourself, and what you have or don't have. It separates that which you desire from that which you will get. As your spirituality increases, your desires that are based upon the desires of God will become manifest. The Spirit of Truth is the beginning of higher spirituality on Urantia; and the hearing of it, moment to moment above all else, is the activation of that spirituality which leads to your individual happiness and fulfillment. Spirituality is a golden box. Within it can be found treasures; treasures that cannot be bought by ascending sons and daughters, for this golden box is owned by the Supreme Deity. Its gifts are bestowed based upon each individual's willingness to seek his or her God in whatever way one can. Based upon that search, and knocking on the door of the heart of God, the golden box begins to be filled. As you become honest, the gift of honesty is given. As you become patient, the gift of patience is given. As you become more giving, the gift of material things is given to you. As you seek wisdom over pride, wisdom is given; and the golden box begins to shine with the light of God. We shall call this box the **heart circuit**. Wisdom, which increases one's spirituality, cannot be purchased. Even when words of wisdom are read, they may not be understood, for wisdom is given by and through the Holy Spirit to those who put others first, for it is written that love should not seek its own welfare but the welfare of others.

"Motives, in harmony with divine ordinance, increase spirituality and bring the body into higher morontia realities and above. Individuals, who are trapped in third dimensional patterns in regard to religious thinking and even livelihood, cannot begin to reach the higher motives, for the higher motives deal with others outside of one's own nuclear family, where most of the people of Urantia are presently obligated. Worse than that, millions do not even have concern for their own families but only concern for themselves as individuals. The more people you can place into the sphere of your responsibility, the higher your spirituality. This is a divine thing; and it is divinely understood at different levels. At whatever level you can now begin to grasp it, it is given to your planet. Certain spiritual leaders of the past have understood this, but it is now available for all to understand. When the mass consciousness of a planet can realize that we are each others' keeper, the suffering of that planet will end. Words can be written and taught, but little understood. For thousands of years, philosophers have philosophized upon lofty spiritual statements written by prophets and wise men of God, but few manifest the power of those words within their own realities for the benefit of the planet as a whole. At certain periods on Urantia at the time of certain renaissances, many ovan souls who had once come to the realization of selfless service to mankind were again brought to this planet and repersonalized as contemporaries, sometimes together and sometimes in other countries. It has been necessary on Urantia for these ovan souls to come back, for they have been the only voices to cry out against the established way of Caligastia.

"What is spirituality? Many may think it is rebellion, and indeed it is. It is rebellion against Caligastia; it is rebellion against Luciferic "reality"; it is rebellion against evil, sin and iniquity. Jesus was a rebel who came against the established norm. Today on Urantia the Spirit of Truth is even more so a rebel. Today the societies of the planet are much worse than they were even in Jesus' time. Then, the people suffered in slavery and poverty. Today the people are also blinded because of materialism and foolish self-pursuit. Spirituality is faith. The faith to be humble, the faith to give of one's talents and abilities to the true spiritual teachers and elders on this planet when they can be found and recognized. Spirituality is gentle when it has to be and forceful when it has to be. It is Father-Mother. It is not just Mother nor can it be just Father; and when the son or daughter is in balance with both, spirituality can be perfected, for the fusion of childish youth then is incorporated with maturated age, and a liveliness of spirit presents itself instead of rigidity and inflexibility. Spirituality enjoys a good laugh, and some of the most highly spiritual personalities of time and space are great comedians. But the comedy is pure and based upon a cosmic fact of the relationships of the evolutionary process which is most humorous on the higher levels. Spirituality is discipline. Discipline and perfection are wonderful as long as within this perfection one does not become so stagnant that one cannot change when necessary. Spirituality, to those who recognize it, commands authority, and we bow to those of higher spirituality because of that spirituality in relationship to the God of All. Spirituality and authority cannot be escaped, neither can spirituality and responsibility. Many refuse to become spiritual because they realize, even at a lower level, that they cannot escape responsibility for themselves or for others. Spirituality begins in knowing one's place with God at any particular moment in that individual's existence. The saints of the past were spiritual, but as they ascended to the higher mansion worlds and above, their spirituality increased, as it does with ovan souls who return to this planet, and others, who do not default in their reasons for being on Urantia or on their missions, if they are cosmic reservists. Spirituality is strong character; and strong character is the fusion of the Universal Father, the Eternal Son* and the Infinite Spirit* in mortal likeness.

"On some planets there are beings you would consider quite obese, but in comparison to any spiritual Urantian mortals at this time they would be like one with a Ph.D compared to a kindergarten child in terms of their spirituality. It is because spirituality is a nontangible thing. You cannot touch spirituality, nor can you always judge it by appearance, and when you do you have erred greatly. On some planets, those who are highly spiritual may be in a body form that would be so different from yours that they would actually frighten you. But those of us who have ascended high enough to sense the essence of God within them, once again, bow to their spirituality at whatever level they have attained it. Spirituality cannot be technically acquired nor scientifically produced. It can be scientifically analyzed in accordance with higher understanding and **Ascension Sci** analysis, but it cannot be programmed, for only God can create a perfect being and the Creator Sons are the only ones given this power.

"There is a difference between courage and foolishness. True courage demands some form of spiritual attainment. The more courageous one becomes in true spiritual alignment, the more one will accomplish for the benefit of all on a particular planet. Spirituality is colorful and creates in the astral realms the purest perceptions of divine colors that can resonate around any one particular individual personality. These colors in turn manifest healing to that individual and to those who are blessed to be near them. On Urantia, the highest spiritual personalities most often become drained of energy, for so many others unknowingly draw from their life force. True spirituality is fragrant with odors that higher celestial personalities can distinguish. This is why, sometimes around high spiritual personalities, flower essences are recognized even by humans. These things, such as color and smell, are a science in themselves and we are just beginning to touch on the subject. The higher the spiritual personality, the more in control of one's self in all respects one needs to become. It is increasingly easier to take into account many wrongs suffered without justifying oneself, for one begins to realize that justification is not necessary and it is only pride that wishes to make itself correct. It is one thing to correct a person's wrong thinking. It is another thing to do it when it is either out of pride or not necessary. The line is so thin that it may take thousands and thousands of years to come to the place of accuracy. Higher spirituality is knowing the difference. Spirituality is knowledge fused with wisdom and applied with experiential reality in the evolutionary worlds and above. It is applied existential* and experiential* reality in relationship to God and to others of God's creation.

"Higher spiritual personalities are social creatures. They are not isolationists. Solitude, although not only a temporal reality, can become a damaging thing when the spiritual personality begins to self-contemplate to the point of misaligning with higher authority or one's peers at any level. Social communication with colleagues within the same realm of spiritual ascension is medicine for the ovan soul. It is within the union of souls that higher spirituality can be manifested and actualized by ascending beings. Higher spirituality in the company of one's elders knows when to voice an opinion and when not to, and higher spiritual teachers know when to ask of those individuals their opinions and when not to. Higher spiritual personalities are ever so absolute. There is no question once they have presented their opinion based upon absolute reality as they know it. If a question arises, it is in the misinterpretation of what the lower individual heard them say, and this is so throughout the ascension process. Truth is often misinterpreted, for it is heard at the level of one's own spirituality and no more. The problem always arises, how does a higher ovan soul or being communicate with a lower one? Therefore, spirituality is the ability to descend to a lower level and make one's self understood at that level of communication. For if you are not understood at any level, you have no value as a teacher of cosmic reality. You may do well in the solitude of the libraries of time and space, but in practical application to the rest of creation you could become a worthless individualist, and at the point where this begins to happen, the personality begins to default. Always in these cases, lack of patience is found in these individuals; and so it is increasingly important that the art of communication to lower-circle individuals be learned and acquired. It begins in the personality when one begins to look at one's own lack of patience and flexibility. These tendencies are common to mortals of time and space who are void of the higher reception of the Holy Spirit, particularly in stronger Father-circuited personalities. In my own ascension to Paradise as a finaliter, it was one of my faults hardest to overcome. It is not in the text of this transmission to give the solutions to the preceding statement, I can only state the possible problem.

"A person with higher spirituality is not envious, nor jealous of those who have acquired what they have not, either materially or nonmaterially. Envy and jealousy are two of the most difficult things to recognize in one's self. It can take thousands of years within the growth of an ovan soul before the degrees of envy and jealousy of an individual can be recognized. These character faults have been described at great length. These unfortunate traits were found in Lucifer, and we have found that it is ever so difficult to open the eyes of those who have followed in his footsteps and acquired these unfortunate traits. Justification of one's own jealousy and envy is quite a thing to measure on our side. There are volumes written on these subjects in the higher schools on the satellite worlds, so it is not a subject you just touch on. The one thing that we have found, where envy and jealousy continues to exist in personalities, is a decrease in their clairvoyant perceptions and of course the reception from their own Thought Adjuster, depending upon the spiritual acquiescence and other attributes of those individuals that determine the many things pertinent to their present reality and certain mandates given them. Mandates can be given to individuals who have traces of envy and jealousy, as mandates can be given to those with other bad habits. It is true, God is the judge of these things; and it should be left to the Creator Son and personalities of Paradise origin to contemplate and decide these things. We at lower levels can discuss these things and contemplate as to why mandates are given to the imperfect, but it is much easier for us to do so, for our memory circuits are more open at higher levels, and we remember our imperfect selves more clearly. It is written that ascending mortals at times often think too highly of themselves. Spirituality and humility are siblings. They balance each other out and indeed are from the same parents. Humility cannot be known unless some form of spirituality exists, but spirituality can exist at a lower level where no humility at all exists. Spirituality comes first; humility follows and grows and grows and grows. Throughout eternity humility is a learning process which increases one's spirituality.

"Spirituality is visionary. It is not crippled by fear. It is prophetic and finds its purpose in the recognition of the divine purposes of others as well as of one's self. The more one can recognize the function of others in the divine plan and can recognize another's individual placement in the divine time-table, the higher the spirituality within the personality. Spirituality is adventurous. It begins to build when it begins to take risks because of its increased faith, not only on the defaulted worlds of time and space, but in relationship to other unknowns. It first learns to plant the seeds; then it learns to find the correct soils and what seeds to plant for the various beings of time and space; it learns the particular foods that need to be digested in body, mind and spirit. Spirituality does not always feel good to the individual, who learns to do what feels good to God, and learns to recognize that one's own feelings may interfere with the perfect will of God. A person learns to separate one's likes and dislikes for the higher good of all. Higher spirituality is not based on always catering to your feelings; it discerns the will of God through the combina-tion of mind and heart fused with the mandated purposes of God as given first through the Thought Adjuster, Spirit of Truth and Holy Spirit within, and agreed upon then by Celestial Overcontrol at various levels, and on evolutionary worlds, by mortal eldership. Higher spirituality learns not only to listen to the inner self, but to the inner selves of others who are their spiritual elders, human or celestial personalities, who are all together hearing the same divine mind. Higher spiritua-lity understands the difference between rest and slothfulness and can discern the same in others and can make use of idle time for the purposes of God wherever it may find itself. Moment to moment, it is always useful to God; even in periods of rest and relaxation, it is in divine will.

"Higher spirituality does not overwork itself to the point of indifference to family, social or union-of-soul responsibility. Whatever it does, its purpose is within the divine will; and it has learned to accept each moment as a gift of divine origin and looks upon the moment as a continuing learning ex-perience.

"The previous comments on spirituality are just a beginning of the comments that could be made, and is not complete by any standard of time and space. They are presented here to clarify some misconceptions on Urantia of who and what is spiritual; but before you can begin to understand any of this at the level necessary, I suggest that you turn your life over completely to God and request the Holy Spirit to make itself known within you, and this begins by accepting Christ Michael, your Universe Father, who became Jesus and left behind his Spirit of Truth for your education. Begin your registration now at the University of Salvington so that your circuits can be opened to the capital of this universe of Nebadon, and align yourselves properly with the absolute truths which are the foundation and stepping stones to Paradise. If you have not taken this first step, please do.

February 6, 1992

"Paladin, Chief of Finaliters; in cooperation with Christ Michael, Creator Son of Nebadon; in the **adjudication by the Bright and Morning Star versus Lucifer** for the implementation of the Planetary Prince, Machiventa Melchizedek, and his government on Urantia; as transmitted through the Audio Fusion Material Complement, Gabriel of Sedona."

This is part of Paper 210 of *The Cosmic Family, Volume I*

Others of the first century have met us through the mail; others met us in our former lives, and some have actually come for a seminar, or joined us for a period of time and left. Many others from various parts of the world can't wait to get here. Those who left the community for whatever reason, could not grasp fully what is taking place. I always know a little more about them, than they know about themselves, because Paladin tells me. He gives me certain information about their past lives, or present one if necessary, that I need to know, but they are not ready to know. I have met several cosmic sons, for instance, who were not ready to hear that I am their cosmic father. Many sons and brothers don't want to humble themselves to the spiritual authority of an elder brother or elder sister, especially if in this life that elder is chronologically their same age or even younger. Few recognize the older soul inside the body, pride gets in the way. Some come half way until something is said that goes against their opinions. We know that we have met Luke and John Mark, the writers of two of the books in the New Testament; Salome, mother of James and John the apostles; a son of John; a son of Thomas; Ruth and Miriam, the sisters of Jesus; Stephen, the first martyr; Susanna, the leader of the first-century women's corps; Joanna, their treasurer; and Rebecca, the daughter of Joseph of Arimathea, who also was a member of that corps. The opening of the memory circuits is a very slow process for ovan souls on Urantia at this time. It is God's reciprocation for the act of your submission to his will. It is the practice of humility. So you see, because we are so proud and arrogant, these past memories come gradually as we deserve the bits and pieces to the puzzle. We can compare humility to a complicated instrument, like a violin. The more you practice the better you get. At some point, certain notes and chords become clear, pure and true. With each act of humility the character becomes more Godlike. Although at times it may come more naturally, you still have to use that free will and continue to practice or you will lose, perhaps, what you previously gained. After a season of applied experience you will begin to become a more accomplished student of virtue and perhaps one day even be recognized by others as a virtuoso. True humility is a treasure in the making.

CHAPTER 23

THE BRIGHT AND MORNING STAR WALKS IN, AND THE REALITIES OF COMMUNITY LIFE AT PLANETARY HEADQUARTERS

In early 1989, the Bright and Morning Star first came to speak to Niánn and me, and three others who were close to us. We did not realize it at the time, but it takes five ascending sons or daughters of one cosmic family, together geographically, closely aligned to the purpose of God, to bring his presence through and enable interdimensional audio communications. To prepare me for this experience Paladin first fused with my body as I was hiking up Thumb Butte in Prescott while carrying one of the twins on my back. I was about ready to give up when he came in. The change in my body energy easily took me to the top. Celestial Overcontrol had been preparing me for his presence, saying to expect Paladin to fuse in the near future during day time. When these personalities first came to me, I couldn't open my eyes or make any movements. I progressed to where Paladin could actually drive the car. It was and still is fascinating. They can do anything in my body: eat, relieve itself, brush teeth etc. Paladin would stay in for hours at a time. Those who say that beings come in and stay for months at a time and then another one takes over, are not of the light forces, or more properly stated, of the loyal administration of Christ Michael. *The Cosmic Family, Volume I* begins to explain interdimensional communication in detail. Needless to say much teaching is needed in this area. One Friday evening the Bright and Morning Star came with more power, more fusion. It's hard to explain, but now I know it has to do with molecular and subatomic reality. He came in at 8 p.m. and taught for several hours, walking around the house. He was still in when I went to sleep, and Niánn was asked to sleep on the far side of the bed. When I woke up around 5 a.m., three hours earlier than usual, the Bright and Morning Star was still in. He first took me outside and walked around the property. He seemed to be blessing the land and giving orders to unseen entities. I know that he created some kind of vortex around the house. (Weeks later, I surrounded the house with quartz rock; no doubt he programmed me to do so that morning). Next he took me into the bathroom and asked my permission to shave off my beard. I don't like myself without my mustache and beard. I knew he had a good reason, so I complied. When everyone woke up, they met the Bright and Morning Star who made breakfast for everyone. I usually have to be coaxed to do that. His other visitations had always been at night, so this was a new experience. He said he wanted to change the furnishings in the house to open it up. He created a sacred room in which we all ate, sitting on the floor, for the next nine months, until we moved to Sedona. He took Jonathan and me into town that day to buy cloth material for the sacred room and hallways. He took us into a retail store and the owner, a woman in her sixties, said to him, "Are you an angel?" He said, "It is written 'Never turn away a stranger for you never know when you might be entertaining an angel visitor.'" He invited her to his Sunday night visitations at our home, but she never came. She probably was told later by her husband, pastor or a friend that she was crazy and lost faith in her own experience of truth. So often we are talked out of God's will by well-intentioned but ignorant loved ones. We had been looking for some time for a wood cookstove. Prescott is full of antique shops and secondhand stores. He gave us directions to drive to a certain one. The owner was just getting back from California with a shipment of goods, he still had the cookstove in the truck, and was willing to trade for it. The next day we went back to pick it up.

That afternoon the Bright and Morning Star took all of us to our favorite Mexican restaurant. Outside the door we ran into a woman who was a proud and arrogant soul. When she looked at me she intuitively knew it was not me in the body, and was very nervous. The Bright and Morning Star did not speak to her but smiled and moved us all inside quickly. I thought of Jesus' teaching to us, "Do not cast your pearls before swine." Then began the strangest ten minutes of my life. When we entered the restaurant, which was full to capacity, everyone suddenly stopped talking. An energy came into the room that was unmistakably not of this world. The four of us and the twins walked down the aisle together and sat near the front. Everyone began talking again after we were seated. They knew me there by my name, Gabriel. The manager came up and whispered in my ear that I didn't have any shoes on, a fact I, as the human Gabriel, didn't realize until that moment. The Bright and Morning Star didn't like to wear anything on his feet. The manager informed the Bright and Morning Star that he would have to put shoes on or leave. He responded politely with a smile, "Sometimes we must obey God's rules above man's," and slowly and gently got up and motioned for us all to leave. Niánn, Evening Star, Jonathan and the twins started walking out. However, the Bright and Morning Star, almost in slow motion, began walking backwards out of the restaurant, using his hands to bless everyone and saying out loud over and over again, "God bless you all, peace be unto you." Again the whole restaurant was quiet and a divine energy came into the room until we all walked out of the restaurant, the Bright and Morning Star last. I fully expected to hear something about this incident in the next few days or even read about it in the newspaper, perhaps something like "Angel refused service at local Mexican restaurant," or "People become spellbound by an angel who likes Mexican food," but we never heard anything about it. I now wonder if the event was blocked out of the minds of all who experienced it except us five who knew more of the reality that was taking place. When I asked Paladin he said, "I cannot give information on that incident." Needless to say, Niánn and I never went back to that restaurant. He ate no meat and very little else. He wore only loose flowing clothes and a headband. Since that experience I feel lost without one. After three full days, the Bright and Morning Star left my body.

I began to connect more with my past lives, particularly those of royalty. I must confess, I began to feel the prince and king in me, not in any egotistical way, but in having a sense of responsibility for many beyond my immediate family. I had felt responsibility as a pastor, but this was different. I was just beginning to learn about the mandate of the Bright and Morning Star and what it would mean to be his human reflection, his human Audio Fusion Material Complement. A new gentleness was a part of me. I even talked a little differently. For the three days the Bright and Morning Star was in my body, Niánn and I of course could not be intimate, but even after he left, for many months I had little sexual desire. However, I began to love Niánn more purely. I realized I loved her spirit. I began to appreciate her more and see more of her godly quality. It was weeks before the Father circuits in my astral self balanced out the strong mother circuitry of the Bright and Morning Star, and I was ready to grow back my beard. I was also told I had become stabilized on the second psychic circle. Peter the apostle, Francis, the friar, and Gentle Eagle, the Apache warrior, were becoming the more balanced, ascending son, Gabriel of Sedona.

As of this date, July 27, 1993, I am still learning what it means to be a spiritual leader in the context of humans in divine administration. I feel God wants me to share some thoughts based on the experience of community relationships thus far, so that perhaps you who are reading this chapter and coming here in the future will not fall into some of these negative patterns. If anything, our experience should make it easier for those coming. We elders and individual community members alike, should be able to help others avoid the pitfalls of their lower natures and to function within the higher procedures of the divine mind and divine government. Here I can only give in generalities what *The Cosmic Family* volumes teach in specifics.

1. We are not just community members or cosmic family. We are all called by God to be representatives of the Divine Government, which functions like the mechanism of a clock. Foremost, each of us is a vital working part of that clock. When one cog malfunctions, the whole clock either stops completely or loses time.

2. Quite often some think they can do certain things better than the leader, that this should have been done this way or that way. Ten people could have ten different opinions about the same thing or procedure. The leader is damned if he does or damned if he doesn't. In short, people need to learn to acquiesce, and trust the decisions of leadership, i.e. students to Second Assistants, Second Assistants to First Assistants, First Assistants to elders, elders to those over them, and up the administrative ladder. Honor must be given to those with overcontrol mandates. Some quality in them has earned them recognition by Christ Michael; can we do less? It takes a good year of being here at Planetary Headquarters to really understand the reasons for certain procedures and how Overcontrol works with me and everyone else. If you become too quickly opinionated or critical without knowing all the facts, you do yourself harm by becoming disappointed in me, Overcontrol, another elder, other mandated Assistants or the whole process by not being here long enough to understand why I and others make certain decisions, teach certain things or say certain things. Patience can truly pay off in your own character growth and be a wonderful antidote to many of your own frustrations. Many of your perceptions need to be understood in the light of a spiritualized mind, which is one of the reasons you are a student at the Extension Schools of Melchizedek.

3. Individuals can be blindly selfish, putting themselves first or using their children in family quarrels, or taking their children out of school when the parents are mad at a teacher because of an interpersonal dispute that has nothing to do with education.

4. Students must realize that elders, particularly those more active in the process of bringing Continuing Fifth Epochal Revelation to Urantia, just can't be a personal "buddy" to them. We are just too busy. If we spent our time socializ-

ing with all who want to, that's all we would be doing. I look forward to the future on our new planet when I can have more free time to just enjoy others. Right now on Urantia, I and others are quite busy helping to bring about that world.

5. All must learn the law of reciprocation (Paper 202 of *The Cosmic Family, Volume I*) and give what they can of their time and finances. There is so much to do and little help or money with which to do it. Everyone wants to eat of the garden. Few want to work it. Also, you cannot be lukewarm (Rev. 3:16) or serve two masters; you can't serve God and the world. (Mat. 6:24) As Paladin says "You must get off the cosmic fence. In all areas of your life you need to be in the perfect will of the Father."

6. When you arrive here, after the romance period of being awed at the beauty of the area and new friendships, you begin to realize that the trials and tribulations of life will still occur. You must realize that you have need of growth. It may not be as easy as you think to change those old thought forms and habits. People need to own up to their own baggage. God is still using the circumstances of your reality to perfect you.

Many prophets today claim divine inspiration from God. For a few, on some level, this is true. But, Overcontrol states that, since December of 1989, I am the only vessel being used as a level one Audio Fusion Material Complement. I'm not the only one, God or his administration, is talking to in the various ways he does. Celestial Overcontrol has been working with me from a first-circle standpoint for over one and a half years now. To better understand the psychic circles, please read page 1209 of *The URANTIA Book* and Paper 209 of *The Cosmic Family, Volume I*.

It is a written that judgment first starts in the household of God. This is the adjudication. Perhaps we here at Planetary Headquarters who are older starseed, older souls with more ingrained wrong thought patterns, are the biggest hardheads; and they chose the biggest hardhead of all, me, to directly speak through. I certainly am not claiming to be better than anyone else in any way. The mandate of the Bright and Morning Star is an awesome responsibility. For whatever reasons they chose me, I can think of other reasons why they should not have. All I can say is, that I do seek to be perfect and try to own up to my shortcomings. We ask people to come from all over the world and spend a few days with us to get to know us. If you can't discern the fruits of the spirit functioning, particularly in us elders, then I advise you to get away quickly. Those fruits of the spirit are: love, joy, peace, patience, kindness, temperance, honesty and unselfishness, just to name a few. But if you do see them and in a marvelous way... wow! perhaps this whole book and *The Cosmic Family* volumes of the Continuing Fifth Epochal Revelation are all true... wow! wow! And Machiventa Melchizedek, the Planetary Prince and staff is really on the planet. Wow! wow! wow! And the head administrator of our local universe, Gabriel of Salvington, walks in his human Audio Fusion Material Complement once a month and teaches all of us. Wow! wow! wow! wow! wow! Jesus is coming back to this planet soon. Just like he said he would.

CHAPTER 24

TIME FOR PERFECTION[16]

by Machiventa Melchizedek

DEO / DIO INTEGRATION, DEO / DIO DICHOTOMY, HOMOGENEOUS ZONES, HETEROGENEOUS ZONES, CELLULAR MEIOSIS, FUNCTION ZONES, DEOFUNC- TION POWER, IN RELATIONSHIP TO ALL MANDATES GIVEN AT PLANETARY HEADQUARTERS IN AND THROUGH MY JURISDICTION AS PRESENT PLANE- TARY PRINCE AS ONE UNDER AUTHORITY TO THE MANDATE OF THE BRIGHT AND MORNING STAR

Jesus said, "Be ye perfect as your Father in heaven is per- fect." For two thousand years now, those who followed the Master have contemplated these words. You have such sayings as "Nobody's perfect," or "Only one was perfect." Many self-ap- pointed prophets claimed to be perfect; many others have really tried. All have failed because the time had not come. The subatomic reality on Urantia prior to the first seal of *The Book of Revelation* being opened, simply made perfection on Urantia im- possible. Now at Planetary Headquarters, this perfection is not only possible but totally expected and divinely commanded. It is commanded of the **change agents** of the twenty-first century; and it is first commanded of the apostles, sons and daughters of apostles, and the first-century family of Jesus. *The URANTIA Book* states on page 360:3:

---

[16]Paper 291 from *The Cosmic Family, Volume III*. This Paper was first published in the November/December, 1993, issue of *The Salvington Circuit*.

The only creation that is perfectly settled is Havona, the central universe, which was made directly by the thought of the Universal Father and the word of the Eternal Son. Havona is an existential, perfect, and replete universe, surrounding the home of the eternal Deities, the center of all things. The creations of the seven superuniverses are finite, evolutionary, and consistently progressive.

"Ascending mortals need to be consistently progressive in associate **reflectivity** at some cellular level to higher universe creatures. *The URANTIA Book* on page 360:5 states:

Except in the central universe, perfection is a progressive attainment. In the central creation we have a pattern of perfection, but all other realms must attain that perfection by the methods established for the advancement of those particular worlds or universes. And an almost infinite variety characterizes the plans of the Creator Sons for organizing, evolving, disciplining, and settling their respective local universes.

"Many ascending mortals and other will creatures fell from a higher state to a lower one. Many who may have reached **Deo-atomic** reflectivity to an **angel of enlightenment** fell to a pre-emergent state. It has taken thousands of years to get them back even to an **aonic** level. *The URANTIA Book* states on page 361:2:

The personalities of a given universe are settled and dependable, at the start, only in accordance with their degree of kinship to Deity. When creature origin departs sufficiently far from the original and divine Sources, whether we are dealing with the Sons of God or the creatures of ministry belonging to the Infinite Spirit, there is an increase in the possibility of disharmony, confusion, and sometimes rebellion—sin.

Excepting perfect beings of Deity origin, all will creatures in the super-universes are of evolutionary nature, beginning in lowly estate and climbing ever upward, in reality inward. Even highly spiritual personalities continue to ascend the scale of life by progressive translations from life to life and from sphere to sphere. And in the case of those who entertain the Mystery Monitors,* there is indeed no limit to the possible heights of their spiritual ascent and universe attainment.

"All who fell into rebellion have lost the ability to manifest into their reality level that which is needed for higher service to God.

Therefore, they have become, in a sense, a part of the curse of Genesis 3:17-19:

> And unto Adam he said, "because thou hast harkened unto the voice of thy wife and hast eaten of the tree of which I commanded thee saying, 'Thou shalt not eat of it,' cursed is the ground for thy sake. In sorrow shalt thou eat of it all the days of thy life. Thorns, also thistles, shall it bring forth to thee and thou shalt eat the herb of the fields. In the sweat of thy face shalt thou eat bread till thou returneth unto the ground, for out of it wast thou taken, for dust thou art and to dust shalt thou return."

"This is the message to all fallen entities, not just those on Urantia. Besides the more accurate account in *The URANTIA Book*, Continuing Fifth Epochal Revelation teaches that in this Bible story Adam represents all who fell from the first law—to love your God with all your heart, mind, and soul. The woman represents any voice you listen to outside of God's perfect will. Those who try to do right things at the wrong time, such as the Material Son and Daughter, Adam and Eve, or others in error, will still suffer the consequences of having to work hard for survival. Those in rebellion who seemingly become successful and powerful because of fame and greed, only end up sick and dying, and usually they are unhappy when they reach the so-called "top." Because in God there is no limit of service to others, you cannot reach the top in God, you can only go higher. You are only capable of giving more to others and of having more to give to others. There is no limit to your service. If you have not begun to associatively reflect a being higher than yourself, then you remain in spiritual kindergarten. *The URANTIA Book* states on page 362:3:

> The divinely perfect creature and the evolutionary perfected creature are equal in degree of divinity potential, but they differ in kind. Each must depend on the other to attain supremacy of service.

"Since Pentecost, fallen entities cannot completely possess fallen man and woman on a cellular level. But they can partially **dio-integrate** from aonic to molecular levels and up, just like **Deo-integration**. Those who have fallen into iniquity at some point in their past, have a terrible time coming back to cosmic sanity. This is because a real **Deo/dio dichotomy** exists. Dioparticles remain in the life force, even though you may be walking in higher areas of **Deopower** in much of your life during every repersonalization. If all of it is not removed, it can surface and exist in the life force of souls in physical bodies and in part of the brain where certain chemical reactions in the body can trigger them. One of the problems of stabilization is that dioparticles that do find themselves meshed in a certain part of the life force in starseed are carried on in the astral reality from one repersonalization to the next and could crop up thousands of years later. That is what we are trying to do here at Planetary Headquarters and why it is so hard to be here. We make it resurface, even if you don't want it to resurface. That is what the adjudication is all about. Then when it does come up, people can't handle it. They don't want to deal with it, they don't see it and blame it on the other person, and so they leave and they never get healed. Welcome to rebellion.

"In biology there exists a *diatom*, which is any of various minute unicellular algae consisting of two halves overlapping each other. In physics there is also *diatomic*, which means:

1. having two atoms in the molecule
2. having two replaceable atoms or radicals in the molecule.
   (*Webster's New World Dictionary*)

"Continuing Fifth Epochal Revelation states, the Ascension Sci scientist or morontia physicist, depending upon the level of their morontia ascension, can look into a free-will creature subcell, and determine, to name just a few observations:

1. Order of creature.
2. Sex (male/female) or Paradise Trinity[*] physical association.
3. Various Trinity personality traits.
4. Ascension level.
5. Rebellion level of evil, sin, and iniquity.
6. Age of soul.
7. Present time-space location.

"When your subcellular system begins to become **aonic homogeneous,** as opposed to **aonic heterogeneous,** then you are nearing the next level of associative reflectivity. These homogeneous levels are called **homogeneous zones.** Partial heterogeneous zones occurred in cellular life after the rebellion of Lucifer in Satania. Scientists are trying to make evolutionary sense of this phenomenon, however they are greatly limited looking with unspiritual and nonrevelatory eyes. In the book called *The Beginnings of Cellular Life,* by Harold J. Morowitz, on page 9 it states:

> One of the primary features that characterizes the approach of this monograph is its strong focus on the notion that membrane and vesicle formation constituted one of the earliest stages and involved an abrupt transition from the homogeneous to the heterogeneous domain. Homogeneous systems are random mixtures, such as solutions where only one thermodynamic phase can be observed. Heterogeneous systems exhibit at least two distinguishable phases. I shall argue that the transition to vesicles led to the directed chemistry or vectorial chemistry necessary for biogenesis, as well as to other features requiring surfaces larger than the dimensions of small molecules. ...It is the closure of an amphophilic bilayer membrane into a vesicle that represents a complete transition from nonlife to life.

"Continuing Fifth Epochal Revelation emphatically states that evolutionary life, as well as spiritual progression, never reverses itself or its forward progression. If this seeming phenomenon exists, it is not a part of the *divine* plan; it takes place within the *permissive will of God.* **Cellular meiosis** is a product of rebellion that God uses for the ultimate good. Thus, displayed in a microscope is the mercy of God. If the rewritten laws of God can be used to turn the most iniquitous of souls full circle, it is like turning a black widow spider into a butterfly. It must be remembered that even the butterfly goes through the metamorphosis of first being the caterpillar. To be able to fly, so many first have had to crawl for a long time in this rebellion. Metamorphosis is a slow process, and the mercy of God in Orvonton allows the process of a diamond in the making.

"Since Gabriel of Sedona had reached his hoped-for aonic reflectivity to the Bright and Morning Star of Salvington in early 1989, (hoped for by Overcontrol thousands of years ago when they first saw his light shine so brightly) it was decided by Christ Michael that his firstborn son, Gabriel of Salvington, would begin to fuse with this human complement. The number of mortals in Nebadon to reach this level in the pre-stages of light and life are few. Usually virtue does not match mindal ability, nor do ascending sons reach Father/Son/Mother circuit balance in a pre-stage of light and life. It was this accomplishment that led the way for the present Planetary Prince, Machiventa Melchizedek, to come to Urantia. This human mortal's reflectivity to the Bright and Morning Star opened the final door for the upstepping of the adjudication of the Bright and Morning Star versus Lucifer. It opened the cellular door for other ascending sons and daughters to become Liaison Ministers, Elders, First Assistants, Second Assistants and future Vicegerent First Ambassadors. Gabriel of Sedona reached a higher balanced Melchizedek level when he was Alexander of Greece, who was called Alexander the Great. Thus he was able to bring knowledge, philosophy, and higher culture to the world. The **Melchizedeks** are a teaching order. Thus, Alexander, at the Deo-atomic reflectivity of a Melchizedek, brought higher learning to Urantia. At that time this was his mandate, the Deo-atomic mandate of Machiventa Melchizedek. He therefore was able to conquer the world. The city of Alexandria, which was founded by him, later became a great center of learning because he was able to implant his vision into the mind of one of his most loyal followers, who afterwards founded the world's greatest library. Thus in the evolution of this soul came the balance of mind, courage and purpose, or Father/Mother Son/Mother circuitry as he brought higher government, culture and learning to the known world. His accomplishments then led many who followed him to aonic levels of the Melchizedek order and the Lanonandek[*] order, by which administrative cellular reflectivity to Lanonandek beings was then established in cosmic actuality on Urantia. These reflective levels are called **function zones.**

1. VICEGERENT FIRST AMBASSADOR MANDATES
1989 - 2040 AD
FIRST AMBASSADORS
2040 - 2050 AD

"Reaching a Melchizedek level in aonic reality means that you first have opened up your circuits to higher understanding. On Urantia you most likely have become a teacher of Continuing Fifth Epochal Revelation or, before that, of the fulcrum, *The URANTIA Book*, but not being a fundamentalist in either, for an open mind is most important. No matter what era you are living in, you must have come to the latest of epochal revelations* to be reflective to a Melchizedek on an aonic level. Although you may still have iniquitous ways about you, some virtue is necessary to reach that aonic level. The remaining iniquity we will hopefully knock out of you eventually.

"Thus, the Vicegerent First Ambassadors to be chosen, will be those whose mind and circuitry can open to higher and continuing revelation. Thus these first ambassadors and future ambassadors will be found to become aides to Gabriel of Sedona. They will be able to grasp lower-level truth, apply it to the latest epochal revelation, and identify with more people and their religious views without compromising their own higher religious convictions. Ambassadors must be able to accept people where they are, persuade them to like them by being friendly, and then teach these people a higher truth or revelation[17]. This is an art. It is a learned practice.

"On Urantia there are many persons more virtuous than some who are mandated at Planetary Headquarters. However, this will change, for those mandated will have to come into perfection very

---

[17]Santeen with the higher mandate of Liaison Minister is the only example of the office of Ambassador functioning at the time of editing this book, May 1995.

quickly, and they will. Many more virtuous souls, do not have this acquired ability to understand, assimilate, and formulate higher truths, and resonate them with God. Gabriel of Sedona is actually the highest 'Sananda' on the planet in relationship to the human reflectivity of Machiventa Melchizedek. If he was, thousands of years ago, how could he not be now? With the mandate of the Bright and Morning Star, he is also Gabriel/Sananda. Santeen/Sananda is next. Both of these and other male Liaison Ministers to Gabriel in Overcontrol will, ascension-wise, quite naturally carry this dual title, as they will always function as ambassadors of the Divine Government. The Vicegerent First, Second and Third Ambassadors are in training. This training will last approximately forty to fifty years until the humans in overcontrol leave Urantia, and the Vicegerent First Ambassadors and others are ready to rule as stated in previous papers.

"The open-circuited mind of four of the apostles of the first century, has enabled them to reach aonic levels to the Melchizedek order and to be candidates as a Vicegerent First Ambassador to Gabriel of Sedona[18]. Up until this transmission there was little understanding of what this relationship actually meant. Ascending daughters cannot obtain this position on their own. Ascending daughters who are complementary polarities to ascending sons with a Vicegerent First Ambassador mandate can share this with their husbands. Vicegerent First Ambassadors, who become **Deoultimatonic** and progress upwards to Deo-cellular in that mandate, increase the power of that mandate and their service to God and to Gabriel of Sedona. This is done by being in the will of God more perfectly moment to moment and by attaining higher virtue. All of the Vicegerent First, Second and Third Ambassadors will first be students of virtue. The teachers will be those mandated to be in human overcontrol within the Bright and Morning Star mandate, as

---

[18]In the 40-year trial period for those and other Vicegerent First Ambassadors, none may be able to become full ambassadors. If that is the case ambassadors will be chosen from the next generation of starseed children who will then be adults.

Liaison Ministers and First Assistants to Gabriel and Niánn, who co-share that mandate. Vicegerent First Ambassadors may be elders because of higher mindal abilities over First Assistants, but First Assistants may have higher virtue than some Vicegerent First Ambassador elders. All Ambassadors function under the mandate of the Bright and Morning Star. Second and Third Assistants to the Bright and Morning Star are candidates for future ambassadorship positions when Overcontrol leaves the planet, if they so choose to stay or have to stay. Mandated First Assistants usually remain in those positions, or they could possibly ascend to eldership. Vicegerent First Ambassadors usually become mandated elders or vice versa. Second Ambassadors usually do not become elders. As of this writing there are several candidates who in the very near future will hopefully become Vicegerent First Ambassadors.

"It should be understood by all reading this paper that Caligastia is very active in trying to downgrade the mandate of the Bright and Morning Star or any of the mandated personalities at Planetary Headquarters. He is not as active at this time trying to downgrade the Liaison Ministers because they are not yet quite as well known on Urantia. What is known on Urantia is 'Sananda,' the title of the present Planetary Prince. This name has been greatly confused and misused, and now Caligastia has taken it and said that there will be hundreds and perhaps thousands of Sanandas. Because of this distortion of the name, we can no longer use it. In reality there is only one Sananda on the planet, and that is I, the Planetary Prince, Machiventa Melchizedek. So, as far as we are concerned, from this point on, I am the only one who will be called Sananda. I would prefer you call me Planetary Prince, not Sananda. If we would have allowed the name to continue, Gabriel would have been Gabriel/Sananda, Santeen would have been Santeen/Sananda and so on. But we will not allow it to continue. Some apostles are to receive another cosmic name, the name of a higher potential in the future. For now, for the sake of their ascension, for the sake of the work at Planetary Headquarters, until their higher names are given, they are to be more properly identified at this time by their first-century names. This is because it was the name during their highest ascension.

"Again we emphasize that Caligastia is now trying to downgrade the Vicegerent First Ambassadors. Several potential Vicegerent First Ambassadors have defaulted, but another first-century apostle is soon to be at Planetary Headquarters and will also become a Vicegerent First Ambassador. Please refer to Paper 214. Santeen, as the Liaison Minister has the voice power; Vicegerent First Ambassadors, have to have both voice and pen power. Two first-century apostles have now reached an aonic level in reflectivity to the teaching order of Melchizedek and a Deo-atomic level in virtue. God bless them.

"The subcells of reflective associates during the adjudication basically determine health or sickness, life or death, **diopower** in Caligastia or Deopower in God. There is much that these apostles can give to one another. It is the direct command of Christ Michael for Vicegerent First Ambassadors to begin to transfigure.[19] All Ambassadors can strive for the gift of transfiguration. It is given by the mercy of God, for the purposes of God. Some may become Vicegerent First Ambassadors without being able to be given the gift of transfiguration, but we would prefer that all have it for many reasons, mostly the healing of souls.

---

[19] As of February 17, 1995, there are no Vicegerent First Ambassadors, so there can be no transfiguration by divine appointments. Like many false channelers without a mandate, some may claim to transfigure. If they do so, they will bring through holograms of fallen entities, serpents and lizardlike beings of other worlds. They may deceive you also by pretending to hologram through beings of the light, just as false channelers bring through some truth, with many lies.

2. ORVONTON, THE SUPERUNIVERSE OF MERCY

"During the history of rebellion on Urantia, the plan of Over-control has been to first reach the more powerful but iniquitous starseed with all the help we can, bringing in their more virtuous cosmic relatives to provide an example for them. With the more iniquitous ones, even if we didn't put them into families of royalty by birth, they usually would manipulate themselves into positions of leadership by force or shrewdness or by being evilly sagacious. They became the first dynasties of Egypt, the first kings of Israel, and before that, the medicine men and the tribal elders. Their more virtuous cosmic family relatives were always around them to admonish them as to higher virtue whenever they got the opportunity to be the mirror of the virtue of God. For thousands of years, the more virtuous had no power but that of truth. They had no authority but that of righteousness. These of higher light were not perfect, but they were never continually iniquitous. They never fell into iniquity in their thoughts or actions for long periods of time like their cosmic brothers and sisters, either in the universe of Avalon, Fanoving, Wolvering, or now in Nebadon. They always caught themselves before their iniquity ran a course of danger to them and others. Those who touched on iniquitous moments in Nebadon and Urantia usually recognized divine consciousness within a matter of days and repented before any real harm was done to others. This was the first trisector seed of Avalon, the seed of Paladin, my friend and co-worker with God. This seed never fell to aonic iniquity. Other sons and daughters of Paladin did fall to even a cellular level of iniquity before Pentecost and were possessed by iniquity—possessed by it completely. The results of this former possession in cellular reality exists to this day, but at Planetary Headquarters it no longer can.

"The mercy of God is a most magnificent and beautiful tapestry. Today on Urantia, some of Paladin's seed border on dio-molecular iniquitous behavior for hours and days. These same sons and daughters have been extended the most grace by Michael.

Some, who began to dwell in the molecular reality of the new kingdom, were even by the side of the Master as apostles, disciples, and first followers. For Jesus to choose those who were borderline iniquitous, does indeed give you some idea of the mercy of God. Judas did not make it. Those other starseed, some who were apostles, became worse in successive lives instead of better. Many who were with the Master were conceited, and either became humble permanently, or grew a higher degree of arrogance in their already self-important souls. Such is the danger throughout eternity of being with divinity. Remember that. Let it register *deep* within your soul.

"We are still doing work with some of the apostles of Jesus and his first followers. The plan has always been for the greatest lights to be in the company of those with the greatest darkness. How else would you recognize your own sins? Particularly, how could the iniquitous see where they need to change? God forbid that you become so blind to your own ugliness that you constantly see righteousness, goodness, or forgiveness as a weakness in others, or you are so diopower mad that you would manipulate your own sons or daughters, wives, husbands or friends to get your way. King David wrote in Psalm 37 the following words which parallel the adjudication today,

1   Fret not thyself because of evildoers, neither be thou envious against the workers of iniquity.
2   For they shall soon be cut down like the grass, and wither as the green herb.
3   Trust in the Lord, and do good; so thou shalt dwell in the land, and verily thou shalt be fed.
4   Delight thyself also in the Lord; and he shall give thee the desires of thine heart.
5   Commit thy way unto the Lord; trust also in him; and he shall bring it to pass.
6   And He shall bring forth thy righteousness as the light, and thy justice as the noonday.
7   Rest in the Lord, and wait patiently for him: fret not thyself because of him who prospereth in his way, because of the man who bringeth wicked devices to pass.

8   Cease from anger, and forsake wrath: fret not thyself in any wise to do evil.

9   For evildoers shall be cut off: but those that wait upon the Lord, they shall inherit the earth.

10   For yet a little while, and the wicked shall not be: yea, thou shalt diligently consider his place, and it shall not be.

11   But the meek shall inherit the earth; and shall delight themselves in the abundance of peace.

12   The wicked plotteth against the just, and gnasheth upon him with his teeth.

13   The Lord shall laugh at him: for he seeth that his day is coming.

14   The wicked have drawn out the sword, and have bent their bow, to cast down the poor and needy, and to slay such as be of upright conversation.

15   Their sword shall enter into their own heart, and their bows shall be broken.

16   A little that a righteous man hath is better than the riches of many wicked.

17   For the arms of the wicked shall be broken: but the Lord upholdeth the righteous.

18   The Lord knoweth the days of the upright: and their inheritance shall be forever.

19   They shall not be ashamed in the evil time: and in the days of famine they shall be satisfied.

20   But the wicked shall perish, and the enemies of our Lord shall be as the fat of lambs: they shall consume; into smoke they shall consume away.

21   The wicked borroweth, and payeth not again: but the righteous showeth mercy and giveth.

22   For such as be blessed of him shall inherit the earth; and they that are cursed of him shall be cut off.

23   The steps of a good man are ordered by the Lord: and he delighteth in his way.

24   Though he fall, he shall not be utterly cast down: for the Lord upholdeth him with his hand.

25   I have been young, and now am old; yet I have not seen the righteous forsaken, nor his seed begging bread.

26   He is ever merciful, and lendeth; and his seed is blessed.

27   Depart from evil, and do good; and dwell forevermore.

28   For the Lord loveth judgment, and forsaketh not his saints; they are preserved forever: but the seed of the wicked shall be cut off.

29   The righteous shall inherit the land, and dwell therein for ever.

30   The mouth of the righteous speaketh wisdom, and his tongue talketh of justice.

31 The law of his God is in his heart; and none of his steps shall slide.

32 The wicked watcheth the righteous, and seeketh to slay him.

33 The Lord will not leave him in his hand, nor condemn him when he is judged.

34 Wait on the Lord, and keep his way, and he shall exalt thee to inherit the land: when the wicked are cut off, thou shalt see it.

35 I have seen the wicked in great power, and spreading himself like a green bay tree.

36 Yet he passed away, and, lo he was not: yea, I sought him, but he could not be found.

37 Mark the perfect man, and behold the upright: for the end of that man is peace.

38 But the transgressors shall be destroyed together: the end of the wicked shall be cut off.

39 But the salvation of the righteous is of the Lord: he is their strength in the time of trouble.

40 And the Lord shall help them, and deliver them: he shall deliver them from the wicked, and save them, because they trust in him."

"If you put a powerful weapon in the hands of the wrong person, tragedy will result. If you put it in the hands of someone more stable, odds are that the weapon, whatever it is, will be used for higher good, for instance, the weapon of Deopower. It is written, "If you abuse that which is given to you, that which you have will be taken away from you." It is God who allows some kings to be put on the throne, who puts righteous ones there, but once they have become king, and they are a threat to the ultimate destiny of the planet, then the emergency measures of divine intervention will occur. One needs to study the life of Nebuchadnezzar in the Old Testament to see the judgment of God on an individual, even while he lives. In another instance in the Old Testament, Esau was the son of the birthright. Jacob was the son of the promise. Esau knew God only on the outside; Jacob knew God on the inside. Esau was a hearer of God's word; Jacob was a doer of God's word. Esau had religious rote; Jacob had piety. Esau sold his birthright for a cup of soup. Many sell theirs for a cup of diopower, in whatever form this diopower may come. If individuals have Deopower, it is because they have earned it, and no one can take it away but God.

No weapon formed against you shall prosper. Greater is he that is within you than he that is in the world. (Isa, 54:17; John, 4:4)

"If we put individuals in positions of Deopower, it is because they have earned it according to their virtue assent. Others who work under their mandate, as it is throughout the grand universe, receive **Deofunction power** from aonic to cellular levels. The Deopower or diopower of persons under those of greater virtue and higher mandate is kept in check. Those who work in a Deofunction do not necessarily have to understand an order and its ramifications coming from one in Deopower as long as they can clearly represent it at some level in Deopower. Therefore, the receiver of such an order or command can follow it in function without the higher degree of understanding. If followed in function they will be protected from any harm that could come to them. Deofunction power is somewhat like a power of attorney. One can have the function of the power, but not the power itself.

"In the book, *The Beginnings of Cellular Life,* on page 19 it states,

In a genetic system, a single molecular event—that is, a mutation—can radically alter the system, thus deviating from the statistical domain of pregenetic biology.

Each of the apostles, each of the change agents of the Divine Government here at Planetary Headquarters, each of the Liaison Ministers, each of the Vicegerent First Ambassadors, are an event in the body of God. These Deofunction levels are powers given only because of the higher virtue ascension of those above them. Those above them in Deopower have the responsibility to bless all those under them spiritually and materially, based upon the following criteria:

1. Their loyalty to Christ Michael, therefore their loyalty to his representatives at whatever level over them.
2. The Deofunction level of their own virtue ascension.
3. The combined loyalty of a certain quality and quantity of all aligned Urantian and cosmic seeds, Urantian and cosmic reservists alike, creating a certain level of auhter energy.

"Always and forevermore you are quite interdependent upon one another. Little do you understand the beauty of it all. Don't let it frighten you. Resign yourself to the higher understanding of it. In this higher understanding, you will become more of a servant to those who are less virtuous. You will become more of a teacher to those of less mindal capacity. You will become more patient with frustrations. All involved in this union of souls, in this cosmic family, in this love connection, benefit. As long as any one who has been less than what he or she should or could be wishes to repent and change, God bestows mercy and forgiveness, as should be bestowed by all.

"To those of you in the Urantia movement or otherwise, who knew any now mandated personality when they were less than perfect, please remember that this is the superuniverse of mercy. If God forgives you, you should forgive others. Remember, anyone can change, even you. If this change isn't real, we will be the first to know, and the first to act. Jesus said,

He that is without sin among you, let him first cast a stone...
(John 8:7)

October 14, 1993

"Machiventa Melchizedek, present Planetary Prince of Urantia in jurisdiction-power associative mandate to the Bright and Morning Star of Salvington; for the implementation of the Divine Government on Urantia in and through mandated human personalities, prior to the coming of Christ Michael of Salvington; as transmitted through the Deo-atomic Level Two[20] Audio Fusion Material Complement with the mandate of the Bright and Morning Star of Salvington, Gabriel of Sedona."

---

[20]On July 31, 1994, Gabriel of Sedona became a Level Four Audio Fusion Material Complement

CHAPTER 25

GABRIEL MEETS WALLACE BLACK ELK

One day while I was working down at my office table by the creek, I was just getting ready to go when an Overcontrol voice said, "Sit down and work some more." This happened several times, and I stayed at least one hour longer. Finally I saw a woman walking straight toward me, and I knew she was going to speak to me. She asked me my line of work, and when I told her she seemed to know and said that I should go over and introduce myself to a nearby Native American who was sitting just a few yards from me. I had only noticed the back of his head a few minutes before but still felt the power of his presence nearby. I knew immediately when she told me to go over that this meeting was pre-arranged by the midwayers. They had almost brought him to my table.

I introduced myself as Gabriel of Sedona, the founder of Aquarian Concepts Community, and he took a long look at me before inviting me to sit down. I would have done the same. He began talking right away about the visions of Black Elk, who was his great uncle. His name was Wallace Black Elk. I had read *Black Elk Speaks* years ago. Wallace was a huge man but spoke with gentle authority. A lot of what he said for the next hour and a half sounded like Continuing Fifth Epochal Revelation in relationship to the earth changes, and he mentioned how negative thoughts could actually trigger nuclear bombs anywhere in the world. He spoke of the fire coming from the earth. Continuing Fifth Epochal Revelation teaches that lower-level pre-emergent energy created by negative Luciferic thought causes much distortion on the earth. I let him share the visions which were a confirming of my own visions and CFER. Much of what he said is written in this book. I wish to elaborate on a different level of reality. First, I realized that this event of our meeting was no

186

accident and that part of the message to me was that the prophetic ministry of Wallace Black Elk was now going to be replaced by my own and CFER, i.e, the mandate of the Bright and Morning Star; the old making way for the new. After about forty-five minutes I began to send telepathic messages to Santeen to come join us at the creek. Santeen heard me amidst interactions with people in a New-Age bookstore in uptown Sedona and came right down. Santeen's ability to be in the right place when he is needed is excellent. God uses him greatly. Santeen, who usually has a lot to say, allowed Wallace Black Elk to continue to teach. Wallace liked him, and the three of us conversed for another forty minutes or so. During this time, the real learning happened from what was going on around us. Walking by us were community members who were aligned with the Divine Government at various levels. Some glanced at us but probably did not realize who Santeen and I were talking to. One cosmic son walked by us who was in a state of rebellion. The funny thing was that he had paid to see Wallace Black Elk speak; God sent Wallace to me where I was sitting and working. This cosmic son looked at me and turned his eyes away. I believe he never saw Wallace Black Elk. I realized that this is what happens to rebellious souls. They miss their moments of higher destiny. If he would not have been in rebellion, he probably would have noticed that I was talking to one of his favorite spiritual teachers. He missed meeting this great man because of his own erroneous thinking processes. I personally would have called him over to join us had he been more loyal to Christ Michael and the Universal Father. Many millions of rebellious souls on Urantia have walked right past the moments of destiny which could have changed their whole life for the better. We were not even disturbed by tourists who usually come to take pictures in the very area where we were sitting. Our conversation of destiny was divinely guarded. I thought of another cosmic son in another state who first gave me the book *Black Elk Speaks*. If he had been with us, he too would have met Wallace Black Elk. Higher love wishes to share with others all the best fruit, but others have not learned to be under the tree when the ripe fruit falls, so they miss out. The love and blessings of God can only be received by those who are in the perfect will of God, each moment, each day. They're under those trees catching the ripe gifts of God's moment-to-moment blessings. Many are blessed in a variety of ways; that is the nature of God. But so many miss all the other blessings that the Father is wanting to give his children. The reasons why are pointed out in this book and more specifically in *The Cosmic Family* volumes.

I, naturally, invited Wallace Black Elk to have a transmission with Paladin. It was one of the most powerful we ever had. The apostles, James and John, the son of Peter of the first century (now Santeen), Mary Magdalene (Delphius), were all present. Niánn (Perpetua/Hannah/Peter's wife) typed while I (Gabriel/Peter) listened to Paladin/Sky Hawk. Paladin sometimes spoke the Lakota native tongue. Wallace Black Elk is a second-time Urantian and was a son of Sitting Bull. He is being called to Planetary Headquarters by the Wakan Tanka (Great Spirit) of Nebadon, Christ Michael. **Onamonalonton**, who is now on Urantia, was mentioned as wanting to work more closely with Wallace Black Elk. Wallace Black Elk is being called to be a Vicegerent First Ambassador to my mandate in the Melchizedek order. We are presently praying for his alignment.

After the transmission we took a picture together on my back porch with the great red rock vortex behind us. The middle of it looks distinctively like a Mohawk Indian facing east. Two years before this, God sent Great Bear, an elder of the Seneca nation, to our home, and we took the same picture. He took one look at the middle rock and immediately said, "He's looking for the great prophet to come out of the East." Onamonalonton came from the West, so I wondered who that could be? I didn't realize until Wallace Black Elk and I took the picture that I was that prophet, born where the three rivers meet to form the Ohio River in Pennsylvania, now known as Pittsburgh. This area was once sacred to many native tribes before the white man came. I must say that when I was with Great Bear and Wallace Black Elk, I relived many moments of my more recent past repersonalization as the Apache warrior, Gentle Eagle. I felt the sorrow of the Earth

Mother and her cry to give birth to her new children; spiritual children who would understand the beat of her heart and the feel of her skin, the soil. The Continuing Fifth Epochal Revelation is the fifth world of the Hopi. It is the one language of the Iroquois and Seneca. The coming together of the cosmic families are the regathering of the Bird Tribes. It is the perfected government of the Lakota Sioux Indians. The Continuing Fifth Epochal Revelation teaches the true meaning of the Kachinas of the Hopi, the starseed. The native American way of the heart now must join with the mind. The Continuing Fifth Epochal Revelation calls it Ascension Sci. The fusion of the heart and the knowledge of God and his creation with cosmic science, the wisdom of the grandfathers fusing with the evolutionary minds of their descendants, and the time of purification of the Hopi, is happening now with the adjudication of the Bright and Morning Star versus Lucifer. All the good truths of the old ways are now becoming one in spirit with higher truths. The four directions of the medicine wheel, which form the symbol of a solar cross, speak of the Creator of all the ancestors, Christ Michael; and this planet, known in the universe of Nebadon as "the world of the cross," (*The URANTIA Book*, page 229:5) cries out for the return of the Creator Son, the Great Spirit of all the ancestors in Nebadon.

October 15, 1993.

CHAPTER 26

IF YOU SEE ME, YOU SEE THE FATHER

The Continuing Fifth Epochal Revelation is beautiful in that the word of truth becomes a living expression, right before your eyes. The message of Lucifer separated many families and all had to fend for themselves. Life can be very cruel and lonely on your own, with no one to help you. Our work is calling those lost ones back home, first to God, then to the Creator Son, Christ Michael, and then to their cosmic families. Here at Planetary Headquarters the word of truth in revelation is constantly in front of you in the persons and circumstances of the cosmic families. One such beautiful example is Santeen, my warrior cosmic son and son of Simon Peter. It is hard for me to express the love I feel for him. I have had many sons and daughters. I have had many brothers and sisters, some of which have come to Planetary Headquarters for a while and left. All I have loved and trusted. When this trust is betrayed, you can't let that stop you from loving the next son or daughter, brother or sister. The degree of their alignment to God is the degree of their becoming a great blessing to you or a great heartbreak. There is no doubt in my mind that when you see Santeen of the present day, you see Simon Peter just the way he was 2000 years ago. The good thing now is that Santeen is like the Peter after the resurrection. The Peter of Pentecost. The Peter of the fire of baptism of the Holy Spirit. After his transmission with Paladin, Santeen started bleeding in different areas of his body. Paladin told him that he must become the peaceful warrior. That, I'm sure, was told to him in the first century. Finally, the mother circuits were beginning to be truly activated in Simon Peter's son. Perhaps I, as a pre-Pentecost Peter, wasn't a very good example for Santeen in the first century. I like to believe he finally sees a reflection of the Father/Son/Mother balance in his cosmic father, Gabriel of Sedona, that really means something to him. I, as Francis of Assisi, began to bleed also when I became Mother-fused. Santeen helped me to understand the stigmata of Francis of Assisi by his continued bleeding in various spots on his body, for no apparent reason. Santeen is as much a saint today as Francis was then. His willingness to be what God wants him to be is counted as perfect in God's eyes. When he walked with the Master, Peter, a powerful old soul discovering his God in a higher way and discovering his own balance between the Father/Mother circuits, often blundered. I believe the first-century Peter needed Jesus, like I need Paladin, a stronger voice of God-power authority over me. Santeen needs Gabriel of Sedona, even as Gabriel, needs his loyal son, Santeen, and other loyal children. It's an unravelling story that becomes more evident to me each day—the reflective mystery of our interdependency among the loyal sons and daughters of God. We all must know our individual place in the divine plan. When we do, envy and jealousy are a thing of the past. Divine cooperation takes its place and the plan of God is revealed in full to his most humble sons and daughters. After Santeen read *The Cosmic Family, Volume I* and the first copy of *The Salvington Circuit,* he was off to meet us in Sedona. He needed to come and see us face to face, spirit to spirit. The truth of the book already was a breath of fresh air. Now he had to experience the dedicated souls of Christ Michael who helped bring this *Cosmic Family, Volume I* to Urantia. He came; he met us; he left to pack his bags and returned two weeks later to Arizona, leaving his beautiful beachside home in the San Juan Islands because he heard the call of God. Santeen is my right arm and I am his. I need my left arm son and all the other reflective parts of my seed. The Mandate of the Bright and Morning Star is a gift from Christ Michael to all. It is ever expanding in scope. Now I know that my seed is the safety guard of future Urantia, the reflective right and left arms of all who need us. Men and women should aspire to the reflectivity of the Bright and Morning Star, the first born son of Michael, but know that for the evolutionary creature it is a long, difficult journey through time and space. With God or Deopower comes great responsibility. Up the ascension ladder to God, all must love, honor and obey their superiors. False pride, jealousy, or whatever the sin, breaks the flow of God's blessings to you through

your more ascended family members. This is the divine administration principle. In the world you must fight, worry and
even die to *get* what you need. In God's Kingdom, you must give
to get. Love, to get. Honor, to get. Be loyal, to get. Obey, to
get. By serving those above you in God, you serve God. And the
highest leader is the servant to all.

I feel blessed to be a servant to all, but few understand who
or what I really am or what it means. To give just a few ex-
amples, right now it's 70 degrees and sunny and I'd love to just go
to the creek and be mindless, but this chapter would not get done,
and I feel it will benefit many. Also, I just had to say something
to three very close family members that probably no one else
would have said to them. This is painful. I can trust my female
complements, my brothers and sisters, my most faithful sons and
daughters to speak openly with me. "Love should pull no pun-
ches" is an old expression, meaning: Say what needs to be said
without watering down the message. With Santeen you will never
get a watered down message. Jesus spoke for his Father. Santeen
speaks for me. Individuals in the third dimension give people they
trust the power of attorney. In the fourth dimension and up, we
are just learning what this all means in terms of God's delegation
of his authority to others of his creation all the way down the line
to the human mandate of the Bright and Morning Star, and my
delegation of that Deopower to others under my authority. Some
of my cosmic sons and daughters have let me down tremendously.
A cosmic brother who was put into a position of high authority,
completely misrepresented my mandate. I love and trusted all of
them. Some day they will have to accept me as their elder brother
and father, but for now false pride blinds them. We have to be
reflective of our higher elder relatives, and as *The Cosmic Family,
Volume II* states, we also must begin to reflect our angelic guides.
When we reflect any true Deopower, we in turn represent God and
the power of God. I can trust Santeen, my loyal son and mandated
Liaison Minister, to always have my best interest at heart. Jesus
said, "I and the Father are one." When a mandated soul acts
within the will of God, all subordinates do not totally have to

understand the how and why of the decision. Trust and obedience are necessary. Over a period of time those less ascended will come to understand that the mandated leader has God's best interest at heart. For all of us here at Planetary Headquarters in the years to come, this will be an evolving, learning saga. Some have had Deopower taken away because they wanted diopower. They didn't truly understand the difference. I believe Deopower cannot be taught; it must be experienced. God is the only teacher here. In the third dimension, many who represent official authority abuse or misrepresent their position, such as some law enforcement officers or other government officials. They may get away with it in the third dimension, but even in the beginning stages of the fourth dimension and the Divine Government, they won't last long because they have no real power. God's Deopower operates in the laws of the first commandment which is "Love the Lord your God with all your heart, all your mind, all your soul," and therefore, leads to the second commandment, "Love your neighbor as yourself." The bad seed will be separated in the adjudication because they won't reflect their elder father/brothers who are in Deopower positions over them. Therefore, not being true reflections of God, the motives of the heart/mind are worked out in the circumstances of your life. As *The URANTIA Book* says, "The act is ours; the consequences God's."

October 19, 1993.

CHAPTER 27

A VISIT TO TITUS, THE OLDEST LIVING HOPI ELDER

Paladin, the Finaliter, told me that at some point in the future we would be meeting with Hopi elders, and we would be sharing the Fifth Epochal Revelation with them. We were quite aware of the Hopi views about the times of purification and their understanding of the Earth changes. We knew of their several trips to the United Nations to warn the governments of this world that they must change in relationship to the people and the land in order for true peace and harmony to come once again to our planet. If that did not take place, our planet would self-destruct soon. We were aware that the Hopi elders thought that after their final trip to the United Nations the time of the purification had begun, and the Earth changes would now become worse and worse.

Paladin told us that thousands of years ago extraterrestrials had made contact with the Hopi people and had given them information about the time of purification—the end of this Fourth World and the beginning of a new one. The Fifth World, which is to come, we believe, is the Fifth Epochal Revelation and Continuing Fifth Epochal Revelation, which will be the new common language to all humanity—a language in the sense of a common conceptual understanding of spiritual reality, i.e. God and creation.

In early fall of 1994 we were invited to the oldest living Hopi elder's farm in Hopi land. A sign at the entrance of his farm said, "Serving Under Creator's Law, One Mother, One Humanity." Under the words was a logo of a triangle with a circle inside of it and a solar cross inside the circle. This logo is similar to the logo of the Aquarian Concepts Community, except on our logo the triangle is inside the circle. Obviously, the two logos imply the same message. In our terminology, the four directions symbolize the concept of the master universe, incorporating all of the universes; the triangle is a symbol of the Trinity at the center of the master universe, and the circle is the symbol of infinity, eternity and the oneness of God.

With Niánn and me were Santeen, Kamon, Tarenta, Katrina, and Blue Evening Star. All of us are repersonalized starseed who had past Native American lives. All of us had Hopi lives, although as yet Celestial Overcontrol has not told us much about them. All we knew was that we had Hopi lives, and that we had been in contact at that time with extraterrestrial relatives, our ancestors from Avalon. We feel that gradually, in the next few years as we become more involved with our Hopi brothers and sisters in Hopi land, more information will come from Overcontrol, as we mix our particle reality together, hand in hand, and heart in heart.

It was late evening when we entered Titus' little hut. It was dark, and only a small lantern was lit. He was asleep, so we spoke to his adopted son who is in his late fifties; compared to Titus, who was 106, he is a young man. Titus' adopted son, Sacred Food Man, talked to us about eating the sacred food to nourish our bodies for several hours and about many things that we already understood in relationship to the Earth changes due to occur in about six years. During this time I could not make eye contact with Titus, although he awoke for moments at a time, and looked my way. I could not see his eyes because it was so dark, but I somehow felt his stare upon me, the same kind of feeling I experience sometimes when I know an angel, a midwayer, or the finaliter, Paladin, is nearby. I knew at that moment Titus was in touch with spirit beings, perhaps not in the way I was, but he definitely was in touch with them, and they began to enter the room. I think all of us that evening were taken back a few hundred, perhaps a few thousand, years to our past lives; and we heard the voices of our ancestors, our grandfathers and grand-mothers, calling to us. Sacred Food Man told us to come back in the morning, and we would talk again with Titus.

The next morning, before we went back, we visited Sacred Prophecy Rock, which is one of the most sacred spots in Hopi land. There were various markings that depicted a chronology from creation to the future, and to what we would call the first stage of Light and Life and onward to outer space travel. Somehow I knew that I had been there before, perhaps thousands of years ago, and I and my relatives were the ones who had put this information on the rock. At that moment I felt that the past met the present to coordinate our destinies in the future, that the past is there upon that rock, because in my lifetime as Peter, the apostle, I was called "the rock." Jesus knew that I would be a rock of faith and a prophet in proceeding lives of continued revelation. That rock confirmed the reality of what was happening to us, the extraterrestrial contact that I have in the Continuing Fifth Epochal Revelation and the Fifth World of the Hopi, and of our destiny to go out into the system of Satania and help adjudicate the other thirty-six fallen worlds of Satania. It was very clear that at the end of the earth trail, some of the Hopis would go into the skies. I knew what that meant, for Paladin had told us that the "cosmic family" consisted of all the tribes of the earth and three other universes who were the highest followers of God in his perfect will, and who would ascend to help adjudicate the next fallen thirty-six worlds of Satania.

We left Sacred Prophecy Rock to go to see Titus. As we entered his farm now in the daylight, it again felt like we were taken back a thousand years or more. The simplicity of this land and the small hut gave me tremendous peace, made me wish, in a sense, that I was he, and I had lived his life, the life of a farmer, the life of a teacher of the Massau'u (Great Spirit), a life of simplicity, oneness with the land and with the Earth, and the sacredness of the food that he grew and ate. I knew, indeed, that I was going to visit my brother.

Sacred Food Man brought Titus outside and laid him on his couch, and all of us sat around in a circle as Sacred Food Man talked. Although Sacred Food Man taught many truths about proper eating, we thought that too much emphasis was put on the external rather than the internal purification of the spirit. We gave him a copy of *The URANTIA Book* and hoped that he would read it and become a student at the Extension Schools of Melchizedek. To this date, he hasn't.

Every so often during this talk Titus would awaken. He said nothing, but our eyes exchanged glances several times, sometimes for several moments at a time, and I felt him talking to my spirit. Some of the things that I felt he said to me were to keep the faith, the faith in the Great Spirit, faith in the future, to not be afraid of those who would come against the teaching of the truth, that this was the time of the return of the Great Spirit and the ancestors. He was telling me to believe in my destiny, to believe that peace would come to this planet, and that all men would again walk as brothers on the earth. His eyes kept on encouraging me not to lose heart. Several times I got beside him and held his hand and embraced him. Because I have studied physics and Continuing Fifth Epochal Revelation, I knew at those moments his subatomic particles and mine were exchanging. I felt I was receiving much from him and that this interchange was "meant to be" by celestial beings who had set up this meeting for this physical particle interchange to happen before Titus transcended this earth by the death experience. It was an overwhelming feeling, this fusion between Titus and me. It was almost the same kind of fusion that I feel when Paladin or the Bright and Morning Star enters me. It didn't take long for me to realize that the finaliter, Paladin, was there, involved in this interchange. Then I knew that Paladin wished to come through and speak, and he did. He spoke directly to Titus and told the oldest living Hopi elder that it was time for him to go on to the next world, that he no longer had to stay in this one, and that his ministry would be continued in an even higher way by this group of souls who sat around him. He told Titus that his work was over, and that he no longer had to hang on, and that he could do more good now on the other side. Basically, Paladin very audibly confirmed to Titus that he could move on to the spirit world and join his ancestors.

What we all saw next was one of the greatest serendipities that I have ever seen in my life. Titus became alive, and lit up like a fire was under him, his eyes bright and shining. He began to sing and chant, "He ya, hi yeh, he ya he ya...," and he raised his hand in prayer. I think at that moment, and for the resulting few minutes afterwards, Titus saw many spirit beings surrounding him; it was quite a sight to behold. I knew that I had received some kind of subatomic transference from Titus's body to mine, and that I would now hold within my molecular reality some kind of mandate from this Hopi elder, some kind of responsibility that he wanted me to carry on, some kind of responsibility that he wanted me to fulfill to his people. At the time of this writing, I am not quite sure what all that is, but I know that it will all unfold. I made a promise to Titus and to God, The Great Spirit, that I will not let them down, and I will fulfill Titus' wishes to the Hopi people.

I knew it was time to leave. I looked at his eyes closely one more time, and he said good-bye and then closed his eyes and smiled. (We learned two weeks later that Titus had transcended the planet.) Paladin came though again and spoke to Sacred Food Man and told him some things about who he was and where he came from, and a brief message about his destiny. Then we got into the van and went to First Mesa; I knew that we were to go there. Paladin told us that we had some other Hopi people of importance to meet.

I didn't know it at the time, but we were to acquire a touring company called Dorian Tours, soon to be renamed "Spirit Steps." Spirit Steps would be a link in bringing past repersonalized Hopi ancestors back to visit Hopi land to be around their descendants once again to learn and experience the old ways, and to be taught Continuing Fifth Epochal Revelation, the language of the Fifth World, by our tour guides of Aquarian Concepts Community. Again Overcontrol was setting the stage to bring the past into the present to help create the future.

We met some beautiful Hopi people, which eventually led to Spirit Steps Touring Company receiving permission to visit First Mesa under the blessing of that mesa's eldership, and to this writing and day, April 12, 1995, I am looking forward to the future relationship between Aquarian Concepts Community and Spirit Steps Touring Company, the Hopi elders and the people of Hopi land. We know that these people of peace are a sacred people, a beautiful people. Now I am one with them, and our cosmic family is one with them. I know that I and this community are to help them, and as time goes on, I will know how; it will be revealed.

We have much to learn about "unity without uniformity." On this planet, throughout the ages of the past, when the true God of the universe of universes brought revelation to the pristine lands and people of the new world, all too often that message of the cosmic God was distorted in the consciousness of colonialism as it tried to conform all peoples to its viewpoint of God and culture. The challenge for teachers of higher truth is to help all of the peoples of the planet to understand that cosmic God, who is the God, not only of this planet but of trillions of other inhabited planets, and that somehow all these planets and all the various tribes of these planets can keep their individuality but be united in the oneness of that God who is eternal truth. This is a challenge that I will try to meet with respect to all peoples, their ways and cultures. Our oneness has to go beyond ourselves to a greater unity. I believe sincerely that the concepts of the Fifth Epochal Revelation and Continuing are the cosmic unity that is found throughout all the master universe.

I, myself, being a very multi-dimensional being, like to dress sometimes like a Native American, sometimes like an Egyptian, and at other times an Israeli. Sometimes, I prefer to go barefoot. My outward self may change, but my inward understanding of God remains constant. Too often people judge from the outside. They don't look any further than how a person is dressed. Sometimes it is good to bring some tradition into the present, to beat the drum, to chant the chant, to dance. Today thousands and thousands of young Americans are finding the Native American way, and in the understanding of the old ways, they themselves have become new; they have found a new oneness with Mother Earth and the Great Spirit. We of Aquarian Concepts Community know that they have to take another step; they have to learn the dance of the cosmos, to understand the cosmic God. They have to fuse mind with heart, and expand their minds with cosmic revelation, and come to understand that the concept of the Great Spirit incorporates: God the Absolute, God the Qualified and Unqualified, God the Ultimate, and God the Supreme. In their higher understanding of the cosmic God, and in the greater fusion of the truth of the old ways with continuing revelation, they will then not just be at one with the earth and their ancestors, but they can also begin to be at one with their own destinies and be able to manifest that which will actualize their connection to the ancestors they know about who are now living on other worlds of time and space. Continuing Fifth Epochal Revelation is that link to them, not only to the past, but a link to where they are now. It is not only a connection of mind and heart, but from planet to planet, system to system, universe to universe, and the past to the present and future. It is a higher union with God, and is the link that will bring this planet into the Fifth World, the first stage of light and life and that first millennium of peace that all of us want so badly for our beloved Urantia/Earth.

A Synopsis of Ancient Hopi Prophecy Correlated With
Fifth and Continuing Fifth Epochal Revelation[21]

The Hopi understanding of creation, simply stated, is that there is one Creator of all things or Massau'u (Universal Father). Their God created a Nephew (Creator Son) and Daughter (Universe Mother Spirit) to carry out his creative plan of the life in the universes of time and space.

After the creation of the Hopi First World (First Epochal Revelation, which was the arrival of the Planetary Prince 500,000 years ago) there came "the talker" (Lucifer, the System Sovereign,* and Caligastia, the Planetary Prince, who rebelled with Lucifer) who spread confusion throughout the world and segregated the people with his thoughts and words (the Lucifer rebellion which occurred 200,000 years ago). As a result of the chaos instigated by the "talker", every World of the Hopi has gone through a purification process (an Epochal Revelation) to cleanse the planet of the harm caused by inappropriate thought and deed.

In each World, those walking the highest path ("starseed" and reserve corps) and hearing from the Creator (Creator Son, Christ Michael), were allowed to continue their journeys and begin again on each new World (each new Epochal Revelation). The destruction of each World (the default or human misappropriation of the Epochal Revelations) came about because the group consciousness had reached a point where the majority were no longer hearing from God and choosing his will over their own.

Today, in the Fourth World of the Hopi, the World will be destroyed by earth changes, disease, nuclear holocaust and uncontrollable crime (the adjudication or tribulation) because of man's choices to do his will over the Creator's. Only those good and

---

[21]Everything in parenthesis is Fifth Epochal Revelation terminology.

peaceful "Hopi" people (cosmic family aligned with Divine Government) whether they be yellow, red, black or white, will be spared, and their homeland will be preserved as a safe haven where refugees will flee (Planetary Headquarters, primary and secondary protected areas). Bomb shelters, "digging in", moving back to the land and raising food, is futile for those "non-Hopi" who do not adhere to the revelation of God. This is a spiritual battle being fought on material ground. We (Cosmic Family) are at the front lines. Those who are at peace with their Creator are already in the great shelter of life (stabilized third psychic circlers). There is no shelter for evil.

The Fourth World with its materialism (third dimension) will be destroyed and the Hopi Fifth World (4th and 5th dimensions of the Fifth Epochal Revelation and Continuing Fifth Epochal Revelation) will be created. One world, one nation, under one power, the power of the Creator (Jesus/Christ Michael).

The Hopi believe that the time is near for the emergence of the Fifth World (Continuing Fifth Epochal Revelation—*The Cosmic Family, Volume I*). It is being brought about by many people of many nations who have the courage and humility to follow the "song" of the Creator. All must accept a higher level of perception that will lead into a divine new Fifth World ("The Divine New Order").

BIBLIOGRAPHY

Concise Science Dictionary, Second Edition, Oxford University Press, Market House Books Ltd. 1991.

Gabriel of Sedona, *The Cosmic Family, Volume I* , The Extension Schools of Melchizedek Publishing, Sedona, AZ, 1993.

Morowitz, Harold J. *The Beginnings of Cellular Life, Metabolism Recapitulates Biogenesis*, Yale University Press, New Haven, 1992.

New American Standard Bible, Word Bible Publishers, Iowa Falls, Iowa, 1973.

The New Illuminated Holy Bible, American Bible House, New York, 1897

The Salvington Circuit, Vol. 1, No 4, Nov/Dec 1993, The Extension Schools of Melchizedek Publishing, Sedona, AZ, 1993.

The URANTIA Book, URANTIA Foundation, Chicago, Illinois, 1955.

Webster's New World Dictionary, Third College Edition, Webster's New World, New York, 1988.

Williamson, George Hunt, *Secret Places of the Lion*, Destiny Books, Rochester, Vermont, 1989.

GLOSSARY OF TERMS

NOTE: The definitions in this Glossary are limited. For further information we recommend that the reader also study *The Cosmic Family, Volume I* and *The URANTIA Book*.

"Although these definitions are as exact as they can be in relationship to the students who are studying this revelation, updated information can change the definition to some degree. The content of the meaning will still be there. We are limited, based upon language from our side to yours, and hindered by your own inability to understand such a massive volume of information of specific details. Sometimes a definition has many meanings or two terms are very similar. Whenever we can we will try to introduce them but often are not able to clearly differentiate the terms at the time. If you can somewhat begin to understand 10% of these definitions in total, we can expand on them and go from there. It could take years to completely comprehend these very cosmic technical terms in Ascension Science until it becomes second nature to you. Two-brained types such as are now on Urantia, both native and ovan soul, have the ability of complete comprehension at some point in their future evolution."

Paladin, Chief of Finaliters on Urantia.

Terms in **bold type** are new words or concepts introduced in Continuing Fifth Epochal Revelation (*The Cosmic Family, Vol. I*) or words that are redefined. Added information of most other terms can be found in *The URANTIA Book* or are terms used in science or New-Age terminology.

ADAM AND EVE

The Material Son and Daughter, father and mother of the violet race, who came to our planet almost 38,000 years ago to biologically uplift the evolutionary races. They came from Jerusem, the capital of the system of inhabited worlds to which our world belongs. As long as they were in the perfect will of God they were immortal. They portrayed the concept of the Father of All to the evolutionary people, which was the Second Epochal Revelation to this planet. After more than one hundred years they could see little progress on this backward world in rebellion. Although they had been counseled by the Melchizedeks not to initiate the program of racial uplift and blending until their own family had numbered one-half million, through impatience Eve defaulted, and mated with Cano, a man of the Nodite race, who became the father of Cain. Although Adam realized Eve's mistake and knew that she was no longer immortal, he could not bear the thought of separation from his complement. The day after Eve's misstep, he sought out Laotta, a brilliant woman of the Nodite race, and mated with her. After their default, Adam and Eve left the first Garden of Eden, which was situated on a peninsula in the Eastern Mediterranean, and established a second Garden of Eden in Mesopotamia. Adam and Eve have been rehabilitated and have now returned to Urantia during this time of adjudication. Although invisible to human, third-dimensional eyes, they are stationed at Planetary Headquarters in Sedona, AZ, U.S.A., where the Third Garden of Eden is being established. (See also Epochal Revelation, Garden of Eden, and Material Son and Daughter)

ADAMSON AND RATTA

After the default of Adam and Eve, their first-born, Adamson, left the Garden of Eden and mated with Ratta, a pure-line descendant of the Caligastia one hundred with interuniversal genetics. They gave origin to a great line of the world's leadership and also became the grandparents of the secondary midwayers. Many Urantian reservists have their genetics. (See also Caligastia One Hundred, and Midwayers)

ADJUDICATION BY THE BRIGHT AND MORNING STAR VS LUCIFER

The ending of the Lucifer rebellion on Urantia, a process of adjudication which began in 1911 and will be completed in May of 2000 or 2001 AD. The Fifth Epochal Revelation, which includes Continuing Fifth Epochal Revelation, is a major part of re-opening the universe circuits and the final phase is now in progress in and through the Divine Government of Machiventa Melchizedek and his staff, both celestial and human.

(See also Bright and Morning Star, and Lucifer Rebellion)

AMADON

A native Urantian who belonged to one of the highest strains of the evolutionary Andonite race, 500,000 years ago. He was the associate of Van, the head of the loyalists in the rebellion. Both remained on the planet until the arrival of Adam and Eve. Amadon became the human hero of the Lucifer rebellion. He remained loyal to Christ Michael and has now repersonalized during the final phase of the adjudication by the Bright and Morning Star vs Lucifer.

(See also Caligastia One Hundred, and Lucifer Rebellion)

ANCIENTS OF DAYS

Trinity-origin beings who rule a superuniverse and, as Trinity representatives, are the judges of all personalities of origin in that superuniverse. There are three Ancients of Days in every super-universe. (See also Paradise Trinity and Superuniverse)

ANGEL OF ENLIGHTENMENT

A member of one of the twelve corps of Master Seraphim* in the Machiventa Government. These angels have ascended to Paradise level. They are now on assignment and first arrived on Urantia at Pentecost. At present, some of these angels are tem-porarily assigned as the personal angels for third-circle reservists instead of, or along with, a seraphic guardian of destiny.

(See also Reserve Corps of Destiny,* and Seraphim)

ANTAKARANA

A New-Age term for the central channel in the body. According to the ancient Tibetans the Antakarana connects the chakras or circuits. (See also Chakras, and Circuits)

AONIC

Relating to a subparticle within the ultimaton* pertinent to the astral body and memory circuits. A primordial force coordinating primal circuits in relationship to the energy needed for clairvoyant, clairaudient and clairsentient abilities which can begin to be activated on the third psychic circle. A form of emergent energy. (See also Astral Body, Circuits, and Ultimaton)

AONIC HETEROGENEOUS

A state in which one's subcellular reality is nonhomogeneous in Deo-aonic structure.
(See also Aonic Homogeneous and Chapter 24)

AONIC HOMOGENEOUS

A state in which one's subcellular reality reaches a level of associative reflectivity in homogeneous zones (or uniform fields). (See also Aonic Heterogeneous)

APOSTLES

The first-century apostles (including Matthias and Paul) who have repersonalized in the twentieth century. They are a mixed group of starseed and second-time Urantians. An apostle is one who is in full-time spiritual ministry in contrast to a disciple who is in part-time ministry. Some of the first-century apostles have gathered at Planetary Headquarters in Sedona, AZ. U.S.A., and are working in the Divine Government of the Planetary Prince, Machiventa Melchizedek, under the mandate of Gabriel of Salvington, the Bright and Morning Star of Nebadon.
(See also Machiventa Melchizedek, Mandate of the Bright and Morning Star, and Planetary Headquarters)

ARCHANGELS

They are a high order of local universe personalities created by the Creator Son and Universe Mother Spirit. They are an order separate from angels. "They are dedicated to the work of creature survival and to the furtherance of the ascending career of the mortals of time and space." In recent times a divisional headquarters of the archangels has been maintained on Urantia and is presently located at Planetary Headquarters in Sedona, AZ., U.S.A. There are no archangels communicating with humans at present. (See also Creator Son and Universe Mother Spirit)

ASCENSION SCI

A universe spiritual science which fuses the spiritual with the scientific.

ASHTAR COMMAND

The various celestial and mortal beings in spaceships assigned to Urantia for various duties in relation to the adjudication of Urantia, including physical evacuation by spaceship, and the coordination of activities relating to interdimensional changes, under the command of Ashtar, a finaliter, who has assumed a seventh stage morontia body to work in the physical realm.

ASSISTANTS

Mandated First and Second Assistants to Gabriel of Sedona and Niánn, under the mandate of the Bright and Morning Star of Salvington functioning in various aspects of reflectivity of Celestial Overcontrol. (See also Mandate of the Bright and Morning Star)

ASTRAL BODY

A composite of the bodies a personality has existed in before at any point in time and space. Each existence has a separate body connected to it. The astral body in the present is ever growing, that of the past is an inactive completed form, yet is not separate from the present physical body. The astral body of a second-time Urantian does not begin to form until death.

AUDIO FUSION MATERIAL COMPLEMENT

A term describing a fusion between a celestial being and a mortal, a fusion of one entity with another in the complete aonic-to-cellular reality of the lower being. The fusion takes place within the particle reality of the life force of the existing soul. They co-exist within the life force and the existing soul does not leave. It is a gradual process over many years, and the higher the virtue of the chosen vessel, the higher the fusion, the higher the being, and the higher the level of revelation which can be brought through. Gabriel of Sedona is the only Audio Fusion Material Complement on Urantia. The Bright and Morning Star comes on a once-a-month basis to teach for a few hours. Paladin, Chief of Finaliters, fuses with Gabriel of Sedona several times a week. No beings of light have spoken through anyone but Gabriel of Sedona since 1989. (See also Continuing Fifth Epochal Revelation, Mandate of the Bright and Morning Star, and Finaliters)

AUHTER ENERGY

The higher force-energy synergetic field resultant from cosmic nuclear fusion created by the joining or rejoining of spiritual cosmic families or groups based upon the personality bestowal of the Universal Father and each individual's acquiescence to his personality, and the group consciousness in relation to Celestial Overcontrol. This auhter energy creates a measurable light that is visible light years away. (See also Celestial Overcontrol, Cosmic Family, Union of Souls, and Universal Father)

AVALON

Name of a neighboring universe. Most of the starseed in the First Cosmic Family come from Avalon. Some of the Caligastia one hundred were morontia progressors originally from that universe and because of a different Avalon ascension scheme were on assignments in this universe of Nebadon. When the Caligastia one hundred were rematerialized a team of Avalon surgeons were present. (See also Caligastia One Hundred, Rematerialization, Nebadon and Universe)

BRIGHT AND MORNING STAR

The Bright and Morning Star of Salvington is the Chief Administrator of the Universe of Nebadon and the first-born personality creation of Christ Michael and the Universe Mother Spirit. He visits Urantia in overcontrol of the adjudication by the Bright and Morning Star vs Lucifer, and speaks through his mandated Audio Fusion Material Complement, Gabriel of Sedona, and manifests in reflectivity through this vessel. (See also Adjudication by the Bright and Morning Star & Gabriel of Salvington)

BRILLIANT EVENING STARS

An order of local universe aids, created by the Creator Son and Universe Mother Spirit, who function mainly as liaison officers for and under the direction of the Bright and Morning Star. They frequently also function as teachers. The human Liaison Ministers, which is the second highest mandate on the planet, are in reflectivity to these Brilliant Evening Stars. (See also Bright and Morning Star, and Liaison Ministers)

CALIGASTIA

The former Planetary Prince who arrived on Urantia 500,000 years ago with a staff of 100 rematerialized ascending sons and daughters (the Caligastia One Hundred) to bring the First Epochal Revelation to Urantia. His headquarters was the city of Dalamatia. Caligastia followed Lucifer and Satan in a rebellion 200,000 years ago. Although shorn of all administrative powers he has been allowed to remain on the planet until his adjudication is over. The "devil" is none other than Caligastia.
(See also Caligastia One Hundred, Dalamatians, Lanonandek Son, * Planetary Headquarters, Planetary Prince and Satan)

CALIGASTIA ONE HUNDRED

The physical mortal staff of ascenders from three other universes who came to Urantia 500,000 years ago with Caligastia and Daligastia to bring the First Epochal Revelation to Urantia. They were 50 males and 50 females, who had been transported by seraphic transport from the system capital, Jerusem, and had been rematerialized to be his administrative staff on the physical level. Dalamatia was their headquarters and they were organized for service in ten councils of ten members each. During the Lucifer rebellion 40 remained loyal and 60 fell. The rebellious ones mated with the evolutionary races and created the Nodite race, named after their leader "Nod". Some Urantians have their interuniversal genetics. (See also Caligastia, Dalamatians, and Lucifer Rebellion)

CELESTIAL OVERCONTROL

A term designating orders of beings who function on higher levels of universe administration guiding and overseeing the human mandated personalities on a planetary level functioning in cooperation with the Planetary Prince—the final authority of planetary affairs. (See also Planetary Prince, and Universe)

CELLULAR MEIOSIS

"A type of cell division that gives rise to four reproductive cells (gametes) each with half the chromosome number of the parent cell. Two consecutive divisions occur... In the first, homologous chromosomes become paired and may exchange genetic material... before moving away from each other into separate daughter nuclei. This is the actual reduction division because each of the two nuclei so formed contains only half of the original chromosomes. The daughter nuclei then divide by mitosis and four haploid cells are produced." In CFER it is a product of rebellion that God uses for the ultimate good.
(See also Adjudication of the Bright and Morning Star versus Lucifer, and Lucifer Rebellion)

CFER

An acronym for Continuing Fifth Epochal Revelation, which is now coming through the Audio Fusion Material Complement, Gabriel of Sedona.
(See also Continuing Fifth Epochal Revelation, Epochal Revelation, Fifth Epochal Revelation, and *The Cosmic Family, Volume I*)

CHAKRAS

"In certain forms of yoga, chakras are any of the body centers, usually seven, that are considered sources of energy for psychic or spiritual power." (See also Antakarana and Circuits)

CHANGE AGENT

A CFER term for an apostle in full-time spiritual ministry, who is aligned and functioning under the mandate of the Bright and Morning Star. (See also Apostle, and Mandate of the Bright and Morning Star)

CHANGE POINT

The instant of time in which Urantia moves from the third to the fourth dimension completely, approximately in May of 2000 or 2001. As of 1992, only the one-mile to five-mile radius of Planetary Headquarters reflects fourth-dimensional reality to some degree. After the change point, only those personalities who have also manifested fourth-dimensional bodies will be able to return to and remain on Urantia. (See also Fourth Dimension, Morontia Body, Planetary Headquarters, and Third Dimension)

CHIEF OF SERAPHIM

A primary supernaphim from Paradise stationed at Planetary Headquarters on Urantia and in command of the 12 corps of Master Seraphim of Planetary Supervision and the seraphic hosts. The Chief of Seraphim first arrived on Urantia at the time of Pentecost, accompanying the first Governor General. (See also Master Seraphim of Planetary Supervision, and Planetary Headquarters)

CHRIST MICHAEL

The Universe Father, Sovereign, and Creator Son of this universe of Nebadon. He earned his sovereignty by bestowing himself seven times in the likeness of seven different orders of personalities in his own universe, reflecting the seven aspects of the

Paradise Trinity. In his last bestowal he came to Urantia to portray the nature of the Universal Father. He fulfilled the Fourth Epochal Revelation to this planet 2000 years ago in the life of Jesus of Nazareth. Among the 700,000 Creator Sons in the grand universe he was the only Creator Son that was put to death by his own creatures. After his seventh bestowal, at the time of Pentecost, he poured out the Spirit of Truth for the benefit of his entire universe. CFER teaches that he is expected to soon return to this planet as he promised. "Planetary Prince of Urantia" is one of his titles.
(See also Creator Son, Nebadon, Spirit of Truth, and Universe)

CIRCLES (See Psychic Circles)

CIRCUITS
Of, or relating to, the various Paradise circuits of both upper and nether Paradise which connect, via the Salvington circuit of the Nebadon headquarters world of Christ Michael, to human mortals through the various circuits within the body, the main ones being previously known as chakras in lower teachings. The reopening of these Paradise circuits to evolutionary mortals is CFER.
(See also Father-circuited, Mother-circuited, Paradise Isle, Salvington, and **Son-circuited**)

COMPLEMENTARY POLARITIES
Personalities of similar spiritual status who function in pairs, usually male and female, but in some cases can be two males or two females.
(See also Highest Complementary Polarities, and Twin Flames)

CONSTELLATION FATHERS
An order of local universe sonship, the Vorondadek Sons (normally three), who rule the constellation governments of the universes, "The Most Highs who rule in the kingdoms of men." Our constellation, Norlatiadek, is ruled by twelve Vorondadek Sons. There are one million Vorondadeks in our local universe of Nebadon.

CONTINUING FIFTH EPOCHAL REVELATION

The continuation of the Fifth Epochal Revelation (*The URAN-TIA Book* is only one tenth of it), which is now coming through the Audio Fusion Material Complement, Gabriel of Sedona. Although over one hundred Papers have been transmitted, only *The Cosmic Family, Volume I* has been published so far.
(See also Epochal Revelation and Fifth Epochal Revelation)

COSMIC CHILDREN

The children that one has been the biological parent of in their very first life, whether on this planet or in another universe.
(See also Cosmic Parent)

COSMIC FAMILY

A genetically related family of ascending sons and daughters. They are generally of origin in universes outside Nebadon, but include Urantians with extraplanetary genetics, usually related to a finaliter. At present there are **seven cosmic families** on Urantia coming from four different universes.
(See also First Cosmic Family and Seven Cosmic Families)

COSMIC PARENTS

The parents a soul has in its very first life, whether originating on this planet or on another world. (See also Cosmic Children)

COSMIC RESERVE CORPS OF DESTINY

A group of ovan souls on Urantia who function under the guidance of various entities such as midwayers and seraphim to bring cosmic consciousness to the planet, and are called to serve in the Machiventa Government in various capacities in order to fulfill their destiny purpose. These souls are members of one of the seven cosmic families presently sojourning on Urantia. All cosmic reservists are called to Planetary Headquarters for further training.
(See also Ovan Souls, Planetary Headquarters, Reserve Corps of Destiny)

CREATOR SON

A personality of Paradise origin, created by the Universal Father and the Eternal Son, belonging to the order of Michael. Together with a Creative Daughter, a Creator Son is the creator of a local universe of time and space. There are 700,000 local universes. To gain full sovereignty over his universe, a Creator Son bestows himself seven times in the likeness of the created personalities on various levels in his own creation, reflecting one of the aspects of the Paradise Trinity, after which he earns the title of "Master Son". A Creator Son does not live the life of a mortal man to die for their sins, but to reveal the loving nature of the Paradise Father. (See also Christ Michael, Nebadon, Paradise Trinity, and Universe Mother Spirit)

DALAMATIANS

The inhabitants of the original Planetary Headquarters city founded by Caligastia, Urantia's first Planetary Prince, 500,000 years ago, on a peninsula since submerged in the Persian Gulf. Dalamatia was named after Daligastia, Caligastia's assistant. The many legends about Atlantis and the sons of God mating with the daughters of men go back to the time of Dalamatia. (See also Caligastia One Hundred)

DEO-ATOMIC

A term designating atomic structure in alignment with God, as in Deo-atomic cells, which are cells aligned with Paradise absolutes and are the cells of the morontia or light body.

DEO-INTEGRATION

The integration of Deoparticle reality in proper uninet areas of the body as applied to material complements of spiritual beings.

DEO/DIO DICHOTOMY

The state of imbalance between Deo-atomic structure and diotribe particle structure which causes difficulty in maintaining cosmic sanity.

DEOFUNCTION POWER

Power given to personalities working under those with higher virtue and higher Deopower to carry out certain administrative functions. Those who work in Deofunction power do not necessarily have to understand the order and its ramifications, coming from the one in Deopower so long as they can clearly represent it at some level in Deopower.

DEOPOWER

Power used in accordance with the character and will of God with divine mandates and administration.

DEO-ULTIMATONIC

A term designating ultimatonic structure in alignment with God, as in Deo-ultimatonic cells, which are ultimatonic particle reality within cellular structure aligned with Paradise absolute virtue characteristics.

DIO-INTEGRATION

The integration of diotribe reality from aonic to molecular level and up, which may be due to being partially possessed by fallen entities, or tapping into a lower self of a previous repersonalization, or current Luciferic thinking.
(See also Diotribes, and Repersonalization)

DIOPOWER

The power of self-assertion, self-exaltation, greed, and other rebellious attitudes.

DIOTRIBES

A CFER term from *The Cosmic Family, Volume I* referring to negative or harmful particles in your body due to wrong thinking induced by the individual's acquiescence to Luciferic thought patterns. They are the cause of disease in the human body.

DIVINE NEW ORDER COMMUNITIES

Communities of ascending sons and daughters spiritually aligned with the Divine Government of Machiventa Melchizedek on Urantia and functioning within the seven sacred/protected areas being established as administrative sectors of the planet. All Divine New Order communities will come under the leadership of the eldership of Sedona, AZ., U.S.A.
(See also Sacred/Protected Areas and Sectors)

ENERGY REFLECTIVE CIRCUITS

A CFER term from *The Cosmic Family, Volume I* designating energy fields on a planet which allow for interdimensional communication and transportation. Also known in lower-level terminology as vortexes.

EPOCHAL REVELATION

A revelation designed for the uplifting of an entire planet as distinguished from revelation to specific individuals or groups. There have been only five epochal revelations on Urantia to date, all having to do with the sorting and censuring of the successive religions of evolution, each ever expanding and more enlightening. The First Epochal Revelation was inaugurated 500,000 years ago when the Planetary Prince, Caligastia, established Dalamatia, the first Planetary Headquarters on Urantia. The Second Epochal Revelation occurred 38,000 years ago with the advent of Adam and Eve. The Third Epochal Revelation came approximately at the time of Abraham with the arrival of Machiventa Melchizedek. The Fourth Epochal Revelation was fulfilled when the Creator Son of our local universe, Christ Michael, bestowed himself as a human mortal, Jesus of Nazareth, to portray the nature of his Paradise Father. *The URANTIA Book* is the first one tenth of the Fifth Epochal Revelation to the evolving races of Urantia. Continuing Fifth Epochal Revelation (the other nine tenths) is now in progress through the Audio Fusion Material Complement, Gabriel of Sedona. (See also Fifth Epochal Revelation and Continuing Fifth Epochal Revelation)

ETERNAL SON

The second person of the Paradise Trinity, co-creator with the Universal Father and Infinite Spirit. Not to be confused with a Creator Son of a local universe. (See also Paradise Trinity)

EXISTENTIAL REALITY

Relating to God eternal, without beginning or ending. There is no time that he did not exist and he has full knowledge without experience.

EXPERIENTIAL REALITY

Relating to that part of God which grows through experience. This includes the experiences of all personalities in time and space. The Supreme Being is the personalization of all universe experience.

EXPERIMENTAL PLANET

One planet in ten is used by the Life Carriers for experimental purposes to produce new and improved variations in the evolutionary life plasm. Also called a decimal planet. Urantia is a decimal, experimental planet. CFER teaches that Urantia is unique in having humans who are being trained in divine government administration. (See also Life Carriers)

EXTENSION SCHOOLS OF MELCHIZEDEK

They are the extension schools of the Melchizedek University for ascending souls, which consist of 490 worlds near our universe headquarters on Salvington. At present there is only one extension school on Urantia and it is located at Planetary Headquarters in Sedona, AZ., U.S.A. It is both an academic and practical school, the schools of thinking, feeling, and doing, where students learn Ascension Sci, divine government administration, the personal and social effects of the Lucifer rebellion and how to walk in the perfect will of God on a moment-to-moment basis.
(See also Ascension Sci)

FATHER-CIRCUITED
An entity who is encircuited in, and manifests the essence of, the Universal Father. In humans, both male and female have Father circuitry, but the normal male is more Father-circuited. (See also Circuits, Mother-circuited, Son-circuited)

FIFTH EPOCHAL REVELATION
The URANTIA Book is the first one tenth of the Fifth Epochal Revelation to the evolving races of Urantia. Continuing Fifth Epochal Revelation (the other nine tenths) is now in progress through the Audio Fusion Material Complement, Gabriel of Sedona. The Fifth Epochal Revelation is revealed in the lives of those men and women who have aligned with the divine government of the Planetary Prince, Machiventa Melchizedek, under the mandate of the Bright and Morning Star of Salvington, and are trying to walk in the perfect will of God on a moment-to-moment basis. (See also Epochal Revelation and Continuing Fifth Epochal Revelation)

FINALITERS
Ascending mortal or nonmortal sons or daughters who have ascended from their planet of origin through the local universe, the superuniverse, the central universe of Havona, and have reached Paradise. After having been embraced by the three Paradise Trinity personalities they have been mustered into the Mortal Corps of the Finality. Finaliters are sent off on assignments in the superuniverses of time and space and are always involved when a planet is about to move into the first stage of Light and Life. Paladin became Chief of Finaliters on Urantia in January 1992. he is the head of the First Cosmic Family. (See also Ashtar Command and Cosmic Family)

FIRST COSMIC FAMILY
A family of ascending sons and daughters, mostly of origin in the Pleiades, but containing interrelated members from the other six cosmic families presently on Urantia. The First Cosmic Family is

the most closely involved with planetary administration, is responsible for gathering the other six cosmic families, and is headquartered at Planetary Headquarters in Sedona, Arizona, USA. The finaliter, Paladin, is the head of the First Cosmic Family. (See also Cosmic Family and Finaliters)

FIRST SOURCE AND CENTER

The creator, controller, upholder, and God of all creation is the primal cause of the universal physical phenomena of all space. Without the First Source and Center, the master universe would collapse. He is also the Universal Father of all personalities. He unqualifiedly transcends all mind, matter and spirit. A fragment of the First Source and Center lives within the normal human mind and is the spirit pilot to help find the Father on Paradise. (See also Fragment of the Father, Paradise Isle, and Thought Adjuster)

FIRST-TIME URANTIAN

A new soul whose planet of origin is Urantia, and whose present life is the very first existence of that soul. Most people on this planet are first-time Urantians.
(See also Second-time Urantian and Urantians)

FOURTH DIMENSION

In CFER the fourth dimension on Urantia is the morontia level that could have been achieved during the Fourth Epochal Revelation, but was not actualized. It is now being actualized at Planetary Headquarters in and through the Divine Government of Machiventa Melchizedek and among those souls of the First Cosmic Family who have aligned with that government. After the change point Urantia will be completely in fourth-dimensional reality.
(See also Change Point and Third Dimension)

FRAGMENT OF THE FATHER

An actual fragment of the Universal Father that indwells the mind of every mortal with a normal mind. It is the spirit nucleus that with the cooperation of that mind creates the soul. It is the destiny of the soul to fuse with the Fragment of the Father and ascend to Paradise. (See also Thought Adjuster)

FUNCTION ZONES
Reflective levels of association on aonic to cellular levels with spiritual beings. (See also Aon, and Reflectivity)

GABRIEL OF SALVINGTON
First-born Son of Christ Michael and the Universe Mother Spirit, also called the Bright and Morning Star. It was Gabriel of Salvington who appeared to Mary to announce she had been chosen to become the human mother of Jesus. (See also Mandate of the Bright and Morning Star)

GARDEN OF EDEN
The site of the second Planetary Headquarters on Urantia, founded nearly 38,000 years ago by Adam and Eve, the Material Son and Daughter, on a since submerged peninsula extending into the Mediterranean Sea from the area of present-day Lebanon. After the default of Adam and Eve a second Garden of Eden was established in Mesopotamia, between the Tigris and Euphrates rivers. Now a third Garden of Eden is developing at Planetary Headquarters in Sedona, AZ., U.S.A. (See also Adam and Eve, and Planetary Headquarters)

GOVERNOR GENERAL OF URANTIA
"The resident governor general has no actual personal authority in the management of world affairs except as the representative of the twenty-four Jerusem counselors. He acts as the coordinator of superhuman administration and is the respected head and universally recognized leader of the celestial beings functioning on Urantia.... the first governor general arrived on Urantia, concurrent with the outpouring of the Spirit of Truth... " Since December, 1989, with the announcement of Machiventa Melchizedek as Planetary Prince, the Governor General no longer functions in this capacity.

GRAND UNIVERSE
The inhabited part of the master universe which includes the eternal central universe of Havona of one billion unique and perfect worlds, and the seven evolutionary superuniverses of time and space, which include 700,000 local universes, created by the Creator Sons and Creative Daughters.
(See also Master Universe, Superuniverse and Universe.)

HAVONA
The name of the central universe surrounding Paradise which functions as the pattern for the time-space universes. Havona consists of one billion unique and perfect worlds. It is part of the destiny of mortals to go through all these billion perfect worlds before reaching Paradise.

HEART CIRCUIT
The circuit within the body that is connected to Christ Michael, and where the Spirit of Truth is first activated. (See also Circuits)

HIGHEST COMPLEMENTARY POLARITIES
A mortal male or female pair who have reached the highest spiritual relationship, (sometimes called twin flames) usually leading to procreation of higher starseed children. For ovan souls these mates may be on another planet. Usually there is only one highest complement, but not always.

HOLY SPIRIT
The ministering spirit circuit of the Universe Mother Spirit; the first of three distinct spirit circuits to function in the local universe. Not to be confused with the Infinite Spirit on Paradise or the Spirit of Truth, which is the Spirit of the Creator Son, poured out at Pentecost. (See also Spirit of Truth)

HOMOGENEOUS ZONES
Areas of the uniform distribution of subcellular matter.

HOPI'S FIFTH WORLD

The Native American Hopi people believe that the present Fourth World of materialism will be destroyed by disease, crime, nuclear holocaust and cataclysms, and the Fifth World will be created by good and peaceful "Hopis": one world, one nation, under the power of the Massau'u (Creator of All). The Hopis believe that the emergence of the Fifth World has begun with the appearance of people all over the world (the cosmic families), who with courage and humility follow the "song" of the Creator, and that all must come to a higher perception of truth to lead us into a Divine New Order.

INFINITE SPIRIT

Third person of the Paradise Trinity. Not to be confused with Holy Spirit, which is the spirit circuit of the Universe Mother Spirit of a local universe. The Infinite Spirit is the Creator of the local Universe Mother Spirits and the Mother aspect of God.

INTERPLANETARY RECEIVER

A being in the spiritual chain of command who receives interplanetary and interdimensional messages and transmits them to the people on the planet.
(See also Audio Fusion Material Complement)

LANONANDEK SON

An order of local universe Sons who function in system administration. They are best known as System Sovereigns and Planetary Princes. Lucifer, the fallen former System Sovereign, was a Primary Lanonandek Son, and Caligastia, the fallen former Planetary Prince, was a Secondary Lanonandek Son.
(See also System Sovereign and Planetary Prince)

LEY LINES

Grid lines of energy between energy reflective circuits used for communication and transportation.
(See also Energy Reflective Circuits)

LIAISON MINISTERS
Those holding the second highest mandate of the Bright and Morning Star in reflectivity to **Brilliant Evening Stars,** who act as liaison officers in human overcontrol between the Bright and Morning Star mandate and the Machiventa Melchizedek mandated personalities. The seven Liaison Ministers also function as elders on the inner board at Planetary Headquarters.
(See also Brilliant Evening Stars, and Mandate of the Bright and Morning Star)

LIFE CARRIERS
Local universe Sons of God who implant and foster life on the evolutionary worlds. They are created by the Creator Son, Universe Mother Spirit, and one Ancient of Days.

LIGHT BODY   (See Morontia Body)

LUCIFER
A Lanonandek Son, the fallen System Sovereign of Satania, who led a rebellion against his Creator Father, Christ Michael, 200,000 years ago, which involved 37 planets in the system of Satania, including Urantia. Lucifer's Manifesto was about unbridled personal liberty, rejection of universe allegiance and disregard of fraternal obligations and cosmic relationships. Since the bestowal of Christ Michael on Urantia as Jesus of Nazareth 2000 years ago, Lucifer has been imprisoned, and awaits his final adjudication. Although many of today's teachings contain some truth, they are sprinkled with very deceptive Luciferic lies. (See also Lanonandek Son, Lucifer Rebellion, and System Sovereign)

LUCIFER REBELLION
A rebellion led by Lucifer 200,000 years ago in Satania; 37 of the 619 inhabited worlds in the system participated. It involved many personalities of various celestial orders as well as mortals. Although the circuits were cut, the rebellion also spread to neighboring universes by telepathic communication, because of the

presence of interuniversal supermortals on Urantia (the Caligastia one hundred).   On Urantia an adjudication by the Bright and Morning Star began early this century and will be completed in May of 2000 or 2001.   Many fallen starseed had to repersonalize on Urantia at the present time for this adjudication.   The other 36 rebellious planets in Satania will also be adjudicated when the adjudication on Urantia is over.
(See also Adjudication by the Bright and Morning Star)

MACHIVENTA MELCHIZEDEK
Planetary Prince of Urantia since December, 1989.   This same Melchizedek, who belongs to a high order of local universe Sons, incarnated in the likeness of mortal flesh and lived on Urantia for 94 years during the time of Abraham and was known as the Prince of Salem.   He came on an emergency mission when the spiritual light on Urantia was almost extinguished and taught the one-God concept.   He brought the Third Epochal Revelation to this world. He established a school where missionaries were trained who later brought his teachings to all parts of the world.   Now the Extension Schools of Melchizedek at Planetary Headquarters in Sedona, AZ, U.S.A., are again training teachers to bring the Fifth Epochal and Continuing Fifth Epochal Revelation to the rest of the planet.

MANDATE
An authorization to act, given to a representative.   In CFER this refers particularly to human personalities authorized to represent Divine Government authority on the planet.

MANDATE OF THE BRIGHT AND MORNING STAR
The universe directive from Christ Michael, Creator and Sovereign of the universe of Nebadon, authorizing his Chief Administrator, Gabriel, the Bright and Morning Star of Salvington, to adjudicate the Lucifer rebellion, beginning with our planet, Urantia.   Under this mandate is the authority to reinstate Divine Government on the planet through the highest complementary-polarity couple on the planet, his Audio Fusion Material Comple-

ment, Gabriel of Sedona, and Niánn, in cooperation with the present Planetary Prince, Machiventa Melchizedek. This mandate includes bringing through Continuing Fifth Epochal Revelation, healing of the various bodies, and the authority to train and mandate humans to administrative positions in Divine Government. (See also Audio Fusion Material Complement and Bright and Morning Star.)

MANSION WORLDS
Morontia training worlds that souls who come from planets that have not been settled in Light and Life go to some time after their physical death. They are situated near the system capital and have been provided to overcome mortal deficiencies. After the change point Urantia will also function as a Mansion World.
(See also Morontia)

MASTER SERAPHIM OF PLANETARY SUPERVISION
Twelve corps of administrative seraphim, who have graduated on Seraphington, a Paradise satellite world for angels, and been assigned to certain special planetary services under the immediate direction of the Chief of Seraphim and the Planetary Prince. They accompanied the governor general when he arrived on Urantia at the time of Pentecost and the outpouring of the Spirit of Truth. The master seraphim insure planetary progress against vital jeopardy through the mobilization, training, and maintenance of the reserve corps of destiny.
(See also Chief of Seraphim, Governor General, Reserve Corps of Destiny and Spirit of Truth)

MASTER UNIVERSE
The universe of universes, including the eternal central universe of Havona, the seven evolutionary superuniverses of time and space, plus the presently mobilizing, but uninhabited four outer space levels.
(See also Grand Universe, Superuniverse and Universe)

MATERIAL SONS AND DAUGHTERS

The highest type of sex-reproducing beings in a local universe, the Adams and Eves, who are the biological uplifters of the evolutionary races, physically present in administrative capacity under a Planetary Prince. They are the founders of the violet race. Usually only the progeny of the Material Sons and Daughters procreate with mortals. (See also Adam and Eve)

MEDIUMSHIP

The lowest and least accurate form of interdimensional communication, which since 1989, is entirely limited to contacts with fallen entities.

MELCHIZEDEKS

A high order of local universe Sons. They function in many capacities, but mainly as teachers and emergency ministers. Since the Lucifer rebellion and the Caligastia betrayal 200,000 years ago, twelve Melchizedeks have been guarding the spiritual evolution on Urantia. In 1989 Machiventa Melchizedek became our new Planetary Prince. (See also Machiventa Melchizedek)

MICHAEL

An order of Paradise Creator Sons, created by the Universal Father and the Eternal Son, who, in cooperation with the local Universe Mother Spirits, create the 700,000 evolutionary universes of time and space. (See also Christ Michael, and Creator Son)

MIDWAYER COMMISSION

A delegation of midwayers officially assigned to portray the Life and Teachings of Jesus (Part IV of *The URANTIA Book*).

MIDWAYERS

Unique beings about midway between mortals and angels. They are the permanent citizens of an evolutionary world. Primary midwayers are the offspring of the rematerialized staff of the former Planetary Prince, Caligastia. Secondary midwayers on Urantia are descendants of **Adamson** (firstborn of Adam and Eve) and **Ratta** (pure-line descendant of the Caligastia one hundred). They ably assist the angels on Urantia. They have definite power over things and beasts. Midwayers do not sleep or procreate. On Urantia midwayers have often been mistaken for angels. The midwayers are actively involved in guiding destiny reservists to Planetary Headquarters in Sedona, AZ. U.S.A. During the time of the Lucifer rebellion the majority of the primary midwayers went into sin. Many of the secondary midwayers also failed to align with the rule of Michael of Nebadon. At the time of Pentecost they were interned and held into custody, but since 1989, and the arrival of Machiventa Melchizedek as the new Planetary Prince, they have been freed and given another chance to align with the divine government. Unfortunately not all have done so, and many are still communicating with lower channels, teaching Luciferic concepts in a very deceptive way, causing much confusion even among some URANTIA Book readers, who refuse to align themselves with the Machiventa Government. They are soon to be adjudicated. (See also Adamson and Ratta)

MIGHTY MESSENGERS

A class of perfected mortals who have been rebellion tested or otherwise equally proven as to their personal loyalty; all have passed through a definite test of universe loyalty. After having ascended to Paradise and having been embraced by the Paradise Trinity, they are sent out on assignments of all phases of universe activities. Several Papers of *The URANTIA Book* were authored by a Mighty Messenger.

MORONTIA

A level of local universe reality between the material and spiritual levels of creature existence. The human soul is an experiential acquirement that is created by a creature choosing to do the will of the Father in heaven. This new reality that is created by the cooperation of the mortal mind with the divine spirit is a morontia reality that is destined to survive mortal death and begin the Paradise ascension. (See also Morontia Body)

MORONTIA BODY

The various body forms of the 570 ascending morontia levels of creature existence an ascending soul uses within the local universe. It is also known on Urantia as the light body, but this concept would be applicable only to the lowest level morontia body.

MORONTIA COMPANIONS

Children of the local Universe Mother Spirit who have been created especially to serve as friends and associates of all who live the ascending morontia life after death. These companions are touchingly affectionate and charmingly social beings.

MOTHER-CIRCUITED

Encircuited in and exhibiting the characteristics of the Universe Mother Spirit. In humans, both male and female have Mother circuitry, but the normal female is more Mother-circuited. (See also Father-circuited)

MYSTERY MONITORS

Another term for Thought Adjusters—fragments of the Universal Father, that indwell normal minds of mortals after they make their first moral decision.

NEBADON

The name of our local universe, the creation of Christ Michael, Universe Sovereign, and the Universe Mother Spirit. Salvington is its headquarters. (See also Universe)

ONAMONALONTON

"A far-distant leader of the red man and the one who directed this race from the worship of many gods to the veneration of 'The Great Spirit'." Onamonalonton is one of the twenty-four counselors (John, the Revelator, called them the four and twenty elders), an advisory control body of Urantia, whose headquarters are on Jerusem, our system capital. This council is made up of the great, spiritual Urantian leaders of the past in all the eight races of this planet. Onamonalonton has returned to Urantia to help in the establishment of the divine government of the Planetary Prince, Machiventa Melchizedek.

ORVONTON

The name of the superuniverse in which our local universe of Nebadon exists. It is superuniverse #7 of the seven superuniverses which make up the grand universe, and is roughly equivalent to what Urantia astronomers call the Milky Way galaxy. Uversa is its headquarters. Orvonton is ruled by three Ancients of Days. Orvonton is destined to reflect the nature and wills of the three Paradise Deities. Because it is more difficult to attain a balanced reflectivity of the threefold spirit, this seventh superuniverse has had more rebellions in it than the other six superuniverses. It has also been granted more mercy and has been called "the super-universe of mercy." (See also Superuniverse and Grand Universe)

OVAN SOULS

Souls who have survived the initial experience of mortal planetary existence and who have attained the morontia conscious-ness equivalent of the first mansion world and the realization of Paradise circuitry in a morontia body. On Urantia there are approximately 170,000,000 ovan souls from three other universes and approximately 2000 second-time Urantians building their morontia bodies through the process of repersonalization.
(See also Morontia Body)

PALADIN

Paladin became Chief of Finaliters on Urantia in January, 1992, because of the level of spiritual ascension of his cosmic son, Gabriel of Sedona, and others of his cosmic seed. He is head of the First Cosmic Family. He fuses with and speaks through

Gabriel of Sedona and is the chief spokesperson for celestial personalities bringing Continuing Fifth Epochal Revelation to Urantia. He first introduced himself to Gabriel as Sky Hawk because he has had several repersonalizations on Urantia as a Native American. Finaliters always become involved when a planet is about to move into the first stage of Light and Life, which will happen at the change point. (See also Change Point, First Cosmic Family, Cosmic Father, and Finaliters)

PARADISE
The abiding place of the Universal Father, Eternal Son, and Infinite Spirit. This eternal Isle is the absolute source of the physical universes—past, present, and future. It is the universal headquarters of all personality activities and the source-center of all force-space and energy manifestations. It is the geographic center of infinity and the only stationary thing in the master universe. It is the goal of all ascending sons and daughters to ascend to Paradise. (See also Universal Father, Eternal Son, Infinite Spirit, and Master Universe)

PARADISE TRINITY
An association and union of the three infinite persons on Paradise: the Universal Father, the Eternal Son, and the Infinite Spirit, functioning as a corporate entity in a nonpersonal capacity but not in contravention of personality.
(See also Paradise Isle)

PLANETARY HEADQUARTERS
Administrative center of the celestial divine government. The first planetary headquarters was Dalamatia at the time of Caligastia, 500,000 years ago; the second was the Garden of Eden at the time of Adam and Eve, 38,000 years ago; the third were the schools of Salem at the time of Machiventa Melchizedek, approx. 4000 years ago; the fourth was wherever Jesus of Nazareth was, 2000 years ago. At present it is located where the Planetary Prince, Machiventa Melchizedek, resides, in Sedona, AZ, U.S.A. All Destiny

Reservists are called to Planetary Headquarters to receive further training at The Extension Schools of Melchizedek, under the Mandate of the Bright and Morning Star, Chief Administrator of our local universe.
(See also Extension Schools of Melchizedek, Machiventa Melchizedek, and Mandate of the Bright and Morning Star)

PLANETARY PRINCE
The spiritual ruler of an inhabited world in time and space. The first Planetary Prince of Urantia, Caligastia, arrived approximately 500,000 years ago with his assistant Daligastia and a human or corporeal staff of one hundred. Their headquarters was Dalamatia in the Persian Gulf region. "The Planetary staff included a large number of angelic cooperators and a host of other celestial beings assigned to advance the interests and promote the welfare of the human races." Unfortunately Caligastia chose the side of Lucifer and Satan during the Lucifer rebellion. In 1989 AD, Machiventa Melchizedek became Planetary Prince and has his headquarters in Sedona, Arizona, USA. Christ Michael also earned the title of Planetary Prince of Urantia after his seventh bestowal 2000 years ago, during which he lived the life of the human mortal, Jesus of Nazareth. Presently, Gabriel of Sedona is the human representation of the Planetary Prince on Urantia. This divine mandate will increase in Deopower at the time of the change point or upon the return of Jesus. (See also Adjudication of the Bright and Morning Star vs Lucifer, Caligastia, Change Point, Dalamatians, Lanonandek Son, Lucifer Rebellion, Mandate of the Bright and Morning Star, and Planetary Headquarters)

PLEIADES
"A cluster of stars in the constellation of Taurus." CFER teaches that they are not stars but planets settled in Light and Life. Most of the First Cosmic Family come originally from the Pleiades or have Pleiadian genetics.
(See also First Cosmic Family)

PSYCHIC CIRCLES

The seven levels of personality realization on a material world. Entry on the seventh circle marks the beginning of true human personality function. Completion of the first circle denotes the relative maturity of the mortal being. Destiny reservists at Planetary Headquarters who are on the third psychic circle receive an angel of enlightenment. (See also Angel of Enlightenment)

REFLECTIVITY

The reflection in mandated humans of the personality virtues of nondivine celestial counterparts, such as the Bright and Morning Star, Brilliant Evening Stars, Melchizedeks, Seraphim etc. Gabriel of Sedona is reflective of the Bright and Morning Star.

REMATERIALIZATION

One of several techniques providing a physical body for a personality of another dimension. The Caligastia one hundred were rematerialized when they arrived from the system capital 500,000 years ago as the staff of the former Planetary Prince Caligastia. These supermortals came originally from other neighboring universes and were accompanied by an Avalon team of surgeons.

REPERSONALIZATION

A term used in CFER to describe the transfer of ascending ovan souls back into third-dimensional reality through the birthing technique for specific destiny purposes. Some members of the cosmic reserve corps of destiny have repersonalized on this planet in all of the major spiritual renaissances. Gabriel of Sedona writes about some of these in this book. With the exception of about 2000 second-time Urantians, who for undisclosed reasons have for the first time been allowed to repersonalize, these souls come originally from other universes where the ascension schemes are different from that of this universe. In Nebadon souls do, as a rule, *not* return to their planet of origin. Not to be confused with the erroneous earthly concepts of reincarnation. (See also Rematerialization)

RESERVE CORPS OF DESTINY

"This corps consists of living men and women who have been admitted to the special service of the superhuman administration of world affairs as human liaisons, mortal assistants.... The chief function of these reservists is to insure against breakdown of evolutionary progress; they are the provisions which the celestial forces have made against surprise; they are the guarantees against disaster." There are cosmic reservists (originally from other universes) and Urantian reservists (originally from this planet). Since the coming of the new Planetary Prince, Machiventa Melchizedek, all destiny reservists are called to Planetary Headquarters in Sedona, AZ, U.S.A. to receive further training in Divine Government administration at The Extension Schools of Melchizedek. (See also Master Seraphim of Planetary Supervision and Cosmic Reserve Corps of Destiny)

SACRED/PROTECTED AREAS

These are areas of the planet near major energy reflective circuits, set up by people who are aligned with the Machiventa Government. There will be only seven major protected areas on the planet. Some secondary areas will also have a certain degree of protection. The degree of protection depends upon a person's level of alignment and virtue.
(See also Energy Reflective Circuits and Sector)

SALVINGTON

Salvington is the Headquarters sphere of the Universe of Nebadon, home of Christ Michael and the Universe Mother Spirit. Salvington was the first completed act of physical creation in Nebadon and took a little over one billion years to complete. It is situated at the exact energy-mass center of the local universe. It is the destiny of ascending sons and daughters to sojourn on Salvington for a period of time as part of their ascension training on their journey to Paradise. When a soul leaves Salvington he is a full-fledged spirit. (See also Christ Micael, Gabriel of Salvington, and Universe Mother Spirit)

SANANDA

Sananda was the title of Christ Michael on another planet in rebellion when he bestowed himself as a Material Son (Adam) and took the office of Planetary Prince. This was his third bestowal mission when he reflected the combined will of the Universal Father and the Infinite Spirit. Sananda is not the name of Christ Michael and never has been, not on this planet or any other. It is a title of a Planetary Prince, now only given to Machiventa Melchizedek, who became Planetary Prince of Urantia in 1989. Individuals who call themselves by this name have no true connection to the Divine Government of the Planetary Prince, Machiventa Melchizedek. (See also Planetary Prince)

SATAN

First assistant to Lucifer, Satan was an able and brilliant primary Lanonandek Son. Both Lucifer and Satan had reigned on Jerusem for 500,000 years when they fell into rebellion against the Universal Father and his Son, Michael of Nebadon. Satan was sent by Lucifer to advocate the cause of the rebellion on our planet. He was imprisoned after Michael's bestowal on Urantia (as Jesus of Nazareth) and is awaiting the final decision of the Ancients of Days when his adjudication is over. (See also Lucifer rebellion)

SATANIA

The local system of inhabited worlds in which our planet Urantia is #606. It was named after Satan, Lucifer's assistant, long before they both went into rebellion, 200,000 years ago.

SECOND-TIME URANTIAN

A soul belonging to unique group of Urantians numbering less than 2,000 who were sleeping survivors, and who, for the first time in the history of Urantia by decree of Christ Michael, have for undisclosed reasons been allowed to repersonalize on Urantia since the beginning of this century. Some of the first-century apostles have repersonalized and are second-time Urantians.
(See also First-time Urantians and Ovan Souls)

SECTOR

An administrative headquarters area, and on Urantia a protected area in which a Divine New Order community is or will be established before and after the change point. There will be seven sectors on this planet coordinated with the seven cosmic families of Urantia. (See also Sacred/Protected Area)

SERAPHIC TRANSPORT

"All groups of ministering spirits have their transport corps, angelic orders dedicated to the ministry of transporting those personalities who are unable, of themselves, to journey from one sphere to another.... The angels cannot transport combustion bodies —flesh and blood—such as you now have, but they can transport all others, from the lowest morontia to the highest spirit forms.... When enseraphimed, you go to sleep for a specified time, and you will awake at the designated moment." The Caligastia one hundred came here 500,000 years ago by seraphic transport, after which their physical bodies were rematerialized. As material bodies cannot be transported by seraphic transport, they must be evacuated by dematerialization or spacecraft when a planet is no longer safe to live on. (See also Caligastia One Hundred, Morontia, and Seraphim)

SERAPHIM

Local universe angels who are of origin in the Universe Mother Spirit and are designated Ministering Spirits of the local universe. Seraphim are created slightly above the mortal level. Those assigned to the watchcare of ascending mortals are called Seraphic Guardians of Destiny. An angel of enlightenment can also serve as a destiny guardian.
(See also Angel of Enlightenment)

SEVEN COSMIC FAMILIES

The seven cosmic families on Urantia are made up of starseed, and first- and second-time Urantians with genetic links to neighboring universes outside Nebadon, and in particular, Avalon, Wolver-

ing and Fanoving. The head of the First Cosmic Family is the finaliter, Paladin, Chief of Finaliters on Urantia. It is the responsibility of the First Cosmic Family to gather the other six cosmic families and set up communities around the planet.
(See also Cosmic Family)

SON-CIRCUITED

A personality encircuited in the Eternal Son and exhibiting characteristics thereof. In the local universe this is a reflection in and through the Creator Son.
(See also Father-circuited and Mother-circuited)

SOUL MATES

A New-Age term for complementary personalities who serve together harmoniously in some capacity.
(See also Highest Complementary Polarities)

SPIRIT OF TRUTH

The spirit of Christ Michael bestowed on Urantia at Pentecost. It is experienced in human consciousness as the conviction of truth and needs to be continually activated by soul growth through a relationship with God and his will (not man's wishes) as opposed to religious doctrine. The Spirit of Truth should override false *interpretations* of any written scripture or text, be it the Bible, *The URANTIA Book*, or *The Cosmic Family* volumes. The Universe Mother Spirit acts as the universe focus and center of the Spirit of Truth as well as her own personal influence, the Holy Spirit.
(See also Christ Michael)

STAR CHILDREN

Children from other planets or universes who repersonalize on Urantia or on other planets as part of their ascension career.

STARSEED

A term generally used on Urantia to designate mortals repersonalized from another universe. (See also Repersonalization)

SUPERUNIVERSE

One of the seven primary divisions of time and space in the grand universe, which contains 100,000 local universes comprising one trillion inhabited worlds and is presided over by three Ancients of Days. Every superuniverse is divided into 10 major sectors; the name of our major sector is Splandon. Each minor sector is divided into 100 minor sectors; the name of our minor sector is Ensa. Each minor sector is made up of 100 local universes. The name of our local universe is Nebadon. It is the destiny of ascending sons and daughters to receive training on all these various levels on their journey to Paradise.

(See also Ancients of Days and Orvonton)

SYSTEM SOVEREIGN

A primary Lanonandek Son who is the administrative head of a local system of 1,000 inhabited worlds. Although brilliant administrators, Lanonandeks have been prone to rebellion. Our System Sovereign in Satania is Lanaforge, who replaced Lucifer after his fall 200,000 years ago. Lanaforge is a gracious and brilliant ruler who has been rebellion tested.

(See also Lanonandek Son)

THIRD DIMENSION

The dimension of present-day Urantia. It includes the material aspects of height, breadth and depth and only includes a limited level of ascension consciousness. The third dimension consists of choices for self, instead of choices for God and your neighbor.

(See also Fourth Dimension)

THOUGHT ADJUSTERS

Prepersonal fragments of the Universal Father which indwell normal minds of human mortals. It is through the Thought Adjusters that the Universal Father has personal communion with mortal beings. Fusion with the Thought Adjuster guarantees eternal survival. Also called Mystery Monitors.

(See also Fragment of the Father and Universal Father)

TRINITY TEACHER SONS

Paradise Sons of Trinity origin who appear on an evolution-ary world when the time is ripe to initiate a spiritual age. They are the exalted teachers of all spirit personalities.

TRON THERAPIST

Mandated therapist who will use a psychospiritual therapy which will restore broken circuitry within the body, remove diotribes, and will be a touch therapy destined to replace surgery. It will be done only in conjunction with psychospiritual counseling and will involve the permanent healing of all bodies, the astral, etheric and physical, for those who are in alignment with their God. Tron therapy will be available only at Planetary Head-quarters through mandated therapists.

TWIN FLAME

New-Age term for complementary polarity.

ULTIMATONS

The basic units of materialized energy. The first measurable form of energy. Ultimatons have Paradise as their nucleus and respond only to circulatory Paradise-gravity pull. 100 ultimatons are mutually associated in an electron. (See also Aonic)

UNION OF DAYS

Trinity-origin Sons of God who represent the Paradise Trinity as advisors to the Creator Sons of the local universes of time and space. The Union of Days associated with Christ Michael of Nebadon is named Immanuel.
(See also Creator Son, Christ Michael, and Paradise Trinity)

UNION OF SOULS

A group consciousness reflecting the ideals and status of ethical relationships and functioning in the realm of harmonious teamwork. Also the descriptive name of a group of ministering spirits of the order of secondary seconaphim, the Union of Souls.

UNIVERSAL FATHER

The first person of the Paradise Trinity; Creator, Controller and Upholder of all creation. The Universal Father desires to have communion with mortals through the prepersonal fragments of himself, the Thought Adjusters, who indwell the human mind. He also has reserved the prerogative to bestow personality and maintains personal contact with his creatures through the personality circuit. (See also Thought Adjuster)

UNIVERSE

The creation of a Creator Son and Creative Daughter. There are 700,000 local universes in the grand universe. Each universe is subdivided into 100 constellations; each constellation is divided into 100 local systems; each system is destined to have 1000 inhabited evolutionary planets. Our local universe of Nebadon is a relatively young universe and is far from finished. Urantia has seven cosmic families from four different universes: Nebadon, Avalon, Wolvering, and Fanoving.
(See also Avalon, and Nebadon)

UNIVERSE FATHER

A Creator Son of a local universe. Christ Michael of Nebadon is our Universe Father; he was created by the Universal Father and the Eternal Son on Paradise. Nebadon's Universe Father is a Master Son as he has bestowed himself seven times and has reflected the sevenfold will of the Paradise Trinity.
(See also Christ Michael, Creator Son, and Universal Father)

UNIVERSE MOTHER SPIRIT

A Creative Daughter, created by the Infinite Spirit; co-creator of a local universe, and complementary polarity to a Creator Son. Also called the Divine Minister. Not to be confused with the third person of the Paradise Trinity, the Infinite Spirit.
(See also Holy Spirit)

UNIVERSE SUPERVISORS (See Celestial Overcontrol)

URANTIA

The cosmic name of our planet. Urantia is planet #606 in the solar system of Monmatia, in the system of Satania, in the constellation of Norlatiadek, in the universe of Nebadon, in the superuniverse of Orvonton. Urantia is the planet which Michael of Nebadon chose among all the planets in his universe for his seventh bestowal as a human mortal. It is a decimal or experimental planet and is unique in the grand universe in having human mortals who are being trained in divine administration. The ruler of our planet is the Planetary Prince, Machiventa Melchizedek, under the overcontrol of the Bright and Morning Star, Gabriel of Salvington, the Chief Executive of our local universe. The Planetary Headquarters is in Sedona, Arizona, U.S.A.

(See also Experimental Planet)

URANTIA MOVEMENT

A term designating variously organized readers of *The URANTIA Book*.

URANTIANS

A term designating ascending sons and daughters whose planet of origin is Urantia. Contrary to some New-Age teachings, most people on this planet fall into this category and are souls who are experiencing their very first life. There is also a group of about 2000 Urantians who are here for the second time. (See also First-time Urantians, Ovan Souls, and Second-time Urantians)

VICEGERENT AMBASSADORS

Mandated representatives of Machiventa Melchizedek, such as Vicegerent First Ambassadors as well as Second and Third Ambassadors. Up to the year 2040 -2050 AD there will only be Vicegerent Ambassadors. They must be stabilized on the third psychic circle. There are none as of February 17, 1995.

VORTEX

A New-Age term for Energy Reflective Circuit.

WALK-IN

In New-Age terminology generally, a soul who takes over the body completely and the previous soul leaves. Since 1989 no soul ever really leaves a body, even if a fallen or rebellious entity comes in whose sole purpose is to teach false teachings mixed with just enough truth to deceive, if possible, even the very elect of God. No beings of light have spoken through anyone but Gabriel of Sedona since 1989.

(See also Audio Fusion Material Complement)

WATCHER

A Divine New Order community member mandated to oversee environmental concerns.

AQUARIAN CONCEPTS COMMUNITY

Aquarian Concepts Community is a spiritual community located in Sedona, Arizona. The guidelines for the community and its members are based on the teachings found in the Fifth Epochal Revelation, as set forth in *The URANTIA Book* and *The Cosmic Family* volumes, with an emphasis on the life of Jesus of Nazareth, known as Christ Michael, the Sovereign Creator Son of our local universe of Nebadon.

Members come from all parts of the world, with a majority having moved here from within the United States. Founded in 1986, by Gabriel of Sedona and his complement Niánn, the community has about 100 full-time members with new members aligning weekly. *The Extension Schools of Melchizedek*, located at the community center, are for children, teenagers and adults and are unique on this planet. This unique school is not only for mindal development and book learning, it is very much a school for soul growth. Many ovan souls, or souls who have lived previous lives, have been stuck in static spirituality for thousand of years because they took part in the Lucifer rebellion and became trapped in erroneous Luciferic thought patterns. In this school, the elders with the guidance of Celestial Overcontrol, teach how to make the mind and heart connection, correlating science and spirituality in Ascension Sci. "The purpose of all education should be to foster and further the supreme purpose of life, the development of a majestic and well-balanced personality."
(*The URANTIA Book* p. 2086:3)

The community is organizing and developing extensive organic farms and gardens. They are building additional administrative facilities, a new community center and expanding residential housing. Additional land is being purchased and set aside for the long range plans of Aquarian Concepts community which include the establishment of the Third Garden of Eden, the Planetary

Headquarters for the Divine Government of the new Planetary Prince, Machiventa Melchizedek as appointed by Christ Michael of Nebadon.

Aquarian Concepts Community operates a publishing company that distributes the works authored by Gabriel of Sedona, including *The Divine New Order* and *The Cosmic Family* volumes. The community has a music ministry of both live concert tours and the distribution of prerecorded cassettes and compact discs. Healing is a major component of the music ministry and a series of Planetary "Sacred Concerts" are scheduled to begin soon.

There are many forces that influence the causes of disease, but in the majority of cases, the root cause is a spiritual one, a separation from the First Source and Center,* God. True permanent healing cannot begin until an individual aligns with the will of God for his or her life. The Aquarian Concepts Community Healing Team incorporates both spiritual and scientific techniques such as personal transmissions, morontia counseling, future light body hologram, and beginning **Tron therapy.** We also have a medical doctor.

Weekend seminars on Continuing Fifth Epochal Revelation are held at the end of every second month. Classes for community members are held four nights a week and visitors are invited to a weekly social gathering and/or tour of the community by appointment.

For more information, write to:

Aquarian Concepts Community
P.O. Box 3946
West Sedona, AZ.,
U.S.A. 86340

or call (520) 204-1206

Books by Gabriel of Sedona and Community Members

001
☐
The Divine New Order: The autobiography of Gabriel of Sedona, a Level Four A
Fusion Material Complement for the Chief Executive of our local universe
Bright and Morning Star of Salvington. An introduction to Continuing Fifth Epc
Revelation. ($14.95 paper)

002
☐
The Cosmic Family Volume I: The beginning volume of a series whereby Gabri
Sedona is used to bring through Continuing Fifth Epochal Revelation. A serie
Papers authored by various celestial personalities teaching you step by step, pre
upon precept the cosmic absolutes of this great revelation, which is a continua
of the 196 Papers of *The URANTIA Book.* ($19.95 paper)

003
☐
The Salvington Circuit: A magazine-format newsletter written by the membei
Aquarian Concepts Community, containing articles and photographs depicting
and spiritual growth at Planetary Headquarters in Sedona, Arizona. Ong«
features and interviews. (published bi-annually $7.50 per copy; older back is
$5.00 per copy)

004
☐
A Psychological Profile of Gabriel of Sedona: Dr. Marayeh Cunningham, a clii
psychologist, who has been on a spiritual path most of her adult life had
opportunity to observe and work closely for almost two years with Gabrie
Sedona, the Audio Fusion Material Complement through who Continuing F
Epochal Revelation is being transmitted. Using Abraham Maslow's theorie
personality and motivation, she is able to analyze the multidimensional and m
level quality of Gabriel's personality using the criteria of a self-actualizing pe:
as defined by Maslow. ($7.00 paper)

005
☐
Battered Cliff Face: The personal story of Delphius, her struggles and frustrati
dealing with the red tape of bureaucracy in trying to obtain a visa to be able to
her cosmic family at Planetary Headquarters. A humorous immigration experie
in rhyme. ($4.00 paper)

006
☐
Tipis & Yurts; Authentic Designs for Circular Shelters. Blue Evening Star pres«
a variety of habitats which serve during transition and awakening. Expertly cra
tipis and yurts which can be used for homes, temples, children's playhouses, s|
rooms or studios. ($25.00 hardcover) More information about Circle Liv
Workshops on practical preparations for earth changes is available upon request.

007
☐
The Cosmic Family Volume II: The second volume in a continuing serie:
transmitted through the Audio Fusion Material Complement, Gabriel of Sed«
Available in 1996.

Video Tapes

101
☐
A Creekside Visit with Gabriel of Sedona: A unique hour with one of the n
significant visionaries of our time. This video tape offers a rare glimpse into hi§
spiritual realities and presents a cosmic perspective of a world in turmoil.
inspirational dialogue that answers many immediate questions to world problem
well as taking a prophetic look at what could happen if a consciousness shift d
not occur to the mass population of our planet. ($19.95)

dio Tapes

An Introduction to *The Cosmic Family Volume I* as Transmitted Through the Level Four Audio Fusion Material Complement Gabriel of Sedona: A discussion with Gabriel of Sedona about the Forewords and 36 additional Papers that complement many of the unrevealed cosmic realities put forth in *The URANTIA Book*. ($9.95)

An Interview with Gabriel of Sedona and his Complement Niánn: An in-depth discussion with Gabriel and Niánn about Aquarian Concepts Community and Planetary Divine Government. How did they come about? When did they start? Where are they headed? ($9.95)

A Message to the Native American Elders: Niánn presents a message to all respected elders of the various tribes of the North American continent from Paladin / Sky Hawk, an ancient ancestor, concerning the time of purification, earth changes, the change point, the Fifth World / the Fifth Epochal Revelation. ($9.95)

A Three-tape Audio Series with Gabriel of Sedona: Each tape discusses a vital and important theme. Tape #1 is entitled "There Are No Real Leaders." Tape #2 is "What is True Spirituality?" Tape #3 is "The Cosmic Renaissance." ($24.95)

sic

Escape: Music, lyrics, vocals written and performed by Gabriel of Sedona accompanied by The Bright and Morning Star Band. Divine New Order sacred music with mystical vocals and higher-consciousness lyrics. ($9.95 cassettes only)

Wake Up America! and *The Great American Dream:* A two-song CD or cassette single. Music, lyrics, vocals written and performed by Gabriel of Sedona accompanied by The Bright and Morning Star Band. ($6.95 CD, $4.95 cassette)

ts and Crafts

Living Nature Creations: Beautiful hand-made moccasins designed to your exact personal comfort. Many styles to choose from. Native American jewelry. Brochures available upon request.

Cosmic Art & Logos: Send for detailed brochure.

. . . .

ke check payable to:
uarian Concepts
). Box 3946
st Sedona, AZ U.S.A. 86340

YMENT METHOD:

Check / Money order enclosed
Visa / Mastercard Exp. Date:

rd# _____

nature _____

order by phone 1-520-204-1206
 1-520-204-1252

ow 2 - 3 weeks for delivery

☐ **I wish to contribute to the non-profit / tax-exempt 501(c)(3) Aquarian Concepts**

$_____

SHIPPING, TIME AND EFFORT:*

$3.00 first item, $1.50 ea. additional item

$_____

Sales Tax
Arizona residents add 7.25 % $_____
TOTAL DUE $_____

Ship to:_____
_____
_____
_____

*All foreign orders must phone for current USA postage rates

ABOUT THE AUTHOR

Gabriel of Sedona, visionary and soul surgeon, gifted author, and truly humble spiritual leader, was born and raised in Pittsburgh, Pennsylvania. He studied theology at Duquesne University and began his religious career as a student involved in the charismatic renewal of the Catholic Church. His devotion to God has been life long. He sought monastic life in Benedictine and Franciscan monasteries in the Southwest, where he was also introduced to and has continually learned from Native American spirituality. He has spent years ministering to and counseling street youth, students, and individuals in various spiritual communities across the United States. He was a prison chaplain and worked for 11 years providing shelter and counseling for the homeless and destitute. He has studied the Tibetan Master Djwal Khul's writings and all appropriate metaphysical teachings of true spiritual value.

Presently, as a Level Four Audio Fusion Material Complement for the Chief Executive of our local universe, the Bright and Morning Star of Salvington, Gabriel is used by various celestial personalities for interplanetary and interdimensional communication. Holding the highest mandate of the Bright and Morning Star on our planet, he is the head administrator of the Divine Government and the highest spiritual teacher/leader. He is the repersonalized Peter, the apostle, and destined to be the human Planetary Prince of our planet, preceding Amadon who may stay on Urantia after 2040 - 2050 AD if none of the First Ambassadors qualify for Melchizedek leadership. As a serious disciplined scientific student, he has become a theoretical physicist. Gabriel is in contact with and is currently being used by celestial personalities to bring through the Continuing Fifth Epochal Revelation that is a continuation of the 196 Papers of *The URANTIA Book*. These Papers, collectively known as *The Cosmic Family* volumes, are fundamental as a basis for understanding the current state of our planet and our relationship to the cosmic community.

Gabriel lives with his complement, Niánn, and their three children, at Aquarian Concepts Community in Sedona, Arizona. In addition to being the spiritual leader of this community and ministry, he also is an accomplished futuristic lyricist, singer, and songwriter.